English Food

Jane Grigson was brought up in the north-east of England, where there is a strong tradition of good eating, but it was not until many years later, when she began to spend three months of each year working in France, that she became really interested in food. *Charcuterie and French Pork Cookery* (also published by Penguin) was the result, exploring the wonderful range of cooked meat products on sale in even the smallest market towns. This book has also been translated into French, a singular honour for an English cookery writer.

After taking an English degree at Cambridge in 1949, Jane Grigson worked in art galleries and publishers' offices, and then as a translator. In 1966 she shared the John Florio prize (with Father Kenelm Foster) for her translation of Beccaria's *Of Crime and Punishment*. Since 1968 she has been writing cookery articles for the *Observer Colour Magazine*; *Good Things* and *Food with the Famous* are based on these highly successful series. In 1973, *Fish Cookery* was published by the Wine and Food Society, followed by *English Food* (1974), for which she was voted Cookery Writer of the Year in 1977, and *The Mushroom Feast* (1975), a collection of recipes for cultivated, woodland, field and dried mushrooms. Jane Grigson's highly acclaimed *Vegetable Book* (1978) and *Fruit Book* (1982) have both won the André Simon Memorial Fund Book Award and the Glenfiddich Writer of the Year Award. All of these are published in Penguins.

Jane Grigson's reputation rests on elegance, erudition and her infectious enthusiasm for quality and simplicity in food and cooking. The *Sunday Telegraph* has said of her, 'Jane Grigson is one of the best of the British cookery writers' and *The Times* has called her 'the most engaging food writer to emerge during the last few years'. On the publication of *English Food*, the *Guardian* wrote: 'Those who know Jane Grigson's *Good Things*, will know what I mean when I say that this is the perfect English companion. Chiefly notable are her enthusiasm and her discernment. Mrs Grigson will turn the same delightful eye on a Yarmouth bloater as on a wild duck stuffed with apricots.'

Jane Grigson was married to the poet and critic the late Geoffrey Grigson.

English Food

AN ANTHOLOGY CHOSEN BY

JANE GRIGSON

with illustrations by Gillian Zeiner

Penguin Books

Penguin Books Ltd, 27 Wrights Lane, London W8 5TZ (Publishing and Editorial)
and Harmondsworth, Middlesex, England (Distribution and Warehouse)
Viking Penguin Inc., 40 West 23rd Street, New York, New York 10010, USA
Penguin Books Australia Ltd, Ringwood, Victoria, Australia
Penguin Books Canada Ltd, 2801 John Street, Markham, Ontario, Canada L3R 1B4
Penguin Books (NZ) Ltd, 182–190 Wairau Road, Auckland 10, New Zealand

First published by Macmillan 1974
Published in Penguin Books 1977
Reprinted 1979, 1981, 1983, 1987, 1988

Made and printed in Great Britain by
Richard Clay Ltd, Bungay, Suffolk
Set in Linotype Baskerville

For Geoffrey and Sophie, and for my parents in whose house I first learnt about good English food

Contents

Acknowledgements

Thanks are due to the following people for the recipes and information they have provided: Elizabeth Bolgar; D. M. Dickson; Bobby Freeman; Winifred McQuiggen; Joyce Molyneux; Peggy Murray; Breian Lloyd-Davies; Michael Smith; George Willacy; Malcolm Young; H. Horton of the Manchester Library of Social Sciences; Mary Norwak of the *Farmer's Weekly*; Tony Jones of the National Federation of Women's Institutes, and the many secretaries of county branches who sent me their publications; Guy Mouilleron, chef of Le Relais at the Café Royal, London; Mrs Sleightholme and *Woman* magazine; Janet Smith of the Liverpool Record Office. Thanks, too, to Marjorie White, who helped with the cooking and with suggestions, and who kept the household going through a long and difficult winter, and to my daughter, Sophie, who also helped with the cooking and with much vigorous criticism. I am also grateful to the copyright holders of those recipes I have quoted from published sources, and due acknowledgements will be found in the text, as well as in the list of source books on page 311.

Introduction

The English are a very adaptive people. English cooking—both historically and in the mouth—is a great deal more varied and delectable than our masochistic temper in this matter allows. There's an extra special confusion nowadays in talking of good and bad national cooking. The plain fact is that much commercial cooking is bad, or mediocre in any country—it's easy enough to get a thoroughly disappointing meal even in France where there exists an almost sacred devotion to kitchen and table. The food we get publicly in England isn't so often bad English cooking as a pretentious and inferior imitation of French cooking or Italian cooking.

It is also true that a good many things in our marketing system now fight against simple and delicate food. Tomatoes have no taste. The finest flavoured potatoes are not available in shops. Vegetables and fruit are seldom fresh. Milk comes out of Friesians. Cheeses are subdivided and imprisoned in plastic wrapping. 'Farm fresh' means eggs which are no more than ten, fourteen or twenty days old. Words such as 'fresh' and 'home-made' have been borrowed by commerce to tell lies.

In spite of all this the English cook has a wonderful inheritance if she cares to make use of it. It's a question of picking and choosing, and that exactly is what I have done for this book. My aim has been to put in obvious dishes on a basis of quality : even more I have tried to show how many surprises there are. I have also included a number of Welsh dishes because I like them, and because they are linked closely with much

1

English food, while retaining a rustic elegance which we have tended to lose.

No cookery belongs exclusively to its country, or its region. Cooks borrow—and always have borrowed—and adapt through the centuries. Though the scale in either case isn't exactly the same, this is as true, for example, of French cooking as of English cooking. We have borrowed from France. France borrowed from Italy direct, and by way of Provence. The Romans borrowed from the Greeks, and the Greeks borrowed from the Egyptians and Persians.

What each individual country does do is to give all the elements, borrowed or otherwise, something of a national character. The history of cooking is in some ways like the history of language, though perhaps it's harder to unravel, or like the history of folk music. The first mention of a dish, the first known recipe for it, can seldom be taken as a record of its first appearance. As far as origins go, there's seldom much point in supposing that a dish belongs to Yorkshire, or Devonshire, or Shropshire because it's survived in those places and may bear their names. What goes for counties goes for countries. Who's to say whether *Pain Perdu* or Poor Knights of Windsor is really English or French; both in France and England it was a dish of the medieval court. Did the English call it payn pur-dew out of the kind of snobbery we can still recognize, or because they took it from France? And if they took it from France, where did the French take it from? It's a marvellous way of using up stale bread, especially good bread, and who's to say that earlier still the Romans, or the Greeks before the Romans, didn't see the point of frying up bread and serving it with something sweet? In England today *Pain Perdu* has been anglicized into a nursery or homely dish, Poor Knights of Windsor. In France with brioche to hand, or the light *pain de mie*, *Pain Perdu* remains a select dish gracefully adorned with brandied fruit and dollops of cream under such names as *Croûte aux Abricots*.

There's no avoiding the fact that the best cooking has come down from the top. Or if you don't like the word 'top', from the skilled, employed by those who could pay and had the time to appreciate quality. In England on the whole the food descends less from a courtly tradition than from the manor houses and rectories and homes of well-to-do merchants—latterly from a Jane Austen world. It hands down the impression of the social life of families in which the wives and daughters weren't too grand to go into the kitchen and to keep a close eye on the vegetable garden and dairy. This was the world in which the great amateur horticulturalist Thomas Andrew Knight in his Herefordshire manor house diversified and improved so many fruits and vegetables in the late years of the eighteenth century and the early years of the nineteenth.

One thing to note is that the great English cookery writers from Hannah Glasse to Elizabeth David have always been women, in contrast to the French tradition of cookery writing by male chefs. Our classical tradition has been domestic, with the domestic virtues of quiet enjoyment and generosity. Whatever happened when the great mass centres developed in the nineteenth century, English cookery books of the eighteenth century to early Victorian times had been written from an understanding of good food and good eating, a concern for quality. Mrs Beeton had her great qualities, and gave many marvellous recipes. But from the first edition of her book in 1859, you can see the anxiety of the new middle class, balanced between wealth and insolvency, and always at pains to keep up appearances. And keeping up appearances remains the *leitmotiv* of much modern food advertising. Showy photographs in what is called 'full' colour and the message, 'Impress your Friends' or 'Impress his Boss' suggest that without taking any trouble or thought at all, marvellous food will fall out of the packet on to the plate. We need to renew and develop the old tradition of Hannah Glasse, Elizabeth Raffald, Maria Rundell and Eliza Acton as far as we can in our changed circumstances. It is no accident, I hope, that these early writers are being reprinted, often in facsimile, and that their dishes appear on the menus of some of our best restaurants as well as in an increasing number of homes.

Soups

The best English soups are unrivalled, but one might wish there were more of them. Soup is a primitive dish. Such soups as mulligatawny and oxtail and mutton broth are continuing good versions of very old ways of cooking meat, at least as old as the first making of metal pots. All the same, soups are capable of great refinement and delicacy, particularly the fish and vegetable soups. They have the advantage of being easy to make, and variable within quite wide limits.

A soup can be a meal, it can be the introduction to a meal. It can be a comfort in itself, or an appetiser. While it is true that most packet and canned soups are reasonably good in comparison with other manufactured foods, they suffer from a sameness of taste (due, I think, to the presence of monosodium glutamate) and a farinaceous texture. The praise for good home-made soup is out of proportion to the effort involved—and it doesn't cost much.

Perhaps the tradition of Dickens and the workhouse, and little boys' bones in the cauldron, and manor house ladies and rectors' wives has somewhat damaged the notion of soup for the

English. Nearly every Victorian cookery book has a recipe for charitable or beneficent soup, to be trotted round the parish by mother and unmarried daughters to the deserving poor. The French chef of the Reform Club, the great Alexis Soyer, caused a sensation by nobly going over to Ireland in the potato famine to save Irish souls with his soup. But soups are a good thing all the same. Palestine soup, pea soup, smoked haddock soup, proper mulligatawny soup are all excellent. And English eel soup and oyster soup are superb; so is the medieval almond soup—a masterpiece of delicacy.

Stock is not essential for vegetable soups—water does as well or better, if the vegetables are fresh and good. Fish stock can be contrived in half an hour from a couple of pounds of fish bones, heads and skin which the fishmonger will give you for nothing. (They should not be cooked for any longer—unless you like your fish soup flavoured with glue.) Which leaves meat stock. If you put meat—meat on the bones, bone being essential to a good soup—into the pot, you do not need to prepare a preliminary stock. Most hearty English soups are of this type— boiling fowl, boiling beef, boiling mutton or lamb which cook gently for hours in water with a few pot herbs. A stock pot is a bad idea outside a professional kitchen, where it can be properly looked after, skimmed, reboiled and used quickly. This is not to say that using the liquor left over from boiling chicken, beef or fish is not a good idea, if you happen to have it. On the whole stock is essential for French consommé, i.e. clear meat soups and jellied meat soups, and not for the general run of English recipes.

It must be admitted that stock cubes are useful, but they should be employed, if at all, in dilute form, at half strength to avoid the preponderance of monosodium glutamate taste. Think of the chicken or beef cube as a seasoning, and not as a substitute for meatiness. Soup cubes, incidentally, are nothing new to the English. Before the days of canning, meat was simmered, and the liquid boiled down and down to a gluey sediment which was cut into small lumps and known as portable soup. Explorers, sailors, and other people on the move added water, hotted the whole thing up, and drank their instant soup.

Fried cubes of bread or crisply fried scraps of bacon add greatly to the pleasure of most soups, and are well worth the trouble. Brandy and port also make a wonderful addition to meat soups, just as a little dry white wine makes all the difference to several of the fish soups. This has been much more of an English practice than you would suppose, going back at least to the Middle Ages. Cream, chopped parsley, chives, egg yolks, a knob of butter are equally good enrichments for vegetable soups. The Welsh—and Scots—chop leeks and add them to meat soups before they are served. The leek softens slightly in the heat without cooking properly, and so retains an agreeable crispness and a light overtone of onion which isn't aggressive.

Almond Soup

For 6

2 oz ground almonds	1 tablespoon cornflour
4 pts chicken or light veal stock	¼ pt single or double cream
Freshly ground white pepper	1 tablespoon lightly salted butter
1 bay leaf	Salt
½ pt milk	2 oz toasted or fried almonds to garnish, or croûtons of fried bread

Simmer the first four ingredients for 30 minutes. Remove the bay leaf. Add the milk, and liquidize the soup to extract maximum flavour and texture from the almonds (in the old days it was a question of sieving repeatedly). Mix the cornflour with the cream and use to thicken the reheated soup, without allowing it to boil (if you do, the almonds will tend to separate from the liquid and turn gritty). Stir in the butter. Taste and correct seasoning. Pour through a fine sieve into the heated soup tureen. Float the almonds on top and serve. If you have chosen croûtons, put two or three in with the soup and serve the rest in a bowl. With this kind of fine delicate flavour, it is most important that the almonds or croûtons should have been fried in butter.

A beautifully white soup which goes back to the cookery of the Middle Ages, the courtly cookery of England and France (the French name is *soupe à la reine*). Almonds then played an even larger part in fine dishes than they do today. As well as its flavour, this soup has the advantage of being made from the kind of ingredients that most people have in the house in summer or winter: perhaps this is another reason why it has survived so many centuries, not just in palaces but in the homes of people of moderate prosperity.

Apple Soup

For 6

2½ pints beef stock
¾ lb good cooking apples, or Cox's
½ teaspoon ginger
¼ teaspoon pepper

plus *either* some boiled rice, *or* 3 oz pearl barley, soaked, and simmered in a little extra beef stock until cooked

Bring the beef stock to the boil, and add the apples roughly chopped, core and all. When they are soft, push the soup through a vegetable mill or sieve. Season it with ginger and pepper, adding a little extra if you like. Mix in the rice or pearl barley and serve very hot.

It is interesting that this soup of most unusual ingredients—unusual in their combination, that is—tastes very clear and refreshing in a way that seems entirely modern. Yet the recipe comes from Eliza Acton's *Modern Cookery* of 1845. Miss Acton attributed it to Burgundy—perhaps she came across it when she spent a year in France after the Napoleonic wars—but it does not appear in any French collections of Burgundian recipes. In the end I came across the original version, in a reprinted manuscript from the Bodleian Library at Oxford, of the beginning of the fifteenth century. It's called *Apple moys*, or apple mush (from the French *mol*, meaning soft): the apples are cooked and sieved and added to 'good fat broth of beef'.

The seasonings were sugar, saffron, and ginger. On fast days, almond 'milk' and olive oil were used instead of beef stock. The rice or pearl barley are more modern additions from the early nineteenth century, but they do go well with the soup.

Broad Bean Soup

For 4

4 oz chopped onion	Salt, pepper, sugar
2 oz butter	4 tablespoons double cream
½ lb shelled broad beans	Croûtons of fried bread
¼ teaspoon chopped sage, savory or parsley	

Soften the onion in the butter, without browning it. Add the beans together with 1¾ pints of water and bring to the boil. Put in whichever herb you choose, together with salt, pepper and ¼ teaspoon of sugar. When the beans are cooked, remove a tablespoon of them, rinse them under the cold tap and peel off the white skins; set them aside. Sieve or liquidize the soup. Add the skinned beans and reheat. Correct the seasoning and add a little more sugar if necessary. Stir in the cream and serve with croûtons.

Chestnut and Apple Soup

For 4

1 lb chestnuts in their shells	2 oz butter
3½ pts light beef stock or water	4 oz single cream
1 stick celery heart	Salt, pepper
2 large Cox's apples, peeled, cored, sliced	Bread croûtons fried in butter

Nick the chestnuts from the centre to the pointed top, at right angles to the base. Boil them in water for 10 minutes, then turn the heat off and remove the chestnuts one by one to peel them. To do this, put your left hand into an open glove to hold the chestnut, then use a small sharp knife to peel off the shell, and then to remove the inner brown skin. If the chestnuts were a good, fat glossy brown to start with, they should be quite easy to deal with. Making a nick from the centre to the pointed end means that the shell peels off much more easily, and the nut in consequence remains more or less intact (though for this recipe, it doesn't matter if the nuts have crumbled into pieces).

Now cook the chestnuts with the stock and celery for about 20 minutes; meanwhile simmer the apple slices in the butter with a good sprinkling of pepper. Liquidize chestnuts, celery and apple with the stock and the buttery apple juices. Taste and correct seasoning. Add the cream. If the soup is too thick for your taste (the thickness will obviously depend on how many chestnuts had to be discarded), dilute it with water. It should not be too heavy in texture, but light, with a faint sharpness from the apples. Serve with croûtons.

Many European chestnut soups are flavoured with bacon, and made on the heavy side. Understandable, when soup had to be the whole meal. This apple and chestnut recipe is more suitable for soup as a first course only.

Green Pea Soup

For 6

8 oz shelled peas
1 medium onion, chopped
2 oz butter
2 rashers smoked streaky bacon, chopped

2 pts chicken or light ham stock, or more (see recipe)
Salt, pepper
Chopped parsley

This soup can be made in wintertime quite successfully with frozen peas, or with dried split *green* peas which have been soaked (4 oz dried peas). In the latter case, the cooking time will have to be prolonged to an hour.

First cook the onion gently in the butter until it begins to soften and turn gold. Add the bacon and fry for another 2 or 3 minutes. Pour in 1 pt of the stock, add the peas and simmer until they are cooked. Liquidize and dilute to taste with more stock, add seasoning to taste—if you are using dried peas it is particularly important not to add salt before they are cooked. Reheat, sprinkle with parsley and serve.

The peculiarly English thing about this soup is the flavour of smoked bacon. It belongs to the tradition of boiled salt pork and pease pudding.

Palestine Soup

For 6

1 lb large Jerusalem artichokes	2½ pts light chicken stock
4 oz chopped onion	2 tablespoons parsley, chopped
1 clove garlic, crushed (optional)	2 oz double cream
1 oz chopped celery	Salt, pepper
4 oz butter	Croûtons
2 rashers unsmoked bacon, chopped	

Artichokes can be peeled raw like potatoes, but as they are so knobbly it is less wasteful to scrub and blanch them in boiling salted water. After 5 minutes, or a little longer, the skins can be removed quite easily (but run the artichokes under the cold tap first). Keep the water they cooked in, unless it tastes very harsh (it does sometimes when the artichokes are becoming old).

Cook onion, garlic and celery in half the butter until soft. Add the bacon and stir about for a few minutes, then the peeled artichokes and 2 pints of the stock. Simmer until the vegetables are cooked. Liquidize or sieve, adding the remaining stock and some of the original cooking water if the soup needs diluting further. Put the remaining butter together with the parsley and cream into a warm soup tureen. Reheat the soup to just under boiling point, correct the seasoning, and pour it into the tureen. Stir it well as you do this, to mix in the butter, cream and parsley. Serve with the croûtons.

Jerusalem artichokes have nothing to do either with Jerusalem or artichokes. When these delicious, warty tubers were introduced into Europe from Canada early in the seventeenth century, their taste was considered to resemble the unrelated globe artichoke's. In Italy, to avoid confusion, the family name was tacked on : the newcomers were distinguished as *girasole*—sunflower—artichokes. We seem to have corrupted *girasole* to Jerusalem, and from Jerusalem artichokes we naturally made Palestine soup.

The French were more deliberately fanciful. Some members of the Brazilian tribe of Tupinamba had been brought to the French court in 1613, and had been a great success, at about the same time as the new vegetable arrived—also from the New World. The name of one bizarre exotic was borrowed for the other—and the French were soon eating *topinambours*, as they still do. Artichokes took so well to Europe that it seemed at one time as if they might provide a basic food for some of the poorer areas. Their flavour, though, was too strong for daily—sometimes thrice-daily—eating; they were soon ousted as a crop by potatoes, and retreated to the kitchen gardens of the middle and upper classes to provide an exquisite winter soup and the occasional purée.

Tomato Soup, hot or chilled

For 4 (hot), for 6–8 (chilled)

3 oz chopped carrot
2 oz chopped onion
1 clove garlic, chopped
2 oz butter
1 lb skinned tomatoes (or 14 oz can)
1¼ pts light beef or chicken stock

Salt, pepper, sugar
Grated nutmeg
2 teaspoons tomato concentrate
5–8 oz single cream
Chopped parsley

Cook the first three ingredients gently in the butter. Keep the lid on the pan so that they do not brown, and allow about 10 minutes. Halve the tomatoes into the pan (add the juices, too, if you are using a tin). When the carrot is cooked, liquidize the soup, and add seasonings to taste—the tomato concentrate will not be necessary if you are using tomatoes grown out of doors in a really hot summer, neither will the sugar.

If the soup is to be served hot, bring 5 oz of cream to the boil just before the meal starts and add the tomato mixture. Reheat without boiling. If the consistency is too thick, add more stock or water. Sprinkle the parsley on top.

If the soup is to be served cold, allow it to cool down and then chill it in a large basin. Stir in 8 oz of the cream. Check the consistency and seasoning—chilled soups need more liquid and more seasoning than hot ones. Chill again, and sprinkle parsley on top just before serving.

One of the finest of all soups. Its clear-tasting richness will surprise and delight anyone who has only known the canned variety.

Oyster or Mussel Soup

For 6

2 dozen large oysters, or 2 lb mussels	Salt, pepper, Cayenne pepper, nut-
4 shallots, chopped	meg
3 oz butter	¼ pt double cream
2 tablespoons flour	Lemon juice to taste
1¼ pts veal stock, or light beef stock	Chopped parsley

To open oysters, first scrub them under the cold tap. Then wrap your left hand (if you are right-handed) in a cloth, pick up the first oyster flat side up and curl your fingers over it. With your right hand, push the blade of an oyster knife (or a short stubby knife) between the two shells at the hinge end. Lever it open. With the tip of the knife, free the oyster from the shells and tip it into a sieve, placed over a basin, so that the juices are saved and separated from the oyster itself.

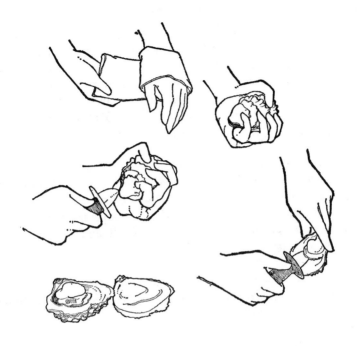

To open mussels, scrub them under the tap, scraping off barnacles, and pulling away the dark thready beard. If any remain obstinately open, or if they are broken, discard them. Put them into a large pan, cover them with the lid and set them over a high heat (no water is usually necessary, but ¼ pt can be added if you like). After five minutes—shake them from time to time—they will have started to open. Remove them with tongs, discard the shells and put the mussels into a sieve set over a basin. Add the juices from the pan to the juices already in the basin.

To make the soup, cook the shallots gently in the butter until they are golden and soft. Stir in flour, moisten with stock and strained shellfish juices. Season with salt, the peppers and nutmeg to taste, and leave to simmer for 20 minutes or so with the lid on the pan. Just before serving, add the shellfish, cream and parsley. Bring up to the boil, pour into a tureen and serve after adding some lemon juice, and checking the seasoning.

Smoked Finnan Haddock Soup

For 4

½ lb Finnan haddock
¾ lb cod, or other white fish
2 oz butter
1 large onion, chopped
Generous tablespoon flour

1 pt milk
3–4 oz cream
Lemon juice, salt, pepper
Chopped parsley

Pour boiling water over the haddock and leave it for 10 minutes. Cut the cod into large cubes. Melt the butter in a large pan, cook the onion in it gently, and when soft add the flour. Cook for a couple of minutes, then moisten with ¼ pt of the haddock water and the milk. Set aside a good tablespoon of haddock flakes, and put the rest—skin, bone, everything—into the pan together with the cod. Simmer for 10 minutes. Remove the bones and liquidize the soup—alternatively leave the fish in pieces, so long as you are fairly confident of having removed all the bones. Reheat the soup to just below boiling point, together with the cream, and more of the haddock water if it needs diluting; fish soups should not be very thick, particularly when they have a delicate flavour like this one. Season to taste with lemon juice, salt and pepper. Stir in the tablespoon of haddock flakes and the parsley. It is important to buy good haddock for a soup of this kind. (See page 76.)

Oxtail Soup

For 6–8

1 large oxtail, cut in pieces
3 stalks celery, chopped
1 onion, stuck with 3 cloves
1 carrot, sliced
1 small turnip, sliced
2 oz butter

1 teaspoon peppercorns
Bouquet garni
4 pts water
2–3 oz port wine
Salt, pepper
1 heaped tablespoon flour (optional)

Always prepare oxtail soup—or oxtail stew, for that matter—the day before it is required. This gives you a chance to skim off the fat completely before finishing the soup; if you do not do this, the flavour is ruined.

Brown the oxtail and vegetables in the butter. Transfer them to a large pan and add the peppercorns, bouquet and water. Season with salt. Bring to the boil and simmer, covered, until the meat is almost dropping off the bones. This can take four hours, or even five.

Strain off the liquor into a bowl. Leave to cool, then place in the refrigerator. Discard the vegetables and bones: keep the pieces of meat, but remove the fat and skin.

Next day, remove the sheet of fat from the liquor. Put the liquor in a pan, with the meat, and bring it to just below boiling point.

If you wish to thicken the soup, mix some of it with the flour, then pour it back into the pan and simmer for five minutes before adding the port, and extra seasoning as required.

Try to avoid buying small, skinny-looking oxtails. They do not take long to cook, it is true, but their flavour is insipid by comparison with an oxtail of decent size.

Cawl (pronounced 'Cowl')

For 6–8

2 lb brisket of beef (or shin, or smoked gammon, or ham, or 1 lb each beef and smoked bacon)
2 large onions
2 or 3 carrots, parsnips, swede, turnips (quantities can be varied according to supply)
1 lb potatoes (preferably new)

2 stalks celery, chopped
small white cabbage, sliced beef dripping or bacon fat
Bouquet garni
2 or 3 leeks
Marigold flowers

Melt the fat in a heavy pan and brown first the meat, then the onions, carrots, parsnips, swede, turnip. Transfer everything to a large pan or casserole when it is nicely browned. Cover with cold water to within 1½" of the rim of the pan;

add a little salt and the chopped celery. Bring slowly to the boil, taking off the scum as it rises. Season with bouquet garni, sea salt and freshly ground black pepper. Transfer to a very low heat and leave to simmer for several hours. The friend from whom I had this recipe says that if the heat is gentle enough, the cawl can be left all day or overnight.

Put the potatoes into the pot half an hour before serving (old potatoes should be cut to new potato size), and the cabbage 10 minutes before serving. Chop the leeks finely, but keep them to one side.

To serve, slice the meat and put it into individual bowls with some of the vegetables and some of the soup. Sprinkle the chopped leeks on top—they will be cooked enough by the time the bowls are on the table—and float a marigold flower in each bowl. Ideally the bowls should either be wooden, or flowery Welsh earthenware.

Cawl may mean no more than soup in Welsh, but as you can see it is more than an elegant mouthful or two as a prelude to a main course. It is soup on the grand peasant scale from the old days of fireplace cookery, a meal in itself. French *pot-au-feu*, *potée* and *garbure* and *hochepot* are its close relatives. This kind of dish has no 'correct' version or original recipe. It varies from region to region, according to the local resources, and from house to house within the same village, even from day to day in the same house. We know who invented Chicken Marengo or Peach Melba, we can never know who made the first cawl or *potée*. We cannot even know in which country they were first made. For most people it was a case of putting into the big iron pot water, and as much else as they could find to flavour it and give it substance. The result in Caernarvon was, and is, obviously different from the result in Gascony or Belgium, but the principle was the same. Cockie-Leekie is the same kind of thing, so is Irish stew. They have survived because they were the best versions of these old one-pot dishes; they were so good that even when families became more prosperous, and had separate kitchens and coal and gas stoves, they did not want to lose them. (The preliminary browning of the meat and vegetables in this recipe is a modern device to enrich the flavour of the cawl—in earlier times, everything went into the pot directly.)

Mutton and Leek Broth

For 4–6

4 oz pearl barley
1½ lb scrag end of neck, chopped in
   pieces
4 pts water
5 oz diced carrot
4 oz diced turnip

1 small stalk celery, chopped
5 oz chopped onion
Salt, pepper, sugar
1 leek, trimmed
Chopped parsley

Wash and soak the pearl barley for 4 hours. Drain it, and put it into a large pot or pan, depending on whether you will be cooking the soup in the oven or on top of the stove. Remove the largest bits of fat from the meat, and add it to the pot with the water. Bring to the boil and simmer gently for an hour. Add the carrot, turnip, celery and onion, with some salt and pepper. Cook for a further hour—longer if you like (this is a good-tempered soup). Towards the end of cooking time, take out the pieces of lamb; the meat will be dropping off the bones, which can be thrown away. Cut the meat up fairly small, and return it to the pot. Skim off surplus fat. Taste and correct the seasoning, adding a little sugar to bring out the flavours; this is a particularly good idea when using lamb, which has less taste than mutton. Finally, chop the leek and put it into the hot soup. Give it a few more bubbles, then sprinkle the parsley on top and serve. The leek will be cooked enough in the heat of the soup, while retaining an agreeable crispness. Wholemeal or granary bread and butter goes well with this kind of broth.

A magnificent soup, quite one of the best and comparable with any of the more famous European soup-stews. Followed by fruit and cheese, it makes a restoring meal at the end of a long, difficult day.

Mulligatawny Soup

For 4–6

1 boiling fowl, or the drumstick and thigh joints of a roasting bird, plus giblets (frozen chickens are no good at all for this recipe)
2 onions, sliced
3 oz butter
curry powder to taste
6–8 oz moist fresh cheese (e.g Gervais 'Jockey' brand fresh cheese) or 1 pot yoghurt
Salt
4 cloves
Juice of 1 large lemon
Boiled rice

Cut the chicken into pieces, brown the onions in 2 oz of butter with the chicken. Stir in the curry, fresh cheese or yoghurt and some salt, and stew for a little while so that the juices turn to a brownish crust on the bottom of the pan. They should not burn, so this needs watching. Pour in 3 pints of water, and leave to cook. Melt the remaining butter in a little pan with the cloves, after a few minutes you will be able to crush them down with a wooden spoon; pour in the lemon juice, mix it all up well and tip into the large pan of soup. Stew for an hour or more depending on the age and toughness of the chicken: the soup is ready when the meat parts easily from the bones, which can then be removed and thrown away. Correct the seasoning, pour into a tureen and serve with a separate bowl of boiled rice. This mulligatawny soup, unlike some of the other recipes, contains no apple, but if you like you can always serve a dish of chopped apple sprinkled with lemon juice to be added to the soup with the rice.

The word mulligatawny means pepper water, and it came into English—like most Indian words—in the eighteenth century, from Tamil, *milakutanni* (*milaku* meaning pepper, and *tanni* water).

CURRY POWDER

If you would like to make a curry mixture of your own, instead of using a proprietary brand, mix together :

4 teaspoons finely chopped onions
1 teaspoon ground turmeric
1 teaspoon ground chili (chili is very hot)
½ teaspoon ground ginger

¼ teaspoon finely chopped garlic
½ teaspoon roasted and ground coriander seed
¼ teaspoon roasted and ground cumin

Turkey and Hazelnut Soup

For 4–6

2½ pts turkey stock
8 oz raw turkey breast, minced
1 large egg yolk
4 oz cream
Fresh or dried chervil

½ teaspoon paprika
Salt, freshly ground black pepper
3 oz grilled, chopped hazelnuts
2 oz butter

Bring the stock to the boil with the turkey breast in it, and simmer for 3 or 4 minutes. Do not allow the turkey to over-cook and become rubbery. Liquidize the soup and then sieve it into a clean pan.

Whisk the egg and cream together, pour in a ladleful of soup, still whisking, and return the whole thing to the pan. Stir over a moderate heat until the soup thickens slightly, but do not allow it to boil. Add the remaining ingredients away from the heat, adjusting the seasonings to your own taste.

Toasted almonds, or peeled boiled chestnuts, both roughly chopped, can be substituted for hazelnuts. At Christmas time, use cooked turkey if you like—for instance, the thigh, which may still be slightly pink—and simmer it for a few moments only so that it is thoroughly reheated but no more.

English Hare Soup

For 6–8

1 young hare, jointed, or head and forequarters of a mature animal
3 oz butter, clarified
4 oz salt belly of pork or green bacon, diced
1 heaped tablespoon flour
½ bottle claret or other red wine
¾ pt beef consommé or stock
1 large onion stuck with a clove

8 oz mushrooms, small if possible
Pinch cayenne pepper
½ teaspoon each mace and black pepper
Bouquet garni, with 4 extra sprigs parsley, plus a sprig each of basil, rosemary, marjoram
Salt

Brown the hare in the clarified butter, together with the pork or bacon. Stir in flour, then wine and stock. Add all the remaining ingredients, except the mushrooms. Simmer until the hare is cooked, 1½ hours for a young animal, 3 hours for an older one. The flesh should be coming away from the bones. Pour the soup into a clean pan through a sieve. Pick out the hare meat and cut into small, conveniently sized pieces. Also remove the pork or bacon. Discard the remaining debris. Simmer the mushrooms in the soup for 10 minutes, correct the seasoning and put in the hare meat and pork or bacon.

If you are using a cheap red wine, a tablespoon of redcurrant jelly, added towards the end of the cooking time, will much improve the flavour. Another alternative is a tablespoon of brown sugar, added gradually to taste.

A recipe from Antonin Carême (1784–1833), the great French chef, who worked for a time for the Prince Regent. He admired several English dishes, including this one, and also gave recipes for sweetbreads on skewers (see page 132), and for cooking sea-kale (page 49).

Cheese & Egg Dishes

English hard cheeses are ideal for cooking, but it is important to use them dry rather than wet, and they are not improved by being purchased in wedges sealed up in plastic. This makes them sweaty and soft and does not improve their flavour. Nor should one put the English hard cheeses into a refrigerator. They are already a specialized form of preserved food. Chilling does not improve the flavour or texture, and they are better kept where it is cool and dry.

Our sad loss throughout England is that we no longer make sheep's milk cheese. In medieval Wiltshire, on the downs, women used to be brought in at the lambing season to milk the ewes and make cheese, and one reason for the Welshness of the Welsh rabbit may be that the Iron Age and Roman Age Welsh were largely a pastoral people moving about and dependent on flocks and herds. Now we have to be content with the small family of hard cow's milk cheeses, excellent as they are.

No other country has developed so rich a variety of excellent hard cheeses as England. We may not have anything so piquant and rich as Parmesan or Pecorino (which is, I agree, a pity), nothing quite so useful and sweet as Gruyère or Emmental, but we do have a marvellous choice—Cheddar, Cheshire, Double Gloucester, Caerphilly, Leicestershire, Derby, Lancashire, Wensleydale, Red Windsor, all with their own character to be learnt and exploited by the cook.

Coming from the north, I find it difficult to be impartial. It must be Wensleydale with apple tart, gingerbread or fruit cake. It must be Lancashire or Cheshire for toasting and making rabbits, or any of the three for a soufflé. If you live in Somerset, and can buy mature farmhouse Cheddar in perfect condition, which is not so easy to do in these days of universal plastic wrappery, your ideas on the subject of cheese for cooking will be very different. And I agree that for a recipe like Little Cheese Puddings (page 26), Cheddar is particularly good.

In fact Cheddar, hard, dry, grated, is the best general-purpose cheese for cooking. For toasting, which includes the rabbits, the cheese to use is white crumbly Lancashire, with Cheshire as second choice. It is worth experimenting with Stilton, particularly in combination with fruit such as pears, because it retains its individuality in cooking.

My own belief is that for eating there is no better English cheese than a farmhouse Double Gloucester in a properly mature and dry condition. Cheese is one of the last substances with individual variations of taste and quality which is worth shopping around for. If possible, go to one of the old-fashioned cheesemongers such as Paxton and Whitfield in Jermyn Street in London, where all the idiosyncracies of cheese are well known and appreciated. On the whole, cheese, like strawberries and celery, is one of the foods which has certainly improved in quality during the nineteenth and twentieth centuries, though it's a pity it is often sold too young.

Eggs, too, have improved, at any rate in size. If you have one of the old egg-shaped steamers which were made for the breakfast tables of 1900 or 1880, you will find that if it was made for four eggs the lid won't fit down over four modern standard eggs. It's worth remembering this difference in the size of eggs if you happen to be making, say, a sponge cake from an old recipe. Such an old recipe may say, in what seems a grandiose manner, 'Take sixteen eggs'. The sixteen eggs of 1840 or whatever the year can safely be reduced to about ten or twelve modern eggs (on top of that you can safely reduce all the quantities by half, eggs included, since there will be half the number of people in your own family). Whether the modern battery egg has improved in flavour is another matter, but it its certainly true that eggs remain one of the best buys wherever you are.

By and large the best accompaniments of eggs, however you cook them, are sea salt, freshly-ground black pepper, cream, good butter and good bread—or toast made from good bread, and not from the pre-sliced flannel variety. Egg dishes should be nothing if not a combination of simplicity, purity and richness. As to omelettes, it shouldn't be thought that if you cook an omelette, you are being French. The omelette (including cheese omelettes) was a regular dish in the English Middle Ages when it was called a fraysse.

The splendid affinity between eggs and cheese hardly needs mentioning. One good point is that they conveniently cook at about the same rate.

Glamorgan Sausages

For 4

5 oz grated Caerphilly or Lancashire cheese
4 oz fresh white breadcrumbs
2 tablespoons finely chopped spring onion, or leek
3 egg yolks
1 heaped tablespoon chopped parsley
½ teaspoon thyme
1 level teaspoon mustard powder
Salt, pepper
1 egg white
Extra breadcrumbs
Lard for frying

Mix the cheese, breadcrumbs and spring onion, or leek. Whisk the yolks, herbs, mustard and seasoning together—use about 1 teaspoon of salt, and plenty of pepper—and add to the breadcrumbs and cheese to make a coherent mixture. If the bread-crumbs or cheese were on the dry side, you may need another yolk or a little water, before everything hangs together as it should. Divide into twelve and roll each piece into a small sausage about 2″ long. Dip them in egg white, roll in the extra breadcrumbs and fry until golden brown in lard.

If you have an electric vegetable chopper of the kind made by Moulinex, this dish can be made very quickly. Reduce the bread, spring onion or leek and parsley to fine crumbs together. Then the cheese, with the thyme and mustard powder. Bind with the egg yolk in a basin and season to taste.

There are many recipes for Glamorgan sausages. The in-gredients are always the same, but the proportions vary. Some-times there is twice as much cheese as breadcrumbs. Sometimes the breadcrumbs exceed the cheese by a third. Sometimes onion is used rather than spring onion or leek. The Welsh serve these sausages with potato, but I think this is too much stodge. They are delicious on their own, or with grilled tomato, as a supper dish, or first course.

Rabbits

WELSH RABBIT

For 2

4 oz grated Lancashire, Cheddar or Double Gloucester cheese	Pepper, salt
3 tablespoons milk or ale	1 teaspoon made mustard, or Tewkesbury, or Urchfont mustard
1 oz butter	2 slices toasted bread

Put the cheese and milk or ale into a small heavy pan. Stir it over a low to moderate heat until the mixture quietly melts to a thick cream. Add the butter, pepper, salt and mustard. Taste, and adjust the seasoning (you may, for instance, like more mustard). Put it back over the heat, until it is very hot but below boiling point. Put the two pieces of toast on to a heat-proof serving dish, pour the cheese over them and place under a very hot grill until the cheese bubbles and becomes brown in appetising-looking splashes. The cheese will overflow the edges of the toast. Serve immediately, with a glass of red wine or ale.

SCOTCH RABBIT (1747)

'Toast a piece of bread very nicely on both sides, butter it, cut a slice of cheese about as big as the bread, toast it on both sides, and lay it on the bread.'

ENGLISH RABBIT (1747)

'Toast a slice of bread brown on both sides, then lay it in a place before the fire, pour a glass of red wine over it, and let it soak the wine up; then cut some cheese very thin, and lay it very thick over the bread, and put it in a tin oven before the fire, and it will be toasted and brown'd presently. Serve it away hot.'

Use the grill; and pile the slivers of cheese up to about $\frac{1}{4}''$ depth on the wine-soaked bread.

GLOUCESTERSHIRE CHEESE AND ALE

Slice single or Double Gloucester cheese into thin pieces. Lay them in an ovenproof dish and spread mustard over them in a thin layer—use Tewkesbury mustard (*La Favorite* brand) if you can, or one of the Urchfont mustards from Wiltshire which have the fieriness of English mustard combined with the attractive mustard-seed texture of French *moutarde de Meaux*. Pour in enough ale just to cover the cheese. Put into a moderately hot oven until the cheese is soft and deliciously melted. Meanwhile toast some wholemeal or granary bread, pour over some heated ale, just enough to moisten the toast slightly, and then spoon the cheese mixture on top. Serve with ale.

Little Cheese Puddings

¼ pt white or granary breadcrumbs
¼ pt grated Cheddar cheese
½ pt milk
2 eggs, beaten lightly

2 teaspoons made mustard (Tewkes-
    bury and Urchfont are good, too)
Salt, freshly ground black pepper
Butter

Mix the crumbs and cheese so that they are evenly distributed—
this is best done with the hands. Mix in the milk, eggs and
seasonings to taste. More mustard is a good idea, if you like
it with cheese. Butter eight small soufflé dishes or ramekins fairly
generously. Divide the mixture between them, leaving room for
it to rise. Put into the oven at mark 3, 325° for 30–40 minutes,
until risen and golden brown on top. Serve immediately. The
outsides of the little puddings should be brown, crisper than a
soufflé, softer than a Yorkshire pudding; the inside is an in-
terestingly granular cream.

In matters of cookery, the English are often their own worst
enemies. I came across this recipe not so long ago in an enormous
undated cookery book, which could have been published during
the first twenty-five years of this century. The leaden syllables
Cheese Pudding, took me back to a war-time childhood, when
this concoction used to appear on the table in a battered enamel
pie dish at supper. Made then with marge, dried egg and
mousetrap, it went down without comment. But made with
butter, fresh eggs and Cheddar, in small pots, it was greeted
with enthusiasm—it looked elegant and tasted delicious.

Lockets Savoury

For 4

8 small slices white bread
1 large bunch watercress
4 ripe pears (Doyenné du Comice
    are best)

12 oz Stilton cheese, sliced
Freshly ground black pepper

Toast the bread and cut off the crusts. Put the slices into four
ovenproof dishes, or one large one.' Arrange the watercress

evenly on top, and then the thinly-sliced, peeled and cored pears. Cover with the Stilton slices. Put into a mark 4, 350°, oven for 5 to 10 minutes, until the cheese begins to melt and the pears release their aromatic flavours. Grind black pepper on top before serving.

In Florence years ago I learnt how delicious cheese is with pears, a combination as popular there as apple tart with cheese in Yorkshire. All kinds of cheese go with pears, Brie, cream cheeses, Gorgonzola, Roquefort and Stilton. And so does black pepper; it was quite commonly used to bring out the flavour of fruit in the Middle Ages (and still is in some parts of France, where they make a peppered pear tart—or rather pie). This recipe, though, is a modern one, and a speciality of Locket's restaurant in London.

Potted Cheese

8 oz grated Cheshire cheese	Pinch Cayenne pepper
3 oz unsalted butter	Walnut halves
About 2 tablespoons port or brown sherry	

Mix the cheese and butter to a paste. Flavour it with the wine and pepper. Pot and decorate with the walnut halves. If the potted cheese is to be kept for a while, omit the walnuts and cover with a layer of clarified butter.

There are many recipes for potted cheese in English cookery books, from Hannah Glasse onwards. She mixed 3 lb of Cheshire cheese with half a pound of butter, and flavoured it with a quarter-pint of rich Canary wine and half an ounce of powdered mace. 'A slice of this exceeds all the cream cheeses that can be made.'

Other writers have flavoured the cheese with dry or made mustard, with Chili vinegar or Worcester sauce. The proportions of butter to cheese have fluctuated from Hannah Glasse's 8 oz to 3 lb of cheese, to Michael Smith's equal quantities and to an equal quantity of sherry (in *Fine English Cookery*, Faber, 1973). I follow the recipe in *Pottery*, by 'A Potter' (in fact, Cyril Connolly's father), which was published by the Wine and Food Society in 1946, but use Cayenne pepper instead of Chili vinegar. 'A Potter' points out that Stilton or Wensleydale can be used—they must be moistened with port. Gorgonzola or Roquefort should be flavoured with chopped chives and pepper: egg yolk and port or sherry provide the softening element.

Rolls filled with Cheese and Tomato Paste

6 bridge rolls, about 4″ long	1 egg, beaten
Paste	2 oz grated Cheddar cheese
1 small onion, chopped fine	Extra breadcrumbs (see recipe)
2 oz butter	Salt, pepper, sugar
3 ripe tomatoes, skinned, chopped	1 tablespoon chopped parsley

Split the bridge rolls, and remove as much of the crumb as you can without piercing the outside of the rolls. Keep the breadcrumbs as you will need them for the paste.

To make the paste, cook the onion gently in the butter in a small pan until it begins to soften. Add the tomatoes, which should be the firm and well-flavoured kind. Simmer for 15 minutes or more, uncovered, until the mixture becomes fairly thick. Whisk in the egg, and continue to cook over a low heat so that the paste thickens further without boiling. Remove the pan from the stove. Stir in the cheese and breadcrumbs from the rolls—if the paste is rather sloppy, add some extra breadcrumbs. Season with salt and pepper, and a little sugar if the tomatoes were the greenhouse kind. Lastly mix in the parsley.

Fill the rolls generously with this mixture. It makes an excellent picnic dish.

Cheese Soufflé

Soufflé:
2 oz butter
1½ oz flour
½ pt milk
4 large egg yolks
3 oz Cheddar or Lancashire cheese, grated
½ teaspoon salt
Freshly ground black pepper
Good pinch Cayenne pepper

5 egg whites
1 tablespoon Parmesan cheese, grated

½ oz butter
1 tablespoon breadcrumbs from stale bread
1 tablespoon grated Parmesan cheese

First choose a dish of about 2½ pts capacity—a soufflé dish, a Pyrex dish, or a charlotte mould. If the capacity is less than 2½ pts, tie a piece of oiled greaseproof paper or foil firmly round the outside, so that it sticks up about 2″. Staple the overlap or tether it with a paperclip. This helps the soufflé to rise dramatically above a too-small dish. It should be removed quickly before the soufflé is served.

Next turn the oven to mark 6, 400°F, and place a baking sheet on the centre shelf.

To make the soufflé, melt the butter in a moderate-sized pan, stir in the flour and cook for a few moments. Keep stirring. Have the milk at boiling point. Remove the flour and butter roux from the heat and tip in the milk all at once. Beat steadily with a small wire whisk until smooth. Still off the heat, add the egg yolks one by one, beating them in thoroughly. Mix in the English cheese and seasonings. Reheat until everything is warmed through, but keep the mixture well below boiling point.

Whisk egg whites with a pinch of salt until they stand in peaks on the whisk. They should also bear the weight of an egg. Or you can turn the basin upside down—needless to say the whites should not fall out.

Stir a tablespoon of white into the soufflé mixture fairly thoroughly to soften it. Then tip in the rest of the whites, and fold the two mixtures gently together with a spatula or metal spoon. Scrape and lift up the mixture from the bottom of the pan. The whites should lose as little of their lightness as possible, so do not go on too long. A *few* small concentrations of white won't hurt.

Turn the mixture into the prepared soufflé dish. Sprinkle the top with the Parmesan and breadcrumbs mixed together. Place the dish on the heated baking tray in the oven. Shut the door and do not open it for 30 minutes—this will give you a delicious soufflé with a creamy inside.

If everyone is not sitting in their places, as they should be, turn the heat down to mark 1, 275°. The soufflé should be all right for another 10 minutes. On the whole, though, it is better to have everyone at table. In a properly-trained household, the cry of 'Soufflé!' should have the same effect of assembly as 'Fire!'

OTHER FLAVOURINGS

Fish

2 oz onion or shallot, chopped and cooked down gently in 2 oz butter. Add 8 oz cooked, minced fish, or soft roes, or shellfish. Season with appropriate herbs. Add to soufflé instead of the grated Lancashire or Cheddar cheese.

Smoked fish

6–8 oz smoked salmon scraps, or any cooked, smoked fish, finely chopped.

Meat

Cook 2 oz onion or shallot in 2 oz butter, as for fish. Add 6–8 oz prepared, blanched and minced sweetbreads, or cooked, puréed brains. Or minced cooked poultry, or ham. Plus herbs.

Vegetables

1 oz onion and 1 clove garlic cooked in butter, as for fish. Mix with 6–8 oz cooked, drained vegetables reduced to a purée. Spinach and turnip are very successful. With mushrooms, chop them, and cook them with the onion and garlic once they are soft and golden.

Little Cheese Soufflés

For 8 as a first course
For 4 as a supper or lunch dish

4 large eggs
¼ pt each single and double cream
8 oz Lancashire cheese, grated
Salt, pepper

Pinch Cayenne pepper
Grated nutmeg to taste
2 tablespoons breadcrumbs

Whisk the eggs thoroughly, then mix in the creams. Set aside two tablespoons of the cheese and add the rest to the eggs and cream. Season with salt and pepper, Cayenne pepper and nutmeg. Grease 8 small soufflé dishes or ramekins with a butter paper. Divide the mixture between them, allowing a half-inch space between it and the rim of the dishes as the mixture will rise. Mix the 2 tablespoons of cheese with the breadcrumbs and scatter them over the top. Bake at mark 6, 400°, for 20–25 minutes, until the soufflés are well risen and slightly browned. Serve immediately with thin slices of bread baked in the oven until crisp.

A Fricassee of Eggs

For 8 as a first course

8 large fresh eggs
8 large sprigs parsley
6 oz lightly salted butter
¼ pt double cream

¼ pt soured cream
Salt, freshly ground black pepper
Slices of baked bread, or triangles of
    toast

Put eggs into fast-boiling water for 8 minutes. Run them under the cold tap, and shell and quarter them. Arrange in 8 little soufflé dishes or ramekins. Meanwhile chop the parsley leaves. Then melt the butter in an 8″ frying pan (do not use an ordinary saucepan, as there must be a large surface for evaporation): when it is melted and gently bubbling, stir in the creams with a wooden spoon. Keep on stirring for a minute or two, until the butter and creams amalgamate and reduce to a thick sauce. Add the parsley, season to taste, and pour over the eggs. Tuck triangles of toast into the dishes, or serve the baked bread on a separate plate. Eat immediately.

This recipe comes straight from Hannah Glasse. All I have added is parsley. In the days before pasteurization, cream rapidly developed a sharp tang, which is why I use a mixture of double and soured cream. Another solution is to use all double cream, plus a final seasoning of lemon juice. The lovely richness of the sauce suggests an idyllic countryside, cows in a pasture with summer flowers, and a steady sound of bees. An interesting thing is that one still finds it on menus in Normandy and the Sarthe, served with trout and other fine fish, or with boiled chicken and rice.

Curried Eggs

For 4–6

12 eggs	1 pt stock
1 large onion, chopped	¼ pt cream
2 oz butter	1 tablespoon arrowroot or cornflour
1 tablespoon curry powder	Salt

Hard boil and shell the eggs. Cut them in half. To make the sauce, cook the onion gently in the butter until soft and golden. Stir in the curry powder, then the stock. Simmer steadily until the sauce is reduced to a good flavour—about half an hour. Mix the cream with the arrowroot or cornflour, add to the sauce and stir until thickened. Taste and add salt if necessary. Put in the eggs to heat, but do not allow them to boil. Serve with boiled rice.

Mrs Raffald's Bacon and Egg Pie

For 4–6

6–8 oz bacon	Salt, pepper
4 large eggs	12 oz shortcrust pastry
¼ pt double cream	Beaten egg to glaze

Cut up the bacon into pieces. Beat the eggs and cream together and season them with salt and pepper. Use a little more than half the pastry to line a flat tin or large pie plate. Put in the bacon, then the egg custard. Cover the pie in the usual way, pressing the edges close together. Brush with beaten egg and bake at mark 6, 400°, for 50 minutes. It is best eaten warm.

Apart from the double pastry crust, this is an exact equivalent of the *quiche lorraine*, and the ancestor of our modern bacon and egg pies (which are ruined by the substitution of milk for cream). The double crust makes this pie very suitable for picnics and packed lunches: at more elegant meals, follow the French example and bake it as a flan without the upper crust.

Wyau Ynys Mon (Anglesey Eggs)

For 4–5

1¼ lb potatoes	2 oz, plus 2 tablespoons grated
6 medium-sized leeks	Cheddar cheese
3 oz butter	8 hard-boiled eggs, shelled, quar-
1 tablespoon flour	tered
½ pt hot milk	Salt, pepper

First scrub and boil the potatoes, then peel them and put them through the vegetable mill. Secondly, trim and clean the leeks. Then chop them roughly and swish them about in a bowl of water to dislodge any remaining grit. Remove them to a colander, then into a saucepan with 1 oz butter—the leeks should retain just enough water to enable them to stew gently with the butter, without burning, *so long as the pan is covered tightly*. When the leeks are done, crush them into their cooking juices which should not be abundant.

Meanwhile, as the vegetables cook, make the cheese sauce. Melt the second ounce of butter in a small pan, stir in the flour, cook for 2 minutes. Tip in the milk, whisking all the time to avoid lumps. Cook for 10 minutes at least—better still 20.

Amalgamate the potato and leeks and beat in the remaining ounce of butter; add salt and pepper. The mixture should be light and a beautiful pale green with green flecks. Put it around the edge of an oval gratin dish, or similar ovenproof dish. Put the eggs in the middle.

Add the 2 oz of cheese to the sauce, correct the seasoning and pour over the eggs. Scatter the remaining cheese over the top and bake in a hot oven until golden brown—mark 6, 400°. Serve on its own as a supper dish; or for lunch with slices of cold ham.

The sauce is improved and lightened by the addition of some grated nutmeg. Anglesey Eggs are a homely dish, uplifted by the mixture of leeks with potato, which is delicious.

Oeufs Mollets Christophe

For 4

4 large fresh eggs	4 oz smoked cod's roe
4 small slices smoked salmon	4 oz double cream
4 slices buttered wholemeal bread	Pepper

Plunge the eggs into fast-boiling water. Leave for 6 minutes precisely (7 if they are extra large). Put under the cold tap, and when they are cool enough to handle, crack them all over gently with a wooden spoon and leave for a couple of hours before peeling. This allows the white to firm up, so that there is less risk of the slightly runny yolk bursting through. Place each egg on a slice of smoked salmon. Cut the bread into circles, and remove a circle of bread from the centre, so that you have four bread rings. Place the eggs and smoked salmon on them and arrange on plates. Beat cream and roe until very thick, season with pepper to taste. Spoon this sauce over the eggs, and serve with extra wholemeal bread and butter.

Occasionally when one goes out for a meal, some dish appears which is so delicious and so simple that one is angry not to have thought of it oneself. This dish is a speciality of a restaurant at Ramsbury, in Wiltshire, called The Bleeding Horse (it was once an old inn). The 'Christophe' of the title is the original owner of the restaurant, and the inventor of the dish, Christopher Snow.

Asparagus and Eggs

½–¾ lb asparagus tips
4 slices bread
Butter

8 eggs
Salt, pepper

Cook the asparagus tips in boiling, salted water (keep the thicker ends of the stalks for soup). Drain them well and put in a warm place. Toast the bread, butter it and lay it on a hot dish. Beat the eggs with salt and pepper. Scramble them with a generous tablespoon of butter, keeping them creamy. Arrange three-quarters of the asparagus on the toast, pour the egg on top and decorate with remaining asparagus.

A favourite dish for people who grow their own vegetables, as this simple treatment shows off their fresh flavour well. Purple sprouting broccoli, tiny new peas, artichoke bottoms can all be used instead of asparagus. French recipes often add a flavouring of mustard, chopped herbs such as parsley and chives, and a spoonful of thick cream. A good variation.

Asparagus Omelette

For 6

¾ lb cooked, trimmed asparagus
Butter
2 tablespoons grated Gruyère cheese

9 eggs
Salt, pepper
Chopped parsley, chives

Set aside a few of the best stalks of the asparagus to decorate the dish. Keep the rest warm in the oven—dot them with butter and sprinkle them with cheese, then put a foil covering over them. To make the omelette, beat the eggs vigorously until not a trace of white remains—this should not take long. Add seasoning and a tablespoon of chopped herbs.

Unless you are used to making omelettes, you will find it easier to make three rather than one large one. And if all you have is an 8″ omelette pan, then you will have no choice in the matter. Heat the pan, run a small knob of butter over it, then pour in a third of the mixture. Allow it to set firm beneath, and brown a little, before placing a third of the asparagus across the centre—which should still be slightly liquid. Flip the omelette in half, slide on to a serving dish, and make the remaining omelettes as quickly as possible. It follows that the first omelette should be really moist in the middle, as it has to wait around for the next two to be cooked, and it will go on cooking in its own heat.

Put the reserved asparagus around the omelettes and serve immediately.

Mushroom Omelette

For 6

¾ lb field or cultivated mushrooms	9 eggs
1 medium onion, chopped	Chopped parsley, chives
2 oz butter	Extra butter
Salt, pepper	

Trim any earthy or blemished bits from the wild mushrooms. Rinse them quickly, and slice them. Cook the onion slowly in 1 oz of butter in a frying pan—it should soften to a golden colour. Add the mushrooms, and, as their juices begin to flow, turn up the heat, so that by the time they are cooked they are bathed in a small amount of liquid only.

Make the omelette, and fill it with the mushrooms, as in the preceding recipe.

Vegetables

The vegetable garden did not become widely important in English life until the eighteenth century, and then under the influence in particular of the Dutch and the French, France and the Low Countries having in turn derived their gardening skills from Italy. There are plenty of vegetable names of foreign origin to remind us of this—Brussels sprouts, savoys, broccoli, artichoke, shallot. Often some of the vegetables from the New World reached us via Spain, Italy and France—at any rate in improved forms.

If England has a poor reputation for cooking vegetables, the fault isn't with the often excellent cookery writers of the eighteenth and early nineteenth century, who well understood the preparation of vegetables with a rich or piquant sauce—and weren't given to drowning them with gallons of water. This was before the era of meat and two veg.—and on the whole before the era of the limp vegetables of the greengrocer. London was once a smallish city surrounded by nursery gardens and asparagus beds. Our great contribution—see page 49—was the transference of sea-kale from the South-country beaches

37

to the garden. Mushrooms were also cultivated in England much earlier than one would think—for instance, in the stone mines around Bath. Carême, the French chef who worked for the Prince Regent, commented on the 'sikel' of the London markets which he found very appetising, and he was impressed, too, by the way the cultivated mushrooms were presented for sale, clean, kept white with lemon juice and their stalks neatly cut around. At present one of the sad things is that, for all our splendid modern diversification of the potato, housewives as a rule can only buy such heavy croppers as King Edwards and Majestic which have a relatively poor taste. Proper salad potatoes with a yellow waxy flesh that holds together are almost impossible to find. Back to the garden, or nothing. That's the story of too many vegetables.

The favourite vegetables of the English and Welsh, or perhaps one should say the most eaten, are leeks, onions, potatoes, turnips, carrots, beetroot, peas and broad beans, and the different kinds of cabbage including cauliflower, which was introduced in the seventeenth century along with celery, Jerusalem artichokes, and much else. The history of the improved garden parsnip is obscure; but the parsnip has been another of the English favourites roasted with beef or mashed with salt cod and Friday fish. It's the fashion to decry parsnip—and to cook it carelessly—but with butter and cream and an edge of onion flavour and parsley, and with proper attention, it is one of the best of vegetables, making a good dish on its own. The point with parsnip is to make modified use of its strong, sweet flavour.

Another vegetable unjustly despised is beetroot, from an excess of cold beetroot submerged in malt vinegar. Beetroot is delicious baked in its skin rather than boiled, and then served hot with orange and lemon juice or a cream sauce which includes cream, or cold with vinaigrette and chopped chives. And though this is a book of English cooking, I may at least mention that beetroot is the basis of one of the better and most beautiful-coloured of all European soups, the bortsch of Russia and Eastern Europe.

There are a few wild vegetables not at all to be despised—

not counting the field mushroom and the equally good horse mushroom—hop shoots from the wild plant or the hop garden cooked in bundles and served with butter like asparagus, young nettles used like spinach for soup or purée, comfrey leaves cooked in batter as fritters—these are first rate. And we may include at least one seaweed—laverbread—as a quality vegetable to serve with roast leg of lamb or lobster. Nowadays it seems to be mostly eaten on either side of the Severn Sea. It can be bought from fishmongers and markets for instance in Barnstaple, Bristol, Cardiff, Swansea. The main Cardiff store, James Howell Ltd, St Mary Street, Cardiff, Glamorganshire, sends it to customers all over Great Britain.

Asparagus and Melted Butter

Per person

10 stalks of asparagus	1 oz melted butter
Salt, pepper	Lemon juice

Trim the asparagus so that the stalks are all the same length (keep the trimmings for soup). Remove the hard outer skin from the stalks with a potato peeler. Tie the asparagus in a bundle with string. Put an inch of boiling water into a pan, with salt and pepper, and stand the asparagus in it so that the delicate heads are steamed. If you do not have a tall asparagus pan, arrange a domed lid of foil over the pan. The asparagus will take between 20 and 40 minutes, depending on its thickness.

You might well copy the French habit of cooking new potatoes with the asparagus, so that they take on extra flavour from the water. The two can be served together with great success, particularly if you are a little short on asparagus.

Flavour the melted butter with salt and pepper, and a squeeze of lemon juice, and serve it in a separate jug. It has also become an English habit to serve asparagus with hollandaise sauce, or with mayonnaise if it is to be eaten cold. Recipes are given on pages 287–8.

Broad Beans in their Pods

For 4

2 lb young broad beans, about 3″ long
Salt, pepper

6 oz melted butter
Lemon juice

Top and tail the broad beans, which should be freshly picked and really young. Boil them in a pan of salted water until they are tender—test them after 15 minutes. Strain off the water, pepper the beans and put them on to a hot serving dish. Sharpen the butter with the lemon juice, heat it to just below boiling point and put it into a separate small jug.

Beans cooked in this way make a good first course. They can be eaten like asparagus, in the fingers, or with knives and forks.

Peas from the garden can be cooked and served in the same way. They should not be too old. With peas the presence of a tough white inner skin means that they really must be eaten in the fingers, so that the outer green part and inner steamed peas can be sucked off all together. A dish for friends who are not too inhibited at table.

Pease Pudding

1 lb dried split peas or whole peas
2 oz butter

1 large egg
Salt, pepper

Nowadays many dried vegetables do not need soaking before they are cooked, so much has the quality been improved. If, though, they have been in your storage cupboard for a few months, it is wise to allow three hours' soaking time and to add 1 level teaspoon of bicarbonate of soda to the water if it is at all hard.

To cook the peas, drain them if they have been soaked, then put them into a pan. Cover them with plenty of water and simmer until tender. Split peas will take from 45–60 minutes,

whole dried peas will need at least 2 hours. Drain off the liquid
—keep it for soup—and put the beans through a mouli-legumes
to make a purée which is not too smooth. Mix in the butter,
then the egg and season it well. Put the mixture into a buttered
basin and steam for an hour. Turn it out and serve it with
boiled salt pork.

In the past, pease pudding would be tied into a cloth, and
cooked in with the boiling meat. It is still a most popular dish
in the north of England. Any left over can be fried and eaten
another day, which makes it a welcome dish in poor house-
holds—

> *Pease pudding hot! Pease pudding cold!*
> *Pease pudding in the pot*
> *Nine days old.*

Purée of Dried Peas with Green Peppercorns

1 lb split, dried *green* peas
1 onion, chopped
1 carrot, sliced
Bouquet garni

Large knob butter
About 1 tablespoon green pepper-
corns
Salt, sugar

Soak the peas if necessary. Drain and put with enough
water to cover them generously into a pan, plus the vegetables
and herbs. But, *do not add salt*, because it hardens dried vegetables. Bring to the boil and simmer until cooked. Drain off the
liquid, put the peas and vegetables through a food mill and mix
in the butter. Season with salt to taste, and a little sugar, and
the green peppercorns with a little of the juice from the can—if
you are not used to them, start by adding a teaspoonful and see
how you like the flavour. Very good with duck and pork.

This very English purée of peas is much improved by green peppercorns, which are sold in tins at good grocers and delicatessen shops. They are the fresh peppercorns from the pepper vine, which are canned green instead of being dried to the familiar aromatic and wrinkled blackness. The flavour is quite different, peppery of course, but far more juicy and green-tasting. If you ever see sprays of the fresh green berries, they are even better than the tinned ones. Peppercorns are an excellent spice, too, for steak, sausages and sausage meat stuffings.

Celery with Cream

Wash, clean and trim three heads of celery. Cut them into pieces about 3″ long, boil them in salted water until just tender, then pour off the water. Beat ¼ pt of cream with 2 egg yolks and seasoning. Add this mixture to the hot celery and stir over a low heat until the sauce thickens without boiling. Serve immediately.

Wild celery is a common plant in many parts of Europe, but it wasn't until the sixteenth century that Italian gardeners had the idea of blanching it to remove the bitter flavour, and make it a good vegetable for the table. It was introduced into England about the middle of the seventeenth century, and soon became a popular salad. This recipe from the middle of the eighteenth century shows how delicious a cooked vegetable celery can be when combined with a rich sauce.

Chestnuts as a Vegetable

For 4

1 lb chestnuts
1 large onion, chopped
1 clove garlic, chopped fine
2 oz butter
2 oz bacon, cut into strips (smoked or green, according to taste and the main item of the meal)

2 Cox's eating apples, peeled, cored, diced
Salt, plenty of black pepper

Peel the chestnuts (see page 8), and chop them coarsely into knobbly pieces about ¼ inch long. Cook onion and garlic slowly in the butter in a covered pan, until they are golden and transparent. Stir in the bacon; raise the heat slightly but be careful that the butter does not burn. When the bacon looks transparent, add the diced apple. Fry for a few minutes until the mixture looks and smells savoury and appetising. Lastly add the chestnuts and cook until they are thoroughly heated through, and the pan juices reduced to a small amount of liquid. Season, particularly with pepper, and serve with chicken, guineafowl, turkey and game—or with pork, salt pork and veal.

This mixture can be used to stuff a bird before it is roasted. Or it can serve as a garnish.

If the apple is omitted, it makes a particularly good dish when mixed with boiled brussels sprouts or lightly cooked cabbage. For a first course, or a supper dish, blanch 20–24 cabbage leaves in boiling salted water for 10 minutes. Put a good tablespoon of the above mixture into each leaf; roll the leaves up into little packages, turning the sides in, and place them in a single layer in a large pan. Pour enough light stock or water to come $\frac{1}{4}$ inch up the pan. Cover and simmer for 30 minutes. Reduce the pan liquid to a few tablespoons and beat in 2 oz butter. Pour over the rolls and serve.

Cucumber Ragoût

For 4

2 cucumbers, sliced, unpeeled	3 tablespoons dry white wine
2 medium to large onions, sliced	Salt, pepper, mace
Butter	1 dessertspoon flour
8 tablespoons chicken stock	

Brown the cucumbers and onions lightly in butter in two separate pans. Drain them and put them together into a saucepan with the stock and wine and seasonings. Cover the saucepan tightly, and simmer the vegetables until they are cooked—about 10 minutes or a little longer. Meanwhile mash the flour to a paste with a dessertspoon of butter. Add this mixture, bit by bit, to the vegetables so that the juices become a thick sauce

which is just enough to bind them together. Correct the seasoning and serve, either on its own or as an accompaniment to
chicken, veal or lamb.

The white wine gives this vegetable dish a light piquancy which
is delicious. An exceptionally good and unusual recipe.

Leek Pie

Pastry   3 oz butter
1 lb puff or shortcrust pastry   1 lb leeks, trimmed and sliced
Beaten egg to glaze   4 oz back bacon rashers
                                        4 oz clotted or double cream
Filling   1 heaped teaspoon flour
1 onion, sliced   Salt, pepper

First prepare the filling: cook the onion gently in half the
butter in a frying pan. When it is soft and golden, add the
leeks (there should be from 10 to 12 oz of them, once the waste
has been cut away), and the remaining butter. Continue to cook
slowly until the leeks are reduced to a soft mass. Take the pan
off the heat, add the bacon cut into $\frac{1}{4}''$ strips. Mix the flour
with the cream and beat the mixture into the leeks so that
everything is smoothly amalgamated. Season thoroughly.

Line an 8″–9″ tart tin, preferably the kind with a removable
base, with just over half the pastry. Put in the filling. Brush the
rim with a little beaten egg and cover with a pastry lid. Make
a hole in the centre for the steam to escape. Decorate in a
restrained manner and brush over the top with beaten egg.
Put into the oven at mark 7, 425°, for about 15 minutes until
the pastry is nicely browned, and in the case of puff pastry, well
risen. Reduce the heat to mark 4, 350°, for a further 20–30
minutes.

Variations of this pie occur in Cornwall, Wales, Burgundy,
Picardy and Flanders. I confess that the onion and the flour are
two additions made by a young French friend in Touraine, but

they are such a good idea it seems a shame not to take them over from her. However, no one can deny that leeks are a thoroughly English dish—think of the many leek place names indicating the existence of the all-important leek-enclosure (a more sympathetic idea than the Scottish kail—cabbage—yard).

A White Fricassey of Mushrooms

'Take a Quart of fresh Mushrooms, make them clean, put them into a Sauce-pan, with three Spoonfuls [tablespoonfuls] of Water and three of Milk, and a very little Salt, set them on a quick Fire and let them boil up three Times; then take them off, grate in a little Nutmeg, put in a little beaten Mace, half a Pint of thick Cream, a Piece of butter rolled well in Flour [Beurre Manié], put it all together into the Sauce-pan, and Mushrooms all together, shake the Sauce-pan well all the Time. When it is fine and thick, dish them up; be careful they don't curdle. You may stir the Sauce-pan carefully with a Spoon all the Time.'

This recipe comes from Hannah Glasse, When using the beurre manié, i.e. a tablespoon of butter mashed with the same of flour—add it to the sauce bit by bit. Do not allow the sauce to boil : it will thicken in 5 minutes or even less. The sauce is unlikely to curdle with modern pasteurized cream.

Mushrooms, or the Pearl of the Fields

In his *Shilling Cookery for the People*, first published in 1845, Alexis Soyer, the great chef of the Reform Club, describes a good method of cooking field mushrooms :

'Being in Devonshire, at the end of September and walking across the fields before breakfast to a small farmhouse, I found three very fine mushrooms, which I thought would be a treat, but on arriving at the house I found it had no oven, a bad gridiron and a smoky coal fire. Necessity, they say, is the mother of Invention, I immediately applied to our grand and universal mamma, how I should dress my precious mushrooms, when a gentle whisper came to my ear . . .'

Soyer cooked them on toast, on a stand close up to the fire, with a glass tumbler inverted over them to keep off the taint of the coal smoke. It also kept in all the delicious juices. Here is his method adapted to our happier circumstances.

Wipe the mushrooms, which should be fine large ones, and remove the earthy part of the stalk. Place them, stalks up, on rounds of toast which have been spread with clotted cream. Season them and put a little more cream into the caps. Arrange toast and mushrooms on a baking sheet, and invert one huge or several small pyrex dishes over them. Leave for half an hour in a fairly hot oven, mark 5–6, 375–400°.

'The sight [Soyer again] when the glass is removed, is most inviting, its whiteness rivals the ever-lasting snows of Mont Blanc, and the taste is worthy of Lucullus. Vitellius would never have dined without it; Apicius would never have gone to Greece to seek for crawfish; and had he only half the fortune left when he committed suicide, he would have preferred to have left proud Rome and retire to some villa or cottage to enjoy such an enticing dish.'

I wonder what 'the People' made of such learned flights of culinary fantasy, and hope it didn't put them off the recipe, which is the ideal way of treating our precious field mushrooms.

Comfrey Leaf Fritters

Comfrey (*Symphitum officinale*) grows in damp places alongside streams, rivers and ditches. Its large pointed leaves have a soft thick texture and are covered with slightly prickly hairs. They

make the most excellent fritters, as Hannah Glasse knew in the eighteenth century. Unfortunately we have lost the habit, but as comfrey is common and costs nothing it is worth reviving the recipe.

Remove the stalks from the leaves, wash and drain the leaves in a colander.

Make the batter from 4 oz of flour, a pinch of salt, a table-spoon of oil and about 6 oz of warm water. Finally fold in the stiffly whisked white of an egg.

Dip the leaves into the batter, and fry them to a light golden brown in clarified butter or oil. They make a most elegant looking dish.

Sorrel with Eggs

For 6

¼ lb sorrel
Salt, pepper
3 oz butter

6 eggs
12 triangles of fried bread
6 wedges of orange

Remove the red stalks from the sorrel. Wash it well and tear away any withered bits. Drain it, and place in a large pan over a moderate heat. Cover, and when the moisture starts to bubble, stir it about until it collapses into a dark purée. Add the seasoning and butter, once the wateriness of the sorrel has evaporated. Keep warm while you deal with the eggs. Plunge them into a pan of boiling water, and cook for precisely 6 minutes (7 if they are extra large). Run them under the tap until you can bear to handle them. Crack the shells with a spoon and remove them very carefully because the yolks of the eggs should not be hard (if you crack the whites, the yellow part will run through and mess up the nice appearance). Put the sorrel into a dish, with the eggs on top. The fried bread goes round the edge, and the orange wedges between the eggs.

Latterly we in England have developed a most Athenian characteristic. We are always after some new thing. Which is fine in many ways, but in matters of food often disastrous. We are so busy running after the latest dish, that the good things we've known for centuries are forgotten as quickly as the boring ones. Take sorrel. Most of us have never eaten it, or seen it. Most people with gardens don't grow it. And yet two hundred years ago it was as popular here as it still is in France. No doubt the months-long patch of sorrel, which returns so abundantly every spring, grew near the kitchen door here as it does there, so that even in the rain one can slip out for a handful to liven the soup, or a dish of veal or eggs. Perhaps it is natural that it was valued for its sharpness in the days before lemons were in all the shops, but it gives a different sharpness. Why shouldn't we have both?

Spinach can be used in this way, also, and is good, though less interesting. Allow at least twice as much spinach.

Sea-kale

Sea-kale is delicious; and very English. It is the one vegetable we have developed from a wild species. Along the beaches of Kent, Sussex, and Hampshire sand was piled round the young shoots to blanch away their bitterness. Then the shoots were cut and brought to market. 'Very delicate,' John Evelyn wrote in 1699 of this *Crambe maritima*, this wild sea-cabbage which tastes of anything but cabbage. It was soon found to do well in gardens, blanched under old crocks. Two of the master gardeners of the eighteenth century, Philip Miller and William Curtis, worked out the ways of cultivating sea-kale. It is easier to grow than asparagus; and it is as good to eat by itself. Simply tie it in bundles and cook it in boiling salted water until just tender. Drain it well, and serve with melted butter or with hollandaise sauce, in the same way as asparagus.

Stuffed Tomatoes

For 6

12 medium-sized tomatoes   1 oz butter
Herb stuffing, made without any
   egg, p. 285

Slice off the tops of the tomatoes, scoop out the insides, and turn the tomatoes upside down on a rack to drain. Meanwhile chop the firm part of the inside (discard juice and pips), and add it to the stuffing. Fill the tomatoes with this mixture. Arrange them in a shallow baking pan or dish which has been well greased with the butter. Replace the tops. Bake for 10–15 minutes. The temperature can be between 350° and 400°, mark 4–6, or even higher, so long as the tomatoes are not allowed to burn or collapse : it will depend on what else you are cooking at the same time. Delicious with roast and grilled lamb.

Roast Parsnips

When preparing the parsnips, cut them into quarters and leave them that size, unless they are very large. Blanch them in boiling water for 5 minutes.

Put them round or under a joint of roasting beef, so that they become soft and richly brown in the juices and fat of the meat. Allow one medium parsnip for each person (weighing about 6 oz) if no potatoes are being served.

Alternatively, cook them in a separate pan of beef dripping or oil on a shelf above the beef. They can share a pan with roasting potatoes. This method will make them crisper outside, but one runs the risk that they may become too crusty.

Buttered Parsnips
For 4

1½ lb parsnips	3 oz butter
Salt, pepper	Chopped parsley

Peel the parsnips thinly. Cut off the tops and tails and quarter them into wedges. Remove the inner core if it seems at all woody; divide the wedges into convenient strips. Blanch them for 10 minutes in boiling salted water—they should be almost cooked. Drain them, cut them into smallish pieces and return them to a clean pan with the butter. Shake them from time to time and keep them over a low heat to finish cooking. They should look golden and appetising and slightly soft, but not mushy or brown. Taste and season them again, this time adding plenty of pepper and the parsley.

'Parsnips need butter' should be inscribed in letters of fire in every kitchen. Without butter, or an equivalent fat of quality (which does not mean margarine, but good beef dripping), they can be a depressing vegetable. Cooked this way, they are one of winter's best dishes.

Creamed Parsnips

Complete the recipe above, but before adding the parsley, pour in ¼ pt of double, or double and single cream. Heat through, and turn into a shallow dish. Serve as a first course at a dinner party, or as a supper dish.

Parsnip and Shellfish Salad

Cook the parsnip strips (see above) in salted water. Drain them and mix them with an olive oil vinaigrette. Add shelled prawns, or pieces of lobster (or some cold turbot or monkfish) and arrange on a shallow dish. Scatter with chopped parsley and chives.

Teisen Nionod (Welsh Onion Cake)

For 4

1½ lb firm potatoes, preferably Desiree or waxy new potatoes	4 oz butter
¾ lb onions	Pepper and salt

Peel or scrape the potatoes, then slice them paper-thin, on a mandolin or the cucumber blade of a grater, into a bowl of cold water. Swish them about well to get rid of the starchy juice, then dry them in a clean tea towel. Peel and slice the onions.

Take a shallow dish or oblong cake tin and grease it with a butter paper (if you intend to turn the cake out at the end, it is a good idea to line the dish or tin with bakewell paper or foil before greasing it). Put in a layer of potatoes, then a layer of onions and so on, finishing with potatoes. Season the layers and dot them with butter, leaving about 1 oz to melt and pour over the top layer. Cover the dish with foil—don't worry if the vegetables mount up above the dish, they subside as they cook. Bake at mark 4, 350°, for 1½ hours, removing the foil for the last half hour so that the top can brown. Alternatively bake at mark 6, 400°, for an hour. This is a good-tempered dish, which will cook at most temperatures convenient to your purposes— just allow more or less time.

When the vegetables are cooked but just a little crisp, put a serving dish on top of the dish and reverse it quickly. Ease the paper or foil and remove the tin. Flash under the grill for a few minutes to brown the top. There is, on the other hand, no reason why you shouldn't serve the onion cake in its cooking dish like a French gratin.

I find the texture of this dish very agreeable, but if you want the French combination of softness underneath and crispness on top, pour in ¼ pt of beef stock before cooking starts. Or ¼ pt cream mixed with 2 tablespoons water.

Pan Haggerty
For 4

1 lb firm potatoes
½ lb onions
¼ lb grated Cheddar cheese

Beef dripping
Salt, pepper

Prepare the vegetables as for *Teisen Nionod* (above). Melt about 2 oz of dripping in an 8″–9″ frying pan. Remove it from the heat, and build up the potatoes, onion and cheese in layers, with seasoning, finishing with potato. Put the pan on the heat again and fry the vegetables gently at first, until they begin to cook, then at the end a little faster so that the underneath browns. Invert the pan haggerty on to a plate, put a little more dripping in the pan and slide it back again to brown on the other side. Alternatively leave it in the pan and brown it under the grill.

An appetising north-eastern dish of potatoes and onion, which should be better known all over the country—and might be if it weren't for the insistently homely nature of north-easterners, who would prefer death to appearing grand in matters of food. The cheese and the pan-frying in beef dripping make it taste quite different from the Welsh *Teisen Nionod*, or a French gratin, though in idea and construction it much resembles them.

Glazed Turnips

2 lb young summer turnips   Freshly ground black pepper
2–3 oz butter   Chopped parsley
1 level tablespoon sugar

Peel the turnips, which must be young and sweet, not the kind that is only fit for cattle. Cut them into rough cubes of about $\frac{1}{2}''$. Plunge them into a pan of boiling salted water, and leave them to boil for 5 minutes. Try a cube—it should be almost cooked but slightly resistant. If it is still hard, continue the cooking for another 3–5 minutes. This blanching process is very important, and it can be continued for longer if the turnips are beginning to feel their age. The point is that they should not be strong-tasting, neither should they be mushy.

Strain off all the water, and transfer the turnip to a large frying pan in which the butter has been melted. Sprinkle the sugar over them. Cook over a moderate heat, turning the pieces over regularly so that they begin to caramelize slightly to a pale golden brown. Sprinkle with parsley and serve.

Turnips cooked in this way are delicious with roast duck, or with baked ham.

Laverbread with Bacon

For 4

4 tablespoons of prepared laverbread   Bacon fat
Fine oatmeal

Mix the laverbread with enough oatmeal to make a coherent mixture. Season it and form into little round flat cakes. Fry in bacon fat (with the breakfast bacon, for preference, in a large frying pan) until nicely browned on both sides. These little cakes also go well with a mixed grill which includes bacon, lamb cutlets, sausages and so on.

Although laver, being seaweed, tastes of the sea, it is not fishy or salty as one might expect. The flavour has a hint of oysters (sometimes it is called oyster-green), which goes well with both fish and meat. This sea vegetable is sold washed, boiled to a dark spinach-like purée, and ready to serve. Some people enjoy it spread on slices of thin crisp toast. In cooking it has an important advantage over vegetables of the land—its gelatinous moisture. This helps laverbread, as it is called, to cohere without extra binding ingredients.

Once laverbread was widely eaten in Great Britain—we are, after all, surrounded by sea. Alexis Soyer, the French chef of the Reform Club, was delighted when he discovered this unusual English food in the middle of the last century, and made it a smart society dish for a while. But now it is really a food of the western margins of the British Isles, with only the Welsh exploiting its versatility. Soyer would be disgusted. He always deplored the way in which the English turned their backs on the peasant foods of their past.

Laverbread as a Sauce

½ lb laverbread   Lemon juice to taste
Juice of 1 orange   Salt, pepper
Grated peel of an orange

Heat the laverbread with the orange juice and peel. Season it to taste with a little lemon juice, salt and pepper. Serve with roast lamb—particularly with Welsh roast lamb and new potatoes, and add a few slices of orange to contrast with the deep green of the sauce.

One friend, who ran an hotel at Fishguard, used to serve this sauce with lobster. It was a most successful combination.

Fish

The curious thing about the fact that we live in an island surrounded by seas teeming with fish is that we seem to eat fewer and fewer kinds, and those not always the best. I suppose this is the fault of commerce—the commercial desire being to deal in tons of three or four kinds, rather than in hundredweights of thirty or fifty kinds. To give one example, there is a fair landing of monkfish, which the French rightly regard as a great delicacy (much of the English catch goes to France, at a high price). I have never found a recipe for it in a book of English cookery. Monkfish is mainly eaten and sold in western ports of Cornwall and Devon. Another regrettable thing is our sorry appetite for plaice—though perhaps it has been forced on us: a duller fish never came out of the sea, duller and flatter still by the time it comes to the fishmonger.

There are some parallel mysteries about our appetite for freshwater fish. We neglect pike, one of the best of all fish for firm sweetness of eating, perch, carp, tench, and the crayfish of our limestone streams. Above all, we have taken to a neglect of the eel—except when it's embedded in jelly, which isn't the best way of eating this fish of delicate taste and texture.

Shellfish and smoked fish apart, the prime English fish are turbot, sole, red mullet, sea trout, salmon, pike, eel, trout and herring. Fresh inshore cod is a revelation after cod on ice from the Arctic. Whiting, too, are fresh and pearly, a good dish when they are given the delicate treatment they deserve. There is no possible substitute for that rare species, the conscientious and knowledgeable fishmonger, because fish lose their extra distinction far too quickly, destroyed by delay, freezing and canning (sardines and brisling apart).

Smoked and salted fish are another matter, altogether on their own, the supplementary creation of another edible substance as different from the original as salami is from pork. Luckily we retain these old methods of curing and saving. There are few choicer things to be had than the best kippers and bloaters, the best Finnan haddock or smoked salmon or smoked trout or smoked eel.

Potting fish in butter (which has been the fat for northern fish just as olive oil has been the fat for preserving fish from the Mediterranean) is a practice which goes back to Tudor times, but commercially the potting of fish has lost much of its savour and importance. Whereas potted shrimps before the last war were a delicacy, the modern practice of refrigerating the shrimps and then potting them in butter has been fatal. The only thing is to pot your own shrimps or crab or lobster or trout, if you can come by them in a fresh state. At least it's not difficult (don't forget the spices, particularly mace, and do use lightly-salted butter, as the Lancashire shrimp packers have since the beginning of the century).

The best of the canned fishes are traditional imports—brisling from Norway, sardines from Portugal and Brittany, and of course anchovies, which have been a part of English cooking for hundreds of years. Few fish retain more consistent quality than the tiny brisling which used to go under the name of Skippers sardines. Whitebait are also worth mentioning. Nowadays, it's true, one gets them in frozen blocks, but they're worth eating in the traditional way all the same.

Developments in the farming of fish may change the rather

miserable situation within the next decade or so, and oysters are already 'farmed' commercially of course. Don't expect to get the finest natives, which Caesar conquered Britain for, in the new packets of oysters in batter. The new farm oyster is commonly a different variety, the less sensitive and fine-tasting kind from Japan or Portugal. In general, mussels and crabs are the best of all inexpensive shellfish, but avoid them frozen. Scallops are the sweetest of all shellfish, but not the cheapest. Clams are now being produced in English beds, but are not yet widely on sale. There is nothing to be said for the over-popular scampi as present served in pubs and restaurants. They are little more than egg and breadcrumbs with a chew in the middle.

Baked Carp with Soft Roe Stuffing

There is a world of difference between carp caught from the river and the muted products of a German or Israeli fish farm. For a start they are different varieties, but the freshness of running water with its weeds and tiny forms of floating life are what make the difference. The first carp I ever cooked came from a French river, the Loir. We wrapped it up, with seasoning and butter and a splash of white wine, in a foil parcel, which was laid on a grill over some smouldering charcoal. After 10 minutes we turned the package over to cook the other side. Then we ate it with lemon juice, bread and butter and glasses of white wine. I have persisted with farm carp, but have never found one which came near the perfection of that river fish.

Another way of cooking carp, a recipe for the kitchen, comes from the early nineteenth century :—

For 4–6

A 2½–3 lb carp
4 pts water
6 tablespoons vinegar
6 oz butter
Salt, pepper
¼ teaspoon each mace, nutmeg, cloves

Bouquet garni
1 onion
2 anchovy fillets (or 1 generous teaspoon anchovy essence)
1 pint dry white wine
1 tablespoon flour
Lemon juice

Ask the fishmonger to clean and scale the fish, and also to remove the bitter gall sac at the back of the head. When you get it home, wash it in the water and vinegar very thoroughly.

Choose an ovenproof dish into which the carp will fit closely and snugly. Spread 4 oz of the butter over the base, lay the drained carp on top, and add seasonings, spices, herbs, onion and anchovy. Pour on enough dry white wine barely to cover the fish—you may need less than 1 pt, it depends on the size of the dish. Cover with foil, and put into a fairly hot oven, mark 5–6, 375–400°, until cooked. This will take 30–40 minutes. When the carp is done, put it on to a serving dish and strain the cooking juices into a clean pan. Taste them and correct the seasoning; boil down a little if they seem watery. Mash the remaining butter with the flour, and add it to the barely simmering sauce in little knobs. Keep stirring, and in about 5 minutes the sauce will thicken nicely. Taste and add a little lemon juice to sharpen the flavour. Pour the sauce over the fish and serve.

This method can be applied to any sizeable freshwater fish; or to several small ones—in which case, reduce the cooking time accordingly. The sauce can always be enriched by a spoonful or two of cream, or by a liaison of egg yolk and cream added after the butter-and-flour thickening.

If your carp had a soft roe, use it to make the following stuffing :—

The soft roe, chopped	Heaped tablespoon chopped green
1 oz white breadcrumbs	herbs
Milk	Teaspoonful grated lemon rind
1 small onion, chopped	½ teaspoon anchovy essence
1 oz butter	Salt, pepper, lemon juice

Put the roe in a basin. Mix the crumbs with just enough milk to turn them into a soft paste. Cook the onion gently in the butter until soft. Mix together all the ingredients, with the seasoning and lemon juice last of all, to taste. Stuff and sew up the fish.

Fried Eel with Fried Parsley

For 4

2 lb eel
Seasoned flour
4 oz clarified butter
6 oz lightly salted butter

Juice of 1 lemon
1 dozen large sprigs of parsley
Corn oil

Ask the fishmonger to skin the eel, and cut it into 3″–4″ pieces. Turn them in seasoned flour and fry gently in the clarified butter, until they are golden brown all over, and the flesh begins to part easily from the bone.

Meanwhile melt the lightly salted butter, season it with the lemon juice and pour it into a small jug. Stand it in some very hot water, until it is needed.

Place the cooked eel on a serving dish, and keep it warm while you fry the parsley. To do this pour an inch of corn oil into a saucepan, make it very hot (about 350°) and put in the parsley sprigs a few at a time. They will rapidly turn brown. Remove them and tuck them round the pieces of eel. They taste deliciously sandy yet crisp, and go very well with the mild eel and its sauce. Fried parsley makes a good edible decoration for fish, and it is a pity it has gone out of fashion.

Jellied Eel Mousse with Watercress Sauce

For 6

2 eels, weighing roughly 2½lb in all
3 egg whites
¾ pt double cream
Salt, pepper, nutmeg

Sauce
1 good bunch watercress
¼ pt double cream
Salt, pepper

Ask the fishmonger to skin the eels for you, and, if he will, to cut the fillets away from the back bone. When you get home, cut off ¾ lb of the messiest looking parts. Season the rest, and set it aside, while you make a fish mousse. To do this, put the ¾ lb of eel into the liquidizer with the egg whites, and reduce to a purée : the best way of doing this is to cut the eel into bits and drop them on to the whirling blades. Use the egg white to lubricate the mixture. Transfer the purée to a bowl set over ice. In another bowl whip the cream until thick but not stiff, then work it slowly into the eel purée. It takes about 10 minutes to work the whole thing into a coherent mass. Season it well.

Take an earthenware or stoneware terrine, respectable enough to appear on the table, and layer into it the eel mousse and the eel fillets. Cut a piece of butter paper to fit the terrine, place it on top, then cover the terrine with a double lid of foil. Either steam the mousse for $1\frac{1}{4}$ hours; or put it into a pan with boiling water to come halfway up the side, and bake it in a moderate oven for the same time—mark 3–4, 325–350°. Remove the terrine to a cool place, then, when cold, put it into the refrigerator overnight.

Serve with the following sauce : remove enough leaves from the watercress to make a tablespoon when chopped. Liquidize the rest with the minimum amount of water to reduce the watercress to a murky slush. Push it through a sieve, add the cream and whip until thick. Season and fold in the chopped leaves.

An elaboration of our jellied eel by a French chef, Guy Mouilleron, who is working in London at the Café Royal and enjoys experimenting with English dishes. He had a picture of the silver eel, nosing its way through the thready stems of watercress in a stream, and found that the flavours had an affinity. A beautiful-looking dish, the jellied whiteness of the mousse and the pale green of the sauce, flecked with darker green.

Eel Pie

Cut the skinned eel in pieces $1\frac{1}{2}''$ long. Season them with salt, pepper and a little sage, and lay them in several small or one large pie dish. Add enough water to come about $\frac{3}{4}''$ up the dish—rather less in the case of small pie dishes—and cover with puff pastry in the usual way. Brush with egg glaze. Bake in a hot oven, mark 7–8, 425–450°, for 20 minutes until the crust is well risen and nicely coloured, and the contents boiling. Reduce the temperature to mark 5, 375°, and cook for another half-hour. Protect the crust with a butter paper or brown paper.

Eel pies were one of the popular fair dishes, like pickled salmon, and gingerbread. Dr Kitchiner gives a more elaborate recipe in *The Cook's Oracle*, of 1843. He calls it an 'Eel Pie worthy of Eel-Pie Island', where Londoners went to enjoy themselves and fish and picnic by the Thames.

Eel Pie worthy of Eel-Pie Island

2 eels (preferably from the Thames), cut up	¼ pt dry sherry
	2 oz flour
2 shallots, chopped	Juice of a lemon
4 oz butter	Hard-boiled egg, sliced
1 tablespoon chopped parsley	Puff pastry
Nutmeg, salt, pepper	Beaten egg to glaze

Season the eels. Soften the shallots in half the butter, add parsley, seasoning and sherry, then the eels. Pour on enough water to cover them, and bring to the boil. Remove the eel to a pie-dish. Thicken the sauce with the remaining butter mashed with the flour, season it with lemon and pour over the eel. Scatter the egg on top. Cover with puff pastry, glaze and bake as above.

Eel Stew

For 6

1 eel, about 2 lb	Bouquet garni
2 oz butter	1 carrot, sliced
2½ pts water	Salt
½ teaspoon mace or nutmeg	1 rounded tablespoon of flour
20 peppercorns	3½ oz double cream
1 medium onion, chopped	Croûtons of bread fried in butter

Ask the fishmonger to skin the eel and cut it up into two-inch chunks. Melt the butter in a large saucepan, and add the eel.

Stew it for about 10 minutes, with a lid on the pan. Do not overheat or allow the eel to brown. Pour in the water, and add the spices, onion, herbs, and carrot, with salt to season. Bring to the boil and simmer gently, just a bubble or two gurgling to the surface every few seconds, for 45 minutes. Meanwhile whisk the flour into the cream to make a smooth mixture.

When the 45 minutes are up, strain off liquid through a sieve into a clean pan. Pick out the pieces of eel, removing the bones, and lay them in a soup tureen which should be kept warm while you finish the dish. Bring the strained liquor in the pan up to boiling point, pour some of it into the cream and flour mixture, whisking it well to avoid lumps. Tip this back into the pan and stir over the heat for 5 minutes or until it thickens—do not allow to boil. Correct the seasoning, pour over the eel pieces in the tureen and serve with the croûtons of bread. A delicate and delicious stew-cum-soup.

Elvers in the Gloucester Style

For 4

1 lb elvers	2 eggs, beaten
8 rashers fat streaky bacon	Salt, pepper
A little bacon fat or lard	Wine vinegar

When you go to buy elvers, the tiny eel fry which come swimming up the Severn in the spring, take along an old pillowcase so that the fishmonger can tip them straight into it.

At home, add a handful of kitchen salt to the elvers and swish them about, still in the pillowcase, in plenty of water. Squeeze them firmly to extract as much water as possible, then repeat the washing process again with some more salt. This gets rid of the sliminess.

To cook the dish, fry the bacon until crisp in a little bacon fat or lard. Remove it to a serving dish, and turn the elvers into the bacon fat which remains in the pan. Stir them about for a few seconds until they become opaque, then mix in the beaten egg and cook for a few seconds longer. The important thing is not to cook for too long. Taste and add seasoning. Put the elvers on top of the bacon, and sprinkle with a little vinegar. Serve very hot.

Elvers are tiny eels. Although they have taken three years to make the 2,000-mile journey from their birthplace in the Sargasso Sea, they are no more than an inch or so long, tiny thread-like creatures of a fragile transparency. One might think they had no strength, to look at them, but formed into long cordons or 'eel-fares' (elver derives from eel-fare) they push powerfully upstream, up the Severn, the Loire, the Gironde and many other rivers of Europe, until they reach the streams where for another five to nine years they will live and grow, before making the dark return journey home as full-grown silver eels.

The elver fisherman sets out in the spring on a dark night to catch the turn of the tide. He carries a bucket for the eels, as well as a scoop net and a couple of forked sticks to hold his lantern. The *Illustrated Guide to the Severn Fishery Collection*, on sale at the Gloucester Folk Museum, says that in normal years several tons of elvers are caught between Sharpness and Tewkesbury on the Severn. It also points out that elvers are the only fish fry which may legally be caught as food.

Herrings in Oatmeal
For 6

6 herrings	Salt, pepper
3 oz fine or medium oatmeal	Lemon quarters
4 oz butter	

Ask the fishmonger to fillet the herrings from the back, so that they look like uncured kippers when they are opened out, with the thin part in the centre. Season them with salt and pepper, then press them, skin side and cut side, into the oatmeal so that

they are coated with it. Fry them in the butter until cooked and
lightly browned. Serve them with lemon quarters.

The best way of eating herrings. If you like, rashers of streaky
bacon can be fried first, and their fat used for cooking the
herrings. Bacon and fish go well together.

Welsh Supper Herrings (Swper Scadan)

1 lb herrings, filleted from the belly
1 tablespoon made mustard
2½ oz butter
Salt, pepper
1¼ lb firm potatoes, peeled

2 cooking apples, peeled, cored,
sliced
1 large onion, sliced
½ teaspoon dried sage

Spread the herring fillets out on a board, and remove the heads
if the fishmonger has not already done so. Mix the mustard
with 1 oz of softened butter and spread the cut sides of the
herrings with it. Season them and roll them up. Grease a pie
dish with half an ounce of the remaining butter.

Using a mandolin if possible, slice the potatoes very thinly
(the cucumber blade of a grater can also be used). Put half
of them into the pie dish with seasoning, then half of the apple
and half of the onion slices. Put the herring rolls on top and
sprinkle them with sage. Finish the layers in reverse order,
ending with potato. Pour boiling water to come about halfway
up the dish. Dot the top layer of potatoes with butter, and
season it well. Cover with foil and bake at mark 4, 350°, for
half an hour. Remove the foil, turn up the heat to mark 6,
400°, for another 20–30 minutes, so that the potatoes become
crusted with golden brown flecks.

The combination of herrings, potato and apple is popular all
over northern Europe. When it occurs as a salad, beetroot is
often added as well.

Gooseberry Sauce for Mackerel

½ lb gooseberries
1 oz butter

either 1 egg
or: ¼ pt béchamel sauce
or: ¼ pt double cream

Top and tail the gooseberries. Melt the butter in a pan, add the gooseberries, cover them and leave them until they are cooked. Mash them down; or sieve them, if you like a very smooth sauce (I prefer it slightly knobbly). Mix in one or other of the remaining ingredients, to soften the sharpness of the goose-berries. Add a little sugar if the gooseberries were very young and green, but the sauce should not be sweet like an apple sauce.

This sauce is also good with roast duck, pork, goose, lamb, or veal.

On May 26th, 1796, Parson Woodforde and his niece, Nancy, had for their dinner 'a couple of maccarel boiled and stewed gooseberries and a leg of muton roasted.' In other years, they were not so lucky; the gooseberries did not always ripen for the arrival of the first spring mackerel.

Gooseberry Stuffing for Mackerel

½ lb gooseberries
2 oz butter
4 tablespoons breadcrumbs

Salt, pepper
Pinch of Cayenne pepper

Top and tail the gooseberries and soften them over a low heat with ½ oz of the butter. Mash them roughly; add remaining butter when they are tepid, and mix in the crumbs.

Divide the stuffing between four boned mackerel. Place them in a buttered dish and bake for 30 minutes at mark 5, 375°.

Pike

The best thing with this fine fish is to fillet it, and get rid of the worst of the bones. Cut off the head, and with a very sharp little knife slit along the belly. Clean it out thoroughly, under the tap, but make sure of keeping the roe—the hard roe in particular is delicious as the eggs are large and grainy, caviare-size. With the cut side spread apart, turn the fish back up and press firmly all along the backbone until you feel it give (the same technique as filleting herring). Turn the fish over, and pick out the backbone. Now scrape the two long fillets away from the thick skin; they come away easily because pike is a firm fish like sole. Season the fillets, and cut them into pieces of reasonable size. Put them into a dish, and if you can manage it, sprinkle them with a couple of tablespoons of Madeira and one of brandy—more or less according to the amount of pike, but in that proportion. There should be just enough to make a little juice in the dish. Turn the pieces over occasionally and leave them for several hours.

When you come to cook them, drain the fillets, turn them in flour and fry them in butter with the roe until they are nicely coloured on each side. Serve them with a cream sauce flavoured with the marinade juices, or with a lightly curried velouté sauce finished with cream. If alcohol is out of the question, serve the pike with a purée of sorrel enriched with plenty of cream and butter, or with a hollandaise sauce. Boiled new potatoes are a good addition.

Roach

Roach can be a little dull unless they are cooked very quickly after being caught. They are a beautiful fish, with silver to red scales, and reddish eyes and fins. They seem to have caught a sunset light, which goes, unfortunately, when they are scaled.

Here is a simple recipe which makes the most of them. First of all bring 4 oz of butter to the boil in a little pan. Let it bubble for a moment or two then put it aside to cool, while you scale and clean the fish and season it inside. Strain off the transparent butter through a muslin-lined sieve into a frying pan. Now that the butter has been clarified, it will not burn so easily—very important for the slow cooking of fish.

Turn the roach in seasoned flour. Heat up the butter in the pan, and put in the roach. They should cook gently for about 6 minutes a side. If you keep the heat moderate, they will develop a crisp, golden brown skin, and will not be over-cooked. Serve them with quarters of lemon, and brown bread and butter, or boiled new potatoes turned in butter and parsley.

Salmon in Pastry, with a herb sauce

2½ lb tailpiece of salmon
4 oz butter
4 knobs preserved ginger, chopped
1 heaped tablespoon raisins
1 rounded tablespoon chopped, blanched almonds
1 lb weight shortcrust pastry
Beaten egg glaze

Sauce
2 shallots, chopped
1 heaped teaspoon chopped parsley
1 teaspoon mixed chervil and tarragon
2 oz butter teaspoon flour
½ pt cream (single, or single and double)
Salt, pepper
1 teaspoon Dijon mustard
2 egg yolks, mixed with 2 tablespoons cream from the ½ pt cream above
Lemon juice

Ask the fishmonger to skin and bone the salmon into two roughly triangular fillets. Mix the butter, ginger, raisins, and almonds together; use half to sandwich the two pieces of salmon together and put the rest on top. Season the salmon well, and enclose it in the pastry. Cut away any surplus and use it to make a restrained decoration for the top. Slash the pastry two or three times to allow the steam to escape. Brush over with egg glaze and bake for 30–35 minutes at mark 7, 425°.

Meanwhile make the sauce. Sweat shallots and herbs in butter until soft. Stir in flour, then cream and seasoning. Cook for 10 minutes. Finally beat in the egg yolk mixture and set over a low heat to thicken without boiling—keep stirring. Sharpen to taste with lemon juice.

Place the salmon in its pastry on a hot dish; serve with the sauce in a separate sauce boat.

This is slightly adapted from an excellent recipe from the Hole-in-the-Wall restaurant at Bath. The sauce is French, rather than English, but the whole dish is very much to our taste. It was originally inspired by a medieval recipe, which accounts for the unusual combination of sweetness with fish.

Poached Turbot with Shrimp Sauce

For 6

3 lb chicken turbot	*Sauce*
Milk	½ pt shrimps
Water	1 level tablespoon flour
1 slice of lemon	6 oz butter cut in pieces
Salt, pepper, butter, parsley	Powdered mace or nutmeg to taste
	Pinch Cayenne pepper
	Salt

To stop the fish curving out of shape in the pan, cut it along the backbone on the dark, knobbly-skinned side. Put it, light side up, into a large pan and cover it with half milk, half water. Add the lemon and seasoning. Bring slowly to the boil and simmer for ten minutes or until the flesh loses its transparency and the fillets can be raised from the bone very slightly. Slide the turbot on to a serving dish—use an old-fashioned one with a separate, pierced strainer, if possible, so that the fish is not swilling about in milky wetness. Rub the skin over with a bit of butter, or a butter paper to give it a silky shine, sprinkle on a little parsley and serve with the following sauce :

Pick the shrimps, putting the shells and so on into a pan. Set the meat to one side. Pour ½ pt of water over the debris and simmer it steadily for 10 minutes, then pour it into a measuring jug, through a sieve. Press to extract as much juice as possible. Add water to bring the liquid to ½ pt. Mix smoothly with the flour and heat gently, adding the butter, bit by bit. Simmer for two or three minutes, then put in the shrimps which were set on one side. Season to taste and serve separately.

The milk and water used for poaching the turbot can be simmered with the turbot bones and skin after the meal. This makes a splendid jellied stock for soup next day.

Turbot and other left-over fish can be reheated in butter and cream, and served in small pastry cases. Delicious, if overcooking is avoided.

Whitebait

Whitebait are the small fry of herrings and sprats, a great delicacy of the past, but now a dish for everyone since the arrival of frozen food.

Allow them to thaw if they are frozen. Then pour a little milk over them, drain them and shake them in a large paper bag with some seasoned flour until they are coated. Shake off any surplus and fry them a few at a time in deep oil as if they were chips. Two or three minutes is enough time. Never be tempted to cook a large batch all at once—they will stick together in a most unappetising way. Ideally each tiny fish should be separate from its neighbours, crisp and brown and succulent in the middle.

Put the whitebait on to a serving dish, sprinkle them with Cayenne pepper if you like (for devilled whitebait), and serve with brown bread and butter, and lemon quarters.

Whitebait dinners were held first at Dagenham to celebrate the completion of a vast land-draining scheme in Essex. One year Pitt, then Prime Minister, was invited. He came with several members of the government and soon the whitebait dinners became a political celebration at the end of the parliamentary session. Greenwich replaced Dagenham as the venue, and it became fashionable for people to go there in the summertime when the whitebait were caught in shoals in the Thames off Blackwall.

Water-souchy

For 6–8

5 lb fresh water fish, preferably perch, but a mixture of eel, perch, carp, and so on, does very well
3 oz butter
Two cleaned chopped leeks
2 chopped stalks of celery
Bouquet garni
2 tablespoons chopped parsley
Salt, pepper
Water
Croûtons of bread fried in butter

Pick over and clean the fish, removing the skin from eel, and then cut it into chunks. Spread the butter over a large saucepan, add the vegetables, herbs and seasoning, and put the fish on top with more seasoning. Cover with water. Bring to the boil and simmer for 20 minutes until the fish is done, but not overdone. Serve with croûtons.

The charm of this simple fish stew lies in the freshness of the fish : it is really an angler's way of preparing a mixed bag for his supper. The longer the fish has been caught the less good the water-souchy will be.

The name comes from the Dutch *waterzootje* and the dish has been popular in England since the seventeenth century. It comes in all kinds of spelling, watersoochy, water-souchy, waterzöi, but the formula is always the same.

Kedgeree

For 4

1 lb piece smoked haddock
Olive oil
1 large onion, chopped
6 oz long-grain rice
1 teaspoon curry paste
Butter
3 hard-boiled eggs, sliced
Chopped parsley

Pour boiling water over the haddock and set over a low heat for 10 minutes. It should not boil. Take the haddock from the water, discard the skin and bones, and flake the fish. Meanwhile pour a thin layer of olive oil into a pan and brown the onion in it lightly. Stir in the rice, and as it becomes transparent mix in the curry paste. Pour 1 pt of the haddock water over the rice, and cook steadily until the rice is tender and the liquid absorbed. Watch the pan, and add more water if necessary. Mix in the flaked haddock pieces and a large bit of butter, so that the kedgeree is moist and juicy. Turn into a hot serving dish. Arrange the egg slices on top, sprinkle with parsley, and serve with lemon quarters and mango chutney.

Khichri is a Hindi dish of rice and lentils, which can be varied with fish or meat in all kinds of ways. The English in India worked up their own versions, and soon kedgeree became a popular Victorian breakfast dish. The sad thing is that it became institutionalized as a handy way of using up any left-over fish and rice : it came to table stodgy and tasteless. Left-overs can be used to make a good kedgeree, but the cook's hand should be generous with butter and cream, and the proportion of fish to rice should be more or less two parts to three, cooked weight.

Well-flavoured fish like salmon and first-class kippers and bloaters make a delicious kedgeree. So do shellfish such as mussels : use their liquor to cook the rice.

Anchovy Matchsticks

14 oz puff pastry
2 hard-boiled eggs
1 tablespoon cream

2 tins anchovies
Salt, pepper
Beaten egg to glaze

Roll out the pastry and cut it into two equal-sized oblong pieces. Mash the hard-boiled eggs and mix them with the cream; season with salt and pepper. Drain the anchovies of their oil and arrange the fillets evenly on one piece of pastry in 2 rows—leave 1½″ between each fillet, and between the two rows. Put a little of the egg mixture on top of each anchovy. Brush the pastry between the anchovies with beaten egg, place the second piece of pastry on top, and press down all round the edge and between the anchovies. Cut between the mounds, so that you have a number of matchsticks. Place them on a Bakewell lined metal tray, brush them with beaten egg and bake them for 15–20 minutes at mark 7–8, 425–450°. They should be well risen and light, with an appetising brown top. Eat them straight away if possible, as they lose their charm if they have to be reheated.

To make a nice Whet before Dinner (1769)

Fry some slices of bread, half an inch thick, in butter. Lay an anchovy fillet on each one. Cover thickly with Cheshire cheese, grated and mixed with some chopped parsley. Dribble melted butter over the top and put under a hot grill until brown.

This piquant dish of Elizabeth Raffald's can be served before a a meal, as she suggests, with the drinks, or as a first course, or a supper dish. It is excellent.

Canapés à la crème

Fry the bread in butter as the recipe above, put three anchovy fillets on each slice and place them on a very hot dish. Quickly put a spoonful of clotted cream on top of each one and serve immediately.

A fine mixture of hot, rich, piquant and cold. It was intended as a savoury and the recipe comes from *Savouries à la mode*, by Mrs de Salis, which was published at the end of the last century when savouries were very much the thing at the end of dinner. Nowadays when there is no one in the kitchen to help during a meal, most people prefer to serve a cold pudding or fruit— savouries have become the first course instead.

Smoked Fish

RED HERRINGS

Before the days of refrigeration, red herrings were the food of fast days inland. Their preparation was the great industry of the East Anglian coast from the Middle Ages. One of Shakespeare's contemporaries, Thomas Nashe, even wrote his poetical *Lenten Stuffe* in their honour. Red herrings were thoroughly salted, and then thoroughly smoked, until they became hard and dry and reddish in colour. Although you do not see them in English shops these days, they are still made at Great Yarmouth, and sent out to tropical countries where even the humidity and heat cannot spoil them. Once they were slave food, now they are the food of the poor, a cheap, storable provider of protein.

If you ever manage to buy some, soak them well in water or milk. Then grill them or toast them in front of the fire, basting them with butter or olive oil. Serve them with scrambled eggs or potatoes mashed with plenty of butter. Think of them as anchovies, to be used as a relish rather than a main food.

BLOATERS

The light and savoury bloater cure is only three or four hundred years old. It reflects a more organized and comfortable existence, when luxuries like these could be enjoyed by people in moderate circumstances. The best bloaters come and always have from Yarmouth: they should be eaten within thirty-six hours as the cure of salt and smoke is so light. Of course, with refrigeration they can be stored for longer periods—which is why they are on sale all over the country—but for the best bloaters you must still go to the East coast and eat them straightaway. Bloaters can be grilled with a bit of butter in their bellies, or reheated in the oven. Or they can be mashed with butter and turned into a paste for eating with hot toast (see page 79), a favourite way with the Victorians. However, bloaters, like kippers, are delicious when eaten uncooked: use them in salads with apple and beetroot and celery, or eat them in the Polish way with cream and chives poured over them, and a few onion rings.

KIPPERS

The latest of all the herring cures was developed by John Woodger of Seahouses in Northumberland from an old system of curing salmon (kippered salmon, and so kippered herring, and so kippers). Red herrings and bloaters are cured whole, but Woodger adopted the salmon technique of splitting the fish down the back, before salting them briefly and then smoking them over an oak fire like bloaters, again briefly for a light cure. True kippers are not mahogany brown from dye, but a pale silvery golden colour. They can still be bought in Northumberland, from a firm in Craster, and from the Isle of Man where dyeing is forbidden by law, and from one or two small concerns on Loch Fyne. Fishmongers in other parts of the country who smoke their own fish, will often produce excellent kippers as well. They are usually grilled, sometimes even fried, which works well enough if they are cooked in pairs with a good knob of butter in the middle, but they should be cooked gently, and turned over still in their sandwich form so that only the skin comes in contact with the pan. This prevents the kippers drying out.

My own preference is for jugged kippers: put them into a deep stoneware jug, pour boiling water over them and leave them for ten minutes.

Cut in strips and arranged, without cooking, on slices of brown bread and butter, kippers make a delicious first course which works out a good deal cheaper that smoked salmon.

SMOKED SPRATS

One of the cheapest of luxuries. They can be grilled briefly and served with plenty of brown bread and butter and lemon quarters, or they can be skinned and served as part of an hors d'oeuvre instead of sardines—some dry white wine makes a good dressing.

SMOKED MACKEREL

Tricky to buy as the flesh has often been reduced by the smoking to a pulpy softness which can be unpleasant. Eat with brown bread and butter and lemon quarters in the usual way, if you do manage to find good smoked mackerel. They can also be reheated in the oven and served with mushroom sauce.

FINNAN HADDOCK

Finnan haddock is always cooked. (Recipes on pages 14, 77.) Make sure you buy the proper haddock, and not the unpleasantly dyed 'golden fillet', which is usually whiting. Finnan, which is to say Findon, is the name of a small fishing village near Aberdeen which made a speciality of curing haddocks. The method is now used everywhere in Britain; the results should be silvery and brownish-gold and thoroughly natural in appearance. Smaller haddock and occasionally whiting are left whole and cured in the Arbroath or Eyemouth manner. They are briefly reheated under the grill or in the oven, and eaten with plenty of butter.

SMOKED EEL

Many eels are caught in England, and then sent to Holland for smoking. A strange situation, as smoked eel is one of the finest of the smoked fish, in the smoked salmon class. Skin it and serve it in chunks or filleted with brown bread and butter and lemon juice.

SMOKED TROUT

Another delicacy. As well as the usual brown bread and butter and lemon quarters, horseradish cream is often served with it—double cream flavoured with horseradish, lemon juice and a hint of sugar to taste.

SMOKED SALMON

The greatest of our luxuries, when bought from a first-class curer. The variety of cures and qualities is astonishing, and it is worth paying a little extra when you find a particularly good firm. As a general guide, the best smoked salmon comes from Scotland, with Ireland following a close second—and there are excellent establishments in London which smoke the salmon to individual recipes, so one should not be too doctrinaire. If you buy a side of smoked salmon, the trimmings can be used most successfully as a flavouring for omelettes or scrambled egg; cut them into small evenly sized pieces and add them to the eggs before they are cooked. (See also recipe on page 34.)

Otherwise eat smoked salmon with brown bread and butter —both of the finest quality—and, if you like, a very little lemon juice. Some people claim that the best way of eating it is wrapped round a spoonful of Russian caviare: I have never been in a position to test this claim, unfortunately, and cannot pretend that it is a normal item of good English eating, but I pass the suggestion on nonetheless.

Finnan Haddock and Mustard Sauce

3 Finnan haddock, about 3 lb in all	¼ bay leaf
1 pt milk	1 oz butter
¼ pt water	Rounded tablespoon flour
1 medium onion, sliced,	Mustard to taste, ready-mixed
1 carrot, sliced	English, or Dijon
2 cloves	Salt, pepper

Cut each haddock into two pieces longways. Bring milk, water, onion, carrot, cloves and bay leaf to the boil in a wide shallow pan. Put in the haddock, skin side up, and leave for 10 minutes —the liquid should just simmer. Place the fish on a serving plate, cover with butter papers and keep it warm. Melt the butter in a small pan, stir in the flour and cook for two minutes. Stir in gradually enough of the haddock cooking liquor to make a smooth, fairly thin sauce about the consistency of single cream. Raise the heat and allow the sauce to bubble down gently to a thick consistency. This will also increase the flavour. Finally season to taste with the mustard, starting with a teaspoonful and gradually adding more, and then with salt and pepper. (I confess to a preference for Dijon mustard, or the speckled *Moutarde de Meaux*, as they are less ferocious than English mustard and more agreeable in flavour.)

Pour the sauce over the haddock and serve with some boiled potatoes turned in butter and chopped parsley.   ·

Grilled Bloaters

Per person

1 or 2 bloaters	A lemon quarter
Teaspoon melted butter	

Choose plump, soft-roed bloaters. Ask the fishmonger to chop off the heads and fins. At home, score the fish two or three times on each side. Brush them with butter as you place them on the grill rack. Have the grill well heated. Put the bloaters underneath for 2 minutes. Turn them and give them a further 2 minutes. If the grill was hot enough, they will be crisp and appetisingly brown at the edges; their juices will be sizzling and the rich appetizing smell will ensure that they are eaten immediately. Put the lemon quarter beside them, and serve plenty of unsalted or lightly salted butter to spread on wholemeal bread.

Bloaters can also be baked—though I think that the fierce heat of a grill serves them better. Place them in a buttered dish, dab them with butter and give them ten minutes in a moderate oven, mark 4–5, 350–375°. Squeeze lemon juice over them before serving with wholemeal bread and butter.

If you want something more elaborate, bone the grilled or baked bloaters as quickly as you can, and serve the hot fillets on buttered toast, or in the middle of a creamy ring of scrambled egg.

Another elaboration, with less fiddling at the last moment, is butter flavoured with mustard and chives, or with chopped

parsley and lemon juice. This can be made days in advance if
you like, but remember to remove it from the refrigerator in
time for it to soften to a spreadable consistency. I think that
Dijon mustard is the best kind to use.

Bloater Paste

Pour boiling water over a couple of bloaters, and leave them for
10 minutes. Drain them, remove the skin and bone and weigh
the fillets. While they are still warm, pound them—either by
hand, or in a blender, or with an electric beater—with an equal
weight of lightly-salted butter. Sharpen to taste with lemon
juice, season with freshly ground black pepper and a little salt
if it seems necessary. Serve with hot toast. If you care to smooth
it down in a pot and cover it with a $\frac{1}{4}''$ layer of clarified
butter, bloater paste can be stored in the refrigerator for two or
three days.

As a dish for breakfast and tea, bloaters have acquired a
Dickensian air of fog and domestic stuffiness which is not to
their advantage. This is backed up by the name, which has a
coarseness quite inappropriate to their delicate piquancy. When
Peggotty remarked, in *David Copperfield*, that she was proud
to call herself a Yarmouth bloater, she certainly didn't mean
that she was a fat, hearty creature, but that she was nicely
rounded, and sweet but well-spiced in character, and fit for a
discriminating man (Yarmouth has always had the reputation
for producing the finest bloaters).

The name goes back to the sixteenth century, and for people
in the trade it had a useful accuracy. It meant that these
herrings had been treated so lightly with salt and smoke that
they were still plump and puffy—bloated, if you like—with
moisture, unlike the dry, almost brittle, red herrings. The French
use the equivalent word—*bouffis*—for their Boulogne-cured
harengs saurs : although they are saltier than our bloaters, and
sometimes need a brief soaking, they have the same combination

of sweetness and gaminess, because they, too, have been cured
lightly, with the guts and roes still inside to improve the flavour.
The mild spice of these two cures, the rarely achieved balance
of mildness and piquancy, makes bloaters and *bouffis* two of the
best things to eat in Europe.

Bloater and Potato Salad

For 6 as a first course

3 fine bloaters	Olive oil
1 lb waxy potatoes	Lemon juice
Heaped tablespoon chopped chives	Salt, pepper, sugar

There is no need to cook bloaters. Strip off the skin and remove
the fillets from the bone, having first removed the roes and set
them aside for some other dish. Divide into strips, or cut into
pieces if the fillets look messy, and lay them in the centre of
a dish.

Meanwhile boil the potatoes in their skins. Mix the remaining
ingredients to a vinaigrette in the proportions you like—I use
5 tablespoons of oil to about 1½ of lemon juice. Sprinkle a tablespoon over the bloaters. When the potatoes are cooked, remove
the skins, cut them into cubes and turn them gently in the
remaining vinaigrette. Leave them to cool, then arrange them
round the bloaters, and serve well chilled.

Good kippers can be used instead, but not the mahogany
deep-frozen kind.

This dish gets right away from the high-tea image and shows
how delicious bloaters can be at the start of a dinner party.
The problem here is the potatoes: if you grow Fir apple or
Kipfler varieties, you are all right. And if you can find Desirée
potatoes in your district, you will do quite well as winter
advances. Otherwise you will have to watch the potatoes closely
as they cook, to catch them while they are still firm and not
woolly at the edges. It's difficult to do this, without having a
panful of potatoes which are raw in the middle. Cooking them

in their skins does help, but it doesn't guarantee success. A final snowfall of chopped chives and parsley can be used to disguise a messy potato salad.

Soft Roe Paste

4–5 oz soft herring or mackerel roes
4 oz softened butter, slightly salted is best
1 level tablespoon double cream

Salt, Cayenne pepper
Lemon juice
Chopped parsley

Try to find perfect pairs of roes. The best way of doing this is to buy soft-roed herring or mackerel, and set the roes aside when you cook the fish: they will have a better flavour and consistency than the broken and messy roes which have been flung together on to a separate tray. Season the roes with salt and cook them in 1 oz of the butter. Sieve them and while they are still warm—just tepid, not hot—mix in the butter: the roes should not be so hot that the butter turns to oil. Mix in the cream, then season again, adding a pinch of Cayenne and lemon juice to taste and a little chopped parsley. Serve chilled, but not chilled to hardness, with thin toast or baked slices of bread.

Kipper Paste

1 pair Craster, Isle of Man or Rothesay undyed kippers
Slightly-salted butter
Salt, Cayenne pepper, mace

Lemon juice
1 tablespoon double cream (optional)

Any kippers can be used for this paste, but it is worth choosing the highest quality undyed kippers because the flavour is so much better. Put them in a deep stoneware jug. Pour boiling water over them, and leave for 10 minutes. Drain them carefully, then remove skin and bones. Weigh the fillets and pound them with an equal weight of butter, while tepid but not hot. Season with salt, spices and lemon juice to taste. If you like a particularly light texture, fold in the cream which should first be whisked. This paste will keep for a week in the refrigerator, under a $\frac{1}{4}''$ layer of clarified butter.

How to boil crabs, lobsters, prawns and shrimps

Always boil shellfish in sea water if you can, adding extra salt until the brine will keep an egg floating. If tap water is the only kind available, add salt until it, too, will bear an egg.

With crabs and lobsters, the R.S.P.C.A. recommend putting the creatures into the cold water in a large pan, so that they quietly expire without suffering as the water warms up. Cover the pan and weight the lid down. When the water is at boiling point, allow 15 minutes' simmering for the first pound, then 10 minutes for each subsequent pound. Remove from the water to cool down.

With prawns and shrimps, prepare the same brine as for crabs and lobsters. Bring it to the boil over a high heat, and plunge in the prawns or shrimps. By the time the water boils again, the smaller shrimps will probably be done. Larger prawns take 5 minutes' boiling. But always be guided by colour and flavour. One writer says that prawns lose far less flavour if they are put into a large pan with no water at all, covered, and set over a very high heat to cook in their own juice. This takes about 10 minutes, and one should shake the pan.

Once the shellfish are cool, they are best served as simply as possible. Mayonnaise and brown bread and butter, with lemon quarters, are by far the best accompaniment.

Oyster Loaves

For each person

1 large or 2 small rolls
1½ oz butter, melted
4 oysters
Pinch Cayenne pepper, or 3 drops Tabasco sauce

Salt, black pepper
3 level dessertspoons soured cream
3 level dessertspoons double cream

Cut a topknot from the rolls, scoop out the crumb being careful not to pierce the outside, and brush them and the topknots, inside and out, with melted butter. Place in a hot oven, mark 7, 425°, for 10 minutes, until crisp and golden. Meanwhile scrub and open oysters, and drain off the liquor. Cook them in the remaining butter until they turn opaque (about 1½ minutes). If you are making this dish for several people, use an 8″ frying pan rather than a saucepan for cooking the oysters. Remove oysters from the pan with a perforated spoon, cut them in two or three pieces according to size, and set them aside. To the pan juices, add the oyster liquor, seasonings and cream. Boil down steadily to a very thick sauce, stirring constantly with a wooden spoon at first, then with a small wire whisk if the sauce shows a tendency to separate during the last stages of reduction. Correct the seasoning, reheat the oysters in the sauce, keeping it just below the boil, and pour into the rolls. Replace the top-knots and serve immediately.

When I can buy them, I use part-baked rolls for this dish. Otherwise 2 oz round rolls which have not been baked too brown. Once in France I used brioches, which were particularly delicious : their cost was offset by the cheapness there of oysters. The miniature cottage loaves sold by some bakers could also be used.

Large mussels could be substituted for oysters. They would need to be scrubbed, scraped and opened in the usual way (page 13).

This is one of the best of eighteenth-century dishes. It was taken to America, and became popular in New Orleans in the nineteenth century, where it acquired the endearing name of *la médiatrice*. 'It was the one thing a man felt might effectively stand between his enraged wife and himself when he came home after spending an evening carousing in the saloons of the French Quarter.' He would buy his mediator in the market there, and hurry home with it, all crisp and hot. Now it makes rather an expensive first course for a special meal (though mussels can be used instead), though it should become cheaper as oyster farming develops in Britain. Do not, of course, use the fine natives for this (or any other cooked oyster dish). Portuguese oysters are the thing. Look out for the huge Japanese oyster, which will begin to appear in the shops before long.

Stewed Scallops with Orange Sauce

For 6

¼ pt dry white wine
¼ pt water
1 scant tablespoon white wine vinegar
½ teaspoon ground mace
2 cloves
18 scallops

1 tablespoon butter
1 tablespoon flour
Juice of a Seville orange, or the juice of 1 sweet orange plus the juice of ½ a lemon
Salt and pepper

Simmer the wine, water, vinegar and spices in a covered shallow pan for 5–10 minutes. Add salt and pepper to taste, and more spices if this seems a good idea—their flavour should not be strong but it should hang unmistakably over the dish. Meanwhile slice the scallops in half crossways, then slip them into the simmering liquid and poach them for 5 minutes. They should not be overcooked.

Transfer the scallops to a serving dish and keep them warm. Measure the cooking liquor and if there is more than half a pint boil it down. Mash the butter and flour together and divide into little knobs. See that the liquid is at simmering point, then whisk in the butter and flour knobs to thicken the sauce. Keep it at a moderate heat, without boiling; finally season with the orange juice, or orange and lemon juice, and more salt and pepper if required. Pour over the scallops and serve at once.

A really delicious eighteenth-century dish. The flavour of orange, particularly of Seville orange, goes beautifully with fish. If you want to make a richer sauce, beat an egg yolk with three tablespoons of double cream and stir into the sauce after adding the flour and butter—stir it over a low heat being careful not to boil it. The recipe can easily be adapted to fillets of sole, whiting, etc.

Elizabeth David's Potted Crab

2 lb crab, boiled	Salt (see recipe)
Black pepper, mace, nutmeg, Cayenne pepper	About 8 oz slightly-salted or un-salted butter
Lemon juice	Clarified butter to seal

Pick all the meat from the crab, being careful to keep the firm and creamy parts separate. Season both with spices and lemon juice—salt may be necessary if you bought the crab ready boiled. There will be about 12 oz meat.

Choose an attractive round stoneware pot, or an oval one. Pack the crabmeat into it, in layers. (If you prefer it, use 4 to 6 individual pots or soufflé dishes.) Melt the butter and pour it over the crab meat. There should be enough just to cover it— the quantity required will depend on the amount of crab meat you had the patience to pick out of the shell, and on whether you used one or half-a-dozen pots. It is only fair to point out that Danish—especially Lurpak—or French butter gives the best result with potted meat and fish : it is made in a different way from English butter, and has a milder flavour and better consistency for this kind of dish.

Leave to cool, then cover with clarified butter. A thin layer if the crab is going to be eaten within 24 hours; a $\frac{1}{4}''$ layer if it is being kept for a few days—in this latter case, add a foil covering so that the butter does not dry out and contract from the edge of the pot, so spoiling the seal.

Mrs David has adapted old recipes for potted meat and fish, and published them in a pamphlet, *English Potted Meats and Fish Pastes*. This potted crab is particularly successful as a lunch dish; serve a green salad, or purple-sprouting broccoli salad afterwards. It is a good recipe, too, for lobster.

Elizabeth David's Prawn Paste

1 lb 2 oz prawns in their shells, or
   8 oz peeled prawns
6 tablespoons olive oil
Juice of 1 lime (or ½ lemon)

Cayenne pepper
About ½ teaspoon dried basil
Heaped saltspoon coriander seeds

Remove the prawns from their shells and pound them to a paste with the oil and lime or lemon juice (lime adds the better flavour). If you use a blender, more oil will be required. Season with a pinch of Cayenne pepper. Warm the basil in the oven, crumble it and add to the prawn mixture, along with the crushed coriander seeds. Taste and put in a little salt if necessary. Turn into a small pot and store, covered, in the refrigerator for no longer than thirty-six hours. Eat chilled with thin, hot toast.

An extra good recipe from *Spices, Salts and Aromatics in the English Kitchen* (Penguin, 1970). Potted fish and meat, which were so popular in the nineteenth century, depended on the weary arms of kitchen maids and skivvies. They are becoming popular again now that we exploit electricity instead.

Curried Prawns

1½–2 lb cooked prawns in their shells
1 large onion chopped
2 oz butter
1 heaped teaspoon curry powder

1 rounded tablespoon flour
½ pt fish stock
¼ pt thick cream
Salt, pepper

Shell the prawns first, and use the shells when making the fish stock. Put the prawn meat aside. Melt the onion in the butter until golden and soft, stir in the curry powder and flour, then moisten with the fish stock. Add the cream and reduce to a thick sauce. Season well. Reheat the prawns gently in the sauce for a few seconds and serve in a ring of boiled rice.

Firm white fish can be curried in the same way with great success. The thing is not to overcook the fish in the first place, and not to overheat it in the sauce. Lemon juice can be added for piquancy when cod or haddock are being used.

Shellfish Puffs

For 6

Choux pastry
¼ pt water
Scant teaspoon sugar
2½ oz butter
4 oz strong or plain flour
4 eggs

Filling
1 lb prawns in their shells
  or 1½ lb lobster, boiled
  or 1½–2 lb crab

¾ pt béchamel sauce, fairly thin
2 heaped tablespoons Lancashire
  cheese, grated
2 egg yolks
2 tablespoons double cream
3 oz butter
4 oz mushrooms, chopped
1 small clove, garlic, chopped
Salt, pepper

Make the choux-pastry puffs first, a day or two in advance if you like. They can be stored in an airtight tin, and reheated when required. Bring the first three ingredients to the boil in a moderate-sized pan. Remove from the heat and immediately tip in all the flour. Mix with a wooden spatula, then set over the heat again and cook for a few moments, stirring until the dough forms a coherent waxy ball. There will be a floury film over the base of the pan. Cool the mixture, still in the pan, for five minutes, then beat in the eggs one by one (an electric hand beater is a good idea). The paste will turn a sheeny yellow and hold its shape. Pipe in small mounds on to two or three baking trays lined with Bakewell paper, or on to the base of a confectioner's bun tin. Invert metal biscuit tins over the baking trays, or place the lid on the bun tin. Bake for 35 minutes at mark 8, 450°, without opening the oven door. Take the trays or tin from the oven, raise the lids carefully by the side *away from you* (steam can be very painful). If the puffs are not brown enough they can be returned to the oven for a further five minutes. The point of covering the pastry is that it puffs up to a larger, lighter shape when it cooks in its own steam.

To make the filling, first remove whichever shellfish you have chosen from its shell. Put the shells and general debris into a pan, pour on the béchamel sauce and simmer for 15 minutes. Then sieve the whole thing energetically—it is surprising how much flavour there is in the shells which are so often just thrown away. Add the cheese, egg yolks and cream to the sauce, and stir it over a moderate heat until it is very thick (*don't* boil it). Season and beat in half the butter. Cook the mushrooms in the rest of the butter, together with the garlic. Tip them and their juices into the sauce, together with the shellfish meat. Reheat this filling gently, so that the shellfish is warmed through without further cooking. Season again.

Split the puffs and put a good spoonful or more of the shellfish filling inside. Serve immediately, as a first course.

This filling can also be used for vol-au-vent cases, large or small.

Meat, Poultry and Game

Foreigners have always condescended to admire the range, quality, quantity, and—heretofore—the cheapness of English meat. There have been foreign travellers who have considered that our industrial ills came from the fact that good meat was available to the lower orders, making them uppity and demanding and prone to form trade unions—instead of remaining supine on cabbage water.

Abundance of meat had one bad effect. It made the bourgeois cooks, the Mrs Beetons and the like who dominated English food, despise some of the tastiest and cheapest portions of bullock, sheep and pig. These were left to working-class families, and in time, as they became better off, working-class families began to buy such things only for their cats and dogs. The situation now is that carcases come to the chain butchers as if the animals had never had heads, tails, feet, or insides, or fat. English meat cookery needs to bring back its old ways, its pre-nineteenth-century ways, of dealing with everything from sheeps' heads to pigs' tails and pigs' ears. We're also inclined to forget the point of mixing different cuts, cheap with less cheap—for instance, belly of pork with stewing beef for the sake of the succulent blandness it gives to the gravy, and the contrast of texture—smooth pork fat with fibrous beef. And we need to remember how well some of the cheap cuts of meat combine with poultry—one good example is the serving of boiled salt pork with roast turkey or chicken. Nowadays butchers legitimately complain that their customers want nothing but steak and chops; the butchers themselves begin to know less and less about the finer points of their trade.

Our neglect of veal is probably one odd result of having had such good grazing in winter and summer, as if farmers weren't inclined to rid themselves of calves which their meadows would soon transform into sirloin.

As for game, our modern situation on the whole isn't a very good one. Wild rabbits have become scarce since myxomatosis. Wood pigeons and hares are less commonly seen in the butchers' shops—this applies as well to wild duck, snipe and woodcock, and in most parts of England to partridges. Pheasants and grouse have become a commonplace of the deep freeze, and there's no doubt that freezing takes the edge off their flavour. The only good pheasant is one that has been well hung before plucking, gutting and cooking. The situation is better than it used to be with venison, partly owing to the increase in the feral deer population. It's not too difficult to get hold of cuts of fallow deer, which is an opportunity for reviving old recipes which go back to the kitchens of the medieval castle. There's more venison now in some markets than ever there was in the days of Robin Hood, and there would be more still, if so much of it wasn't exported to Germany.

The poultry problem is to find well-fed, free-range birds (which, remember, also require hanging if their flavour is to develop as it should). Nowadays the neglected bird is the goose which was the bird of winter celebration before the triumph of turkeys. There are other ways of cooking goose than with sage and onion stuffing. I have included a recipe for gooseberry sauce on page 66 which was always served with green goose, i.e. young goose, in springtime, but which can also be served with older goose as well. Green goose is a tender dish, though it's not so easily experienced unless you keep geese yourself or are in a neighbourhood where geese are still kept in large flocks on common land.

The idea of making boxes of pastry, or coffins as they were called in the Middle Ages, and filling them with pork and game, has been with us so long, and so enjoyably, that it is impossible to imagine an English table without them. When decorated with pastry roses and leaves, with diamonds and ornate edgings, when brushed with egg and baked to a rich golden brown, such meat pies have been the set pieces of many fine meals. One surprise, if your main acquaintance with the genre has been the general pork pie, a pie of reduced circumstances, will be the recipe for the great Yorkshire pies which were made until about a hundred years ago and sent down to London, first by coach, and latterly by train, at Christmas time. Layers of boned poultry and game, wrapped one inside the other, were cooked in so much butter and inside so thick a crust, that they lasted well and stood up to the bumping journey. With them would come the York hams, mild cured and delicate, to join the less famous black Bradenham ham, and the Wiltshire ham—still to be had from a first-class grocer even if the Yorkshire pies are now a past glory.

Lamb

First-class lamb has become a problem in England since the importation of cheap, refrigerated New Zealand lamb made it a meat for the most homely occasions (mutton seems to have disappeared altogether—it needs a very knowledgeable butcher, and lost its reputation during the last war, when butchers were not able to carry on their trade in the proper manner). Nowadays I sometimes conclude that our best lamb all goes to France : certainly it is instructive to visit a butchery there and see how highly lamb is regarded—and what a price it is, and how delicious it is.

However, perseverance and a certain obstinacy should lead you to a butcher who can supply local or at least very good English lamb. And remember these lines when you are making your choice :—

> *The mountain sheep are sweeter,*
> *But the valley sheep are fatter,*
> *Therefore we deemed it meeter,*
> *To carry off the latter.*
>
> 'The War-Song of Dinas Vawr'
> *by T. L. Peacock.*

I choose the sweetness of Welsh mountain lamb from Radnor when possible, but that may be because we live near enough to Wales to make an expedition to Cardiff from time to time. There we buy real Welsh lamb in the covered market, and some laverbread to go with it, before sauntering off, our minds at peace, to contemplate the Impressionist paintings in the gallery. (We find that our best expeditions satisfy both body and soul—something that English restaurant keepers do not always understand.)

You may prefer to uphold the honour of your district in Scotland, Northumberland or Devon—so long as you have found a knowing family butcher who cares as much for what he sells as what he takes. Londoners may complain that it's no longer possible for them to choose their lot, arguing preferences at dinner like any Forsyte. But people living around Romney Marsh are worse done by. They have to look across at flocks of sheep feeding on the salt marshes, and know that it will bypass *their* butchers and be served to tourists in Normandy, Brittany and Paris, as *agneau pré-salé, specialité de la maison*, price to match.

Mrs Beeton sternly remarked that Wales was the only part of Britain to have the correct conditions for true *pré-salé* lamb. Half a century later, John Meade Falkner described the reclaimed marshes around Chichester (in *The Nebuly Coat*) and said that sheep grazing behind the dykes had as good a flavour as any *pré-salé* mutton the other side of the Channel. Certainly

French buyers today share his opinion. Now, one may even wonder about the lamb served on Mont St Michel. Customers sit in high restaurants, looking across the bay at the sheep advancing and retreating, with the tides, over the moss-like verdure. Are there really enough of them to feed all those summer visitors? Surely not?

An elegy for *agnus britannicus*? Not entirely, for imported lamb does beautifully when treated with a marinade to taste like venison, or when the shoulder is boned and stuffed with rice and apricots.

Shoulder of Lamb with Rice and Apricot Stuffing

1 boned shoulder of lamb, unrolled
Salt, pepper
Melted butter

Stuffing
8 oz rice, long grain
4 oz dried apricots, soaked, chopped
2 tablespoons seedless raisins

2 tablespoons blanched, split almonds
½ teaspoon cinnamon
½ teaspoon coriander
½ teaspoon ground ginger
Salt, black pepper

Spread out the shoulder of lamb which should have been boned so that a pocket is formed inside the meat. Season it inside and out.

Boil the rice in plenty of boiling, salted water. Drain it well and mix with the remaining ingredients. Use some of the mixture to stuff the lamb, and sew up the pocket with needle and button thread. Brush the lamb over with melted butter and roast it in the usual way—30 minutes per pound (stuffed weight), plus 20 minutes, at mark 5, 375°. When it is done, remove it to a serving dish. Pour the fat from the pan juices, and then mix in the remaining rice mixture to reheat; add a little butter if necessary. Arrange this round the lamb, cut away its thread, and serve.

Since the arrival of frozen, cheap lamb from New Zealand, this type of recipe has increased in common use in England, to compensate for the coarser flavour of the meat. The idea of cooking lamb with dried fruits, originally from the Middle East, has been adapted to our tastes, as curry was earlier on. If I held to the theory of folk-memory, I could say that this and similar recipes fall into the niche once occupied by sweet lamb pies; they were favourite dishes from the Middle Ages until the end of the eighteenth century. A version is said to linger on in southern France at Pézenas. French cookery writers assert that when Clive of India stayed for some time in the town, his chef gave the recipe to a French pâtissier : they are still made there and at Béziers, and include mutton, not very much sugar, and lemon peel. Other versions are found in locally produced cookery books from Wales and the north-west of England. I suspect that they are more honoured in the breach than in the modern kitchens of those parts. I had this recipe from our elderly landlady when we were evacuated during the war to Casterton in Westmorland : her ingredients resulted in a sweet mince pie (the Pézenas pies are eaten as a first course), and very good it is.

Sweet Lamb Pie from Westmorland

1 lb weight shortcrust pastry

Filling
6 oz lean boned lamb
3 oz lamb fat, trimmed from chops etc.
6 oz apples, weighed after peeling, coring and grating
4 oz currants
4 oz raisins
4 oz sultanas

2 oz candied chopped peel
Juice of 1 orange
Juice of ½ lemon
2 oz blanched chopped almonds
4 tablespoons rum
Pinch salt
Freshly ground black pepper
½ teaspoon mace
½ teaspoon cinnamon
¼ nutmeg grated

Make up this pie on a pie plate, the kind that is much used in the north of England. The best ones are tin, but the enamelled kind do quite well. Roll out half the pastry and cover the plate.

Mince the meat, both fat and lean. Put it into a basin and

mix in the remaining ingredients, making sure that everything is well distributed. Taste and add a little more spice if you like. Turn enough of this filling into the pastry to mound up above the level of the rim. Roll out the remaining pastry, and cover the pie, brushing the underneath pastry rim first with beaten egg or top of the milk. Press down and decorate the edge, make a central hole, and brush the lid over with egg or top of the milk. Bake for 30 minutes at mark 6, 400°.

Put any filling left over into a jam jar, cover it and use it up for small mince pies.

Roast Saddle of Lamb

For 10–12

1 saddle of lamb with its kidneys (9–12 lb in weight)	Flour
	¼ pt port or red wine
Salt, pepper, thyme	¾ pt stock made from lamb trim-
Butter	mings and bones

The butcher will have prepared the saddle by slitting the tail and curving it over, with the two kidneys between the tail pieces and the saddle, the whole thing skewered in place with a couple of wooden cocktail sticks. One warning—for this kind of high-class butchery, it is wise to go to an experienced man of mature years, and if his father was a butcher before him, so much the better.

To prepare the joint for cooking, remove the kidneys, but restore the toothpicks to their place so that the tail maintains its curves while cooking. Score the skin into a diamond pattern. Rub the fat over with salt, pepper and thyme (slivers of garlic may be stuck into the meat—this has recently become an English habit). Melt a little butter and dribble it over the joint.

Roast the saddle for 2½ hours at mark 5, 375°, for slightly pink meat. Baste it occasionally with the port or red wine, and the pan juices. After 1¾ hours, add the kidneys to cook under the front of the joint so that they do not dry out. After 2 hours' cooking, dredge the lamb lightly and evenly with flour and a little more melted butter. Leave it to brown—raising the heat if it seems a good idea, but make sure that the tail is protected by foil from burning if you do this.

Meanwhile prepare the gravy. Melt 2 tablespoons of butter in a pan, and cook until it turns golden brown. Stir in 1 heaped tablespoon of flour, and then the stock to make a sauce. Leave this to simmer down gently as the saddle finishes cooking.

Place the cooked joint on a hot serving dish. Spear the kidneys back in place and keep warm while the gravy is finished. Pour off the fat from the pan juices, and set the pan over a good heat. Stir in the sauce, and scrape up all the delicious brown bits which may have stuck to the pan. Taste and adjust the seasoning. Many people like a thick gravy with lamb, others prefer it to be a slightly more runny affair, so adjust the mixture in the pan by adding a little more wine or stock, or by boiling the gravy hard for a few moments to thicken it further. Pour through a strainer into a hot gravy boat.

THINGS TO GO WITH ROAST LAMB

Mint sauce (summer, page 296)

Redcurrant or medlar jelly (winter, page 301-2)

Laverbread, heated with orange and lemon juice (all seasons, page 102)

Young peas and young potatoes, cooked with mint

Asparagus

French beans

Spinach

Cauliflower

Purple sprouting broccoli

Chestnuts and Brussels sprouts

Chestnut purée

Onion sauce

Roast potatoes

TO CARVE A SADDLE

Cut slices parallel to the backbone, or else cut down into chop-like slices at a sloping angle to follow the rib bones. Remove the kidneys and cut them up as fairly as you can.

Guard of Honour

For 7–8

1 best end of neck

Salt, pepper, thyme or rosemary

Butter

Herb stuffing, page 285

Ask the butcher to cut the best end of neck into two, straight down the backbone, and to chine it for easy carving. Be careful he does not trim off the long bones. There will be 7–8 chops in each piece.

At home, turn the joints skin side up, and remove about $1\frac{1}{2}''$ only of skin and fat at the thin end of the joints. This will expose the ends of the bones: scrape them free of meat as well as you can. Score the skin in stripes or diamonds. Rub in salt, pepper and thyme or crushed rosemary. Now stand the joints up on their thick end, skin side out, and push them together so that the exposed bones cross each other alternately. The joints will bristle like a military row of crossed stakes. Very attractive on this scale. Skewer the meat together at the base, and push some stuffing into the cavity (I prefer to fill the cavity, after cooking, with small new potatoes separately cooked, or with mushrooms, because the stuffing has a tendency to fall out in a messy way unless the mixture is made very stiff with egg— and most people prefer a light crumbly stuffing). Roast at mark 5, 375°, for $1\frac{1}{2}$ hours. Protect the exposed bones from burning with a piece of foil pressed into place over them. To carve, cut down between the cutlets, allowing two per person.

Guard of Honour can be served with all the usual things for lamb (see previous page), but the best thing is stuffed tomatoes (page 49), which should be placed round the joint on its serving dish.

Boiled Leg of Mutton (or Lamb) with Caper Sauce

1 trimmed leg of mutton or lamb	*Vegetable*
3 carrots, quartered	3 lb young turnips, peeled, sliced
3 onions, unpeeled	1 level tablespoon flour
2 parsnips, peeled, quartered	1 oz butter
1 turnip, peeled, quartered	$\frac{1}{4}$ pt double cream
Salt, pepper	Nutmeg, pepper, salt
	Caper sauce, page 295

Put the meat into a large pan, with the vegetables and seasoning. Cover it with tepid water. Bring it to the boil, skim well and cover. Leave it for 2½ hours—the liquid should bubble occasionally with a slight burp, it should not be allowed to boil properly. Remove the leg to a large serving dish and cut a paper ruffle to put round the shank bone—see page 123.

Meanwhile prepare the vegetables. The turnips should be cooked in salted water; drain them well, sieve, and whisk in the butter. Stir the cream into the flour and make sure that there are no lumps, and add that to the turnip. Put back over the heat and cook until the purée thickens up nicely. Season with nutmeg, pepper and salt.

When the lamb or mutton is on its dish, take spoonsful of the turnip and put them round it, flat side down. Cut the carrot from the cooking stock into even-sized batons, and put them between the mounds of turnip.

Serve the caper sauce separately.

Boiled leg of mutton is even more delicious if it is allowed to cool in the cooking liquor until next day. Then serve it cold with a plain salad and a bottle of claret.

Leg of Lamb stuffed with Crab

1 large leg of lamb	1 teaspoon curry powder
Salt, pepper	
Carrots, diced	*Stuffing*
Onions, chopped	1 boiled crab, about 1½ lb weight
1 large stick celery, sliced	½ teaspoon curry powder
½ pt dry white wine	1 tablespoon fresh chopped mint
½ pt lamb stock	3 egg yolks
¼ pt double cream	Salt, pepper

Bone the leg of lamb to make a good cavity (or persuade the butcher to do it for you). Use the bones and any trimmings to make the lamb stock. Season the leg inside and out.

To make the stuffing, remove the crab meat from the crab— with patience and application you will get something between 8 and 10 oz. This is a fiddly job, I know, but frozen crab meat will not be nearly so good. Mix with the remainder of the stuffing ingredients, fill the lamb cavity and sew it up.

Chop enough carrots and onions, in roughly equal quantity, to make a good layer in the bottom of a self-basting roaster or similar type of dish. Add the celery and season everything well. Place the lamb on top. Cover with a lid, or a piece of double foil, and leave in a moderate oven, mark 4, 350°, for 2 hours, until the lamb is cooked. Transfer it to a roasting pan and put it back into the oven to brown, while you make the sauce. To do this pour the wine and stock on to the bed of vegetables in the braising pan. Set it over a good heat, and bring to the boil stirring well to scrape up all the meaty bits. Simmer for 5 minutes, then strain into a saucepan. Skim off any surplus fat, add the teaspoon of curry powder and finally the cream. Correct the seasoning and heat through thoroughly before pouring into a hot sauceboat. Serve with hot buttered noodles.

Do not be nervous of the strange sounding combination of lamb with crab: it is delicious, as the crab gives a nutty-tasting piquancy to the meat, and is not in the least fishy. Remember that in the past meat was often 'piqued' with anchovies, or stuffed with oysters, and even cockles, and that anchovy essence still goes into our Melton Mowbray pork pies.

I will tell you how this recipe was invented. It's the habit of foreigners in a strange country to jeer at the food. An English traveller in Italy once complained of the lack of pease pudding and bubble-and-squeak. I have often heard the French laugh at our habit of eating redcurrant jelly with lamb, quite forgetting their own similar combinations of pork with prunes or duck with orange. I suppose it is a sign of insecurity, of the closed mind. This being so, it is not surprising that when our friend Guy Mouilleron of the Café Royal found himself one evening with a group of French chefs working in London, the conversation turned to the odd food habits of the English. Fancy, one of them said, they even eat lamb with crab! General laughter; but Guy Mouilleron thought, Lamb with crab? Why not? So without further suggestions he produced this delicious com-

bination of braised lamb with a crab stuffing. I did not have
the heart to tell him that many English people would be as
shocked as his French friends were at the idea, and that the
combination was left behind with the eighteenth century, as far
as national dishes are concerned. Other recipes that he has based
on our country traditions of the past are to be found on pages
61 and 176.

Spiced Welsh Mutton 'Ham'

6 lb leg Welsh mutton or lamb

Spiced salt
4 oz dark brown sugar
8 oz sea salt

½ oz saltpetre
1 oz black peppercorns
1 oz allspice berries
¼ oz coriander seeds

Crush the spices and mix them with the sugar, salt and saltpetre.
Rub the meat over with this mixture, being particularly careful
to push it down between the meat and bone. Leave in a deep
dish in a cool place for 12–14 days, rubbing the meat each day
with the spiced salt mixture and its juices, and turning it over.

To cook the 'ham', rinse off the bits of spice and place it in
a large pot or ham kettle. Cover with tepid water, bring to the
boil and simmer gently for 3½ hours. Leave to cool down in the
cooking liquor for 2 hours, then remove and drain and finish
the cooling process under a weight.

In the old days, the cured but uncooked 'ham' would be
squeezed free of as much moisture as possible and left under a
weight for 24 hours. It would then be smoked over smouldering
oak chips for 5–15 days. If you have a small, friendly bacon
factory near you, who will smoke your ham, this is something
I can recommend—it is a great luxury.

Lamb to Eat like Venison

Marinade
5 oz chopped onion
5 oz chopped carrot
2 oz chopped celery
3 cloves garlic, chopped
2 tablespoons oil
Bay leaf
2 sprigs thyme
4 sprigs parsley

2 sprigs rosemary
8 juniper berries, crushed
8 coriander seeds, crushed
10 peppercorns, crushed
3 teaspoons salt
1 pt red wine, or dry white wine, or
  dry cider
¼ pt red or white wine vinegar

First make the marinade—brown vegetables and garlic in the oil. Add the remaining marinade ingredients and bring to the boil. Set aside to cool. Remove the outer skin of the leg of lamb, if the butcher has not done so already. Score the fat into a diamond pattern, and place the meat in a deep dish. Pour over it the cold marinade. Leave the whole thing in a cool place for four days, turning the joint over twice a day. Cover the dish between whiles with foil.

To cook the lamb, you will also need

2 onions, sliced
2 carrots, diced
2 stalks celery, chopped
2 leeks, sliced

½ lb unsmoked streaky bacon, cut in
  pieces
2 oz butter
Veal stock

Into a deep pan put the vegetables and bacon which should first have been lightly browned in the butter. Lay the leg of lamb on top. Strain the marinade over it, and add enough veal stock to come about ⅔ of the way up. Bring slowly to the boil, cover the pot and leave to simmer for 2 hours until the lamb is almost cooked—this can be done either on top of the stove or in the oven. Turn the joint over after 1 hour. Shortly before the 2 hours is up, remove 2 pints of the cooking liquor and boil it down to 1 pint of strongly flavoured stock. Put the meat on to a roasting dish and give it 20 minutes in a hot oven to glaze, mark 7, 425°, basting it frequently with the reduced stock.

Serve it with green beans, redcurrant jelly and either the pan juices, or gravy made from them, together with some of the remaining cooking stock.

A leg of pork can be treated in the same way, to taste like wild boar. When one can get it, a leg of mutton is better than lamb : it will need longer braising time, before being put into the oven.

Roast Lamb with Laverbread

1 whole best-end of neck of lamb preferably Welsh	*Laverbread*
	1 lb laverbread
1 clove garlic	3 oz butter
Salt, pepper	Juice of 1 lemon
1 large tomato	Juice of 2 oranges
1 carrot	1 orange thinly sliced
1 pint beef stock	Salt, pepper
1 glass dry white wine or vermouth	
1 tablespoon cornflour	

Ask the butcher to split the neck into two joints right down the centre, then to remove the boniest part of the spine. Do not let him remove the meat from the long bones.

At home, remove a long strip about 1½″ deep from the thin ends; scrape the bones free of meat. Stick slivers of garlic into the joints and season them. All this can be done the day before the lamb is to be cooked. It is also a good idea to make the gravy stock in advance, too; the fat has time to solidify, and can easily be removed before making the sauce. To make the stock, put *all* the meat trimmings, plus the back bone removed by the butcher, into a pan, together with salt and pepper, tomato, carrot and beef stock. Simmer for at least two hours. Strain and leave to cool. When cold, take off the fat, add the wine to the stock and reduce to a good strong flavour. Finally thicken with cornflour in the usual way.

To return to the joints, stand them upright in a roasting pan with the exposed bones interlacing, like the roof ridge of a Danish farmhouse. Cover with a piece of foil to prevent them charring. Cook for 45 minutes at 425°, mark 7, if you like lamb pink; for 60 minutes if you like it well done. When cooked, strain off the fat, and add meat juices to the sauce.

About quarter of an hour before the lamb is ready, prepare the laver. Melt the butter in a saucepan, stir in the laverbread and add the fruit juices to taste. Season if necessary with salt, and pepper.

Spread the laverbread on either side of the joints of lamb on a hot serving dish. Arrange the slices of orange at the edge. Some new potatoes go well with this dish, or old potatoes cut into neat rounds. Pour the sauce into a sauceboat, and serve everything very hot.

If your fishmonger doesn't stock laverbread, and you do not live in the right part of England, you can buy laverbread by post. It travels well, and is already prepared and cooked—it only needs the kind of reheating described above. Address on page 39. Laverbread with orange and lemon also goes well with salt pork or boiled bacon. (There are two more laverbread recipes on page 54.)

Lancashire Hot-Pot

For 6

2 lb best end of neck of lamb chops	Salt, pepper
6 lambs' kidneys (optional)	Water
1 lb onions, sliced thinly	Butter
2 lb potatoes, peeled and sliced thinly	

Using a deep casserole—the traditional kind is glazed dark brown and made in a flower-pot shape, with a rim and lid— put the meat and vegetables into it in layers, seasoning each layer with salt and freshly ground black pepper. Finish off with a nicely arranged layer of overlapping potato slices. Pour in enough water to come about halfway up the pot, and brush the top layer of potatoes over with melted butter. Cover and put into a hot oven, mark 6–8, 400–450°, for about half an hour, then reduce the heat to mark 1, 275°, and leave for $2\frac{1}{2}$ hours. Take off the lid after 2 hours so that the potatoes can brown.

The English cousin of Irish stew, and very good when made

with lamb or mutton of quality. If you want to make econo-
mies, buy scrag end of English lamb, rather than best end of
New Zealand lamb: the flavour will be better. In the old days,
mutton was the meat used. Now it is almost impossible to buy,
but if you do succeed, allow a longer cooking time.

Lamb's Head and Barley, with Brain Sauce

1 lamb's head	1 small turnip
Water	1 leek
Salt, Pepper	½ pt pearl barley
Bouquet garni, including winter savory	1 oz butter
	1 oz flour
Onion, stuck with 3 cloves	¼ pt milk
2 carrots, halved	Rolls of bacon, grilled
1 parsnip, halved	Lemon quarters

Ask the butcher to clean and split the head, being careful to
remove the brain before it is damaged. At home, soak the head
in cold salted water for an hour. Rinse it, and put it into a
cooking pot with enough water to cover it. Bring slowly to the
boil and skim it. Now add seasonings, herbs, vegetables and
pearl barley. Cook for about 1½ hours, at a steady simmer, until
the meat comes easily away from the bones.

Meanwhile soak the brain in cold salted water for 30 minutes,
remove the membrane which nets it and place it in a little
square of cloth. Tie it up and place it in the lamb's head pot
for 10 minutes to cook. Alternatively, remove a large ladleful
of stock from the lamb's head and cook the brain in it. Drain
and chop it. Now make a sauce by melting the butter, stirring
in the flour and moistening this roux with the milk, and enough
lamb stock to produce a thick but not pasty sauce. Stir in the
chopped brains, the parsley and correct the seasoning. Add a
squeeze of lemon juice if you like.

Extract the lamb's head from the pot. Discard the bones and
cut up the meat into nice pieces. Arrange them on a serving
dish with the bacon rolls and lemon quarters. Put the sauce into
a sauceboat. With a perforated spoon remove some of the pearl
barley and put it round the meat. Serve everything very hot.

The liquid in the pan, and remaining pearl barley make a marvellous soup (discard the vegetables and bouquet), which can be eaten before the meat in French peasant style, or at another meal. Personally I think the latter arrangement is preferable. Lamb soup, then lamb's head, is a bit too much of a good thing.

I remember this dish from my childhood with great enjoyment. It is delicious. Do not make the southern-English mistake of thinking it ungenteel food, or even savage food (the title has overtones of those Iron Age chieftains in Ireland who used to pound the brains of their victims with lime, and roll them into balls, to keep as trophies of war). We over-indulge ourselves in attitudes of this kind, and are the losers. Mrs Beeton, for instance, regarded lamb's head as an obscure Scottish dish—'We are not aware whether the custom of eating sheep's heads at Dudingston is still kept up by the good folks of Edinburgh.' Francatelli, at one time chef to Queen Victoria, included an excellent sheep's head broth in his *Cookery Book for the Working Classes*. Which puts it firmly in its place. A century earlier people had more sense. Most eighteenth-century cookery books give one or two recipes for different ways of cooking sheeps'— or rather lambs'—heads. The combination of different textures in this dish is what makes it so good—the different textures of meat, the smooth pearl barley with a slight chewiness, the delicate smoothness of the sauce, and the crispness and sharpness provided by the bacon and lemon.

Roast Pork with Crackling and Baked Apples

For 6

1 shoulder, loin or leg of pork	Bouquet garni
Salt, pepper	Oil
Pork bones	1 oz butter
1 onion stuck with 3 cloves	1 tablespoon flour
1 carrot, sliced	6 large Cox's Orange Pippins

Buy the pork a good 24 hours before you intend to cook it. Ask the butcher to score the rind every half inch, or do it yourself with a very sharp knife of the razor blade variety. Ask the butcher, too, to bone the joint, but not to tie it.

When you get home, season the meat all over and in particular on the boned side. Leave in the refrigerator until it is required for cooking. This pre-seasoning benefits almost all meat for roasting : if you have a brine crock, put the joint into that for 8 hours—but the crackling will not be crisp, after roasting.

Put the bones into a pot with the onion, carrot and herbs. Cover generously with water, and leave to simmer for 3 or 4 hours. Strain off the liquid and boil it down to ¾ pint. Season it.

Before putting the joint into the oven, rub the crackling over with oil, and sprinkle it with salt. Calculate the cooking time at 35 minutes to the lb. Put it into the oven set at mark 7, 425°, then after 20 minutes, lower the heat to mark 3, 325°. An hour before the end of cooking time, score the skin of the apples in a circle an inch below the top (this prevents them bursting), and place them round the pork. To make the gravy, cook the butter in a small pan until it turns golden brown, stir in the flour, and moisten with the stock. Leave to simmer gently for at least 20 minutes.

When the meat is cooked, check the crackling. If it is not crisp enough, put the oven up again to mark 7, 425°, and give the joint another 10 or 15 minutes (without the apples).

Put the meat on a serving dish, surround it with the apples, and keep warm. Skim the fat from the roasting juices, then pour them into the gravy. Correct the seasoning and serve very hot with the meat.

Instead of baked apples, many people serve apple sauce—recipes on pages 292–4.

If you do not care for crackling, ask the butcher to remove the rind (take it home, though, and cut it in squares and use to enrich a beef stew of the kind described on page 109). Half an hour before the joint is cooked, mix up a glaze of :—

1 tablespoon French mustard	½ tablespoon soft brown sugar
1 tablespoon red-currant jelly	½ tablespoon cream

Spread this over the joint, and put back into the oven to turn a beautiful and appetising brown.

The Rev. William Collier, of Cambridge, led a most dissolute life; he was also a notorious *gourmand*.

'An anecdote I had from his own mouth will prove his title to the latter character. "When I was last in town," said he, "I was going to dine with a friend, and passed through a small court, just as a lad was hanging up a board, on which was this tempting inscription :

'A roast pig this instant set upon the table!'

The invitation was irresistible—I ordered a quarter; it was *very delicate* and *very delicious*. I despatched a second and a third portion, but was constrained to leave one quarter behind, as my dinner hour was approaching, and my friend was remarkably punctual." '

From *Reminiscences of Cambridge,*
by Henry Gunning, 1854, 1855.

Stuffed Pork Tenderloin

2 tenderloins	4 rashers streaky bacon
2 large slices cooked ham	2 large onions, chopped
3 oz Lancashire cheese	4–6 oz brown sherry, Madeira or
8 sage leaves, or thyme	port

Slit each tenderloin twice lengthwise, so that it opens out like a book. Cut ham and cheese into flat $\frac{1}{2}''$ wide strips, and put a line of both into each slit (some cheese will be left over). Blanch the sage leaves in boiling water for 1 minute, cut them in half and put along the slits with the ham and cheese; alternatively sprinkle some thyme into them. Tie each tenderloin at $1\frac{1}{2}''$ intervals wtih button thread, to hold them in shape.

Put the onion all over a long narrow dish. Pour in the wine. Lay the tenderloins on top with the rashers of bacon on top to keep them basted with fat. Put into the oven at mark 5, 375°, and leave for 40 minutes. Chop and sprinkle the remaining cheese over them and put back for 5 minutes. The sauce can be left as it is, or thickened with cornflour. Remove the thread before serving, and do not be anxious if the meat still looks pink—this is caused by the saltpetre in ham and bacon cures. At table slice the tenderloins across diagonally.

Beefsteak stewed with Oysters

For 4–5

1½ lb beefsteak (see recipe)	2 oz port
Salt, pepper	1 tablespoon butter, level
18 fine oysters	1 rounded tablespoon flour
2 oz butter	Triangles of bread fried in butter
½ pt water	

Any good beefsteak will do for this recipe, from chuck to rump, but you will have to allow for the stewing time accordingly. Trim off fat and gristle and cut it into neat pieces. Season them and put them aside while you open the oysters, into a sieve set over a basin. Leave the oysters to drain, while you brown the meat in the butter. When it is a good colour on both sides, pour in the oyster liquor and the water, which should barely cover the meat. Put a lid on the pan and leave everything to stew until the beef is tender—this will take from an hour to two and a half hours, depending on the quality of the steak.

When the meat is ready, pour in the port wine. Mash the butter and flour together, and add it to the sauce gradually in little knobs. You may not need it all to thicken the sauce, which should be kept over a moderate heat just below boiling point. Adjust the seasoning, add the oysters to warm through for a minute or two : they should not cook too long or they will become tough. Put the steak and oysters with the sauce into a dish, tuck the bread round the sides and serve very hot.

Shin of Beef Stew

4 lb shin of beef	¾ lb onions, sliced
Dripping	Salt, pepper
2–3 tablespoons of flour	Water
¾ lb carrots, sliced	

'Four pounds of leg or shin of beef cost about one shilling; cut this into pieces the size of an egg, and fry them of a good brown colour with a little dripping fat, in a good sized saucepan, then shake in a large handful of flour, add carrots and onions cut up in pieces the same as the meat, season with pepper and salt, moisten with water enough to cover in the whole, stir the stew on the fire till it boils, and then set it on the hob to continue boiling very gently for about an hour and a half, and you will then be able to enjoy an excellent dinner.'

Francatelli, *Cookery Book for the Working Classes.*

This was substantially the recipe used in our family nearly a century later. The main difference was that the meat was floured before frying, and salt was never added until the end. It was one of our favourite dishes. I remember asking my mother why she bought shin of beef, when other people bought the more expensive—and therefore better, or so I thought—stewing beef. She showed me how the rounded nuggets of meat are patterned with a transparent gelatinous membrane which holds them together, and adds a smooth, jellied texture to the sauce. Nowadays I always buy shin of beef on the bone when I can, and get the butcher to saw it across into slices (like the Milanese *ossi buchi*). This way the sauce is even better, and one has the delicious marrow as well. Or else I buy and cook the meat in one piece, which takes longer of course. The meat is sliced and served on a bed of potatoes and glazed carrots, and sprinkled with parsley. The sauce is reduced by boiling to increase the flavour, and served in a separate sauce boat. It does not look in the least like a stew. I always serve meat and sauce separately, because the older members of the family cannot bear the sight of a stew after their early institutional experiences.

One or two practical suggestions. Stock, or better still stock and red wine, can be substituted for water; the seasonings can be improved by the addition of garlic and a bouquet garni. Always remove the fatty outer skin from the beef, and cook the stew the day before it is needed. Allow it to cool to tepid, then strain off the sauce into a bowl and put it into the ice box of the refrigerator. The fat will rise quickly to the surface—there is always some, however carefully you trim the meat—and can be removed easily. Restore the shin of beef to the sauce, and reheat slowly and simmer for 20–30 minutes before serving.

Garnishes such as olives or mushrooms with glazed onions and triangles of fried bread, enable you to serve the dish a second time without it being too obvious.

Sussex Stewed Steak

For 6

2–2½ lb slice top rump or chuck steak	3 oz stout
Salt, pepper	3 oz port
Flour	2 tablespoons mushroom ketchup or wine vinegar
1 large onion, sliced	

Season the meat and rub it all over with the flour. Put it into a shallow ovenproof dish in which it can lie flat. Put the onion on top in an even layer. Pour in the stout, port and ketchup or vinegar. Cover the dish with a tight-fitting lid of foil, and put it into the oven at mark 1, 275°, for 3 hours. Serve with mashed potatoes, and some field mushrooms if you can get them.

If you do not have a suitable dish, wrap the whole thing in a

double layer of foil, fastening it very securely. It is a good idea
to butter the foil first, and place it on a baking tray.

Roast Beef with Yorkshire Pudding

4–5 lb joint sirloin with undercut,
   on the bone
or 4–5 lb ribs of beef
Beef dripping or oil
1 onion, sliced

Salt, pepper
1 teaspoon sugar
1 teaspoonful of flour
$\frac{1}{2}$ pt beef stock

These are the minimum sizes for joints of beef on the bone, as
far as successful roasting is concerned. Although boned joints
make for easier carving, the flavour is better if the meat is left
on the bone. Rub the meat over with salt and pepper, and leave
overnight.

Next day, weigh the joint and calculate cooking time—15
minutes to the pound for rare meat, 15 minutes to the pound
plus 20 minutes for well-done meat, at mark 7, 425°.

Put enough dripping or oil into the roasting pan to cover the
bottom, and put the pan into the preheated oven. After five
minutes, add the joint which you have placed on a rack or
trivet. 40 minutes before the end of cooking time, pour the
Yorkshire pudding batter into the pan. It will acquire an extra
good flavour from the drippings of the meat.

Cook the onion very slowly meanwhile in a little dripping
in a small pan. Mix in the sugar and let it caramelize to a deep
mellow brown. Stir in the flour, then add the beef stock. Simmer
for at least 20 minutes, and correct the seasoning.

When the meat is cooked, place it on a serving dish, with
the Yorkshire pudding cut in pieces round it. Pour off the fat
from the roasting pan, and add any meat juices which have not
been absorbed by the pudding to the gravy. Strain it into a
hot sauce boat.

Serve horseradish sauce, page 296, and roasted parsnips with
beef. Other suitable vegetables are carrots, courgettes, glazed
onions, roast potatoes.

Yorkshire Pudding

¼ lb flour   ½ pt milk, or ¼ pt each milk and
Pinch salt   water
1 egg

Mix flour and salt, make a well in the centre and break the egg
into it. Add a little milk. Beginning at the centre, stir these
ingredients into a batter, gradually pouring in the remainder
of the milk, or milk and water.

This recipe has remained unchanged since the eighteenth
century when it first became popular. Here is Hannah Glasse's
version for cooking under spit-roasted meat—it can be adapted
for a modern spit-roaster :—

> 'Take a quart of milk, four eggs, and a little salt, make it
> up into a thick batter with flour, like a pancake batter. You
> must have a good piece of meat at the fire, take a stew-pan
> and put some dripping in, set it on the fire; when it boils,
> pour on your pudding; let it bake on the fire till you think
> it is high enough, then turn a plate upside-down in the
> dripping pan [i.e. the pan under the joint] that the dripping
> may not be blacked; set your stew-pan on it under your meat,
> and let the dripping drop on the pudding, and the heat of the
> fire come to it, to make it of a fine brown. When your meat
> is done and sent to table, drain all the fat from your pudding,
> and set it on the fire again to dry a little; then slide it as
> dry as you can into a dish, melt some butter, and pour it into
> a cup, and set it in the middle of the pudding. It is an
> exceeding good pudding; the gravy of the meat eats well
> with it.'

On roast-beef Sundays, my mother's father, who had reached
heights of power and respectability in the Bank of England,
forgot what was due to his position and remembered the ways
of the Northumbrian farm at Old Bewick which his family had
come from. The roast beef went back to the kitchen after the
main course, but the Yorkshire pudding remained to be finished

up with sweetened condensed milk. I do not know how my
grandmother took this—she prided herself on her elegant
desserts—but my mother shared his delight in the crisp and
sticky pudding. When she had a home of her own, and a family,
she passed his taste on to us who only remembered him, in spats
and spectacles and pin-striped trousers, from old photographs.

Try it. But the pudding should be roasted *above* the beef,
and you will have to forgo the meaty juices, at least as part of
the pudding. There is, of course, no reason why you shouldn't
just make the Yorkshire pudding on its own, as a straightfor-
ward second course.

The Prize-Winning Chinese Yorkshire Pudding

½ pt milk
4 eggs
Just under ½ teaspoon salt
Dash of pepper

½ teaspoon *tai luk* (from oriental stores)
½ lb plain flour, sifted

Mix all ingredients except the flour, beating them well together.
Let them stand for 15 minutes, then whisk in the flour. Heat a
roasting pan and some dripping from the meat in the oven,
which should be at mark 8, 450°, then pour in the batter and
leave for 20 minutes 52.2 seconds.

Several years ago, six chefs competed at Leeds in the 'Great
Yorkshire Pudding Contest'. To the chagrin of native cooks, the
winner was Mr Tin Sung Chan from Hong Kong, who runs
the Chopsticks Restaurant. 'His methods were unorthodox,'
wrote the *Guardian* reporter, 'his ingredients oddly arranged,
but his pudding swelled to the height of a coronation crown and
its taste, according to one of the judges, was superb.'

According to Mrs Anne Wilson, again of Leeds, who wrote
Food and Drink in Britain (Constable, 1973), the first recipe
for what we now call Yorkshire pudding comes from *The Whole
Duty of Woman*, published in 1737. The frugal intention was to
make use of the dripping and juices which fell from joints of

meat roasting on a spit (these, in grand houses at any rate, were
the semi-official perquisites of the kitchen boy whose job it was to
turn the spit : he dipped his fingers into the pan to help him
keep going). The interesting thing is that the author instructs us
to place the batter under a joint of mutton. Ten years later,
Hannah Glasse gives us her recipe, the batter identical with
ours today, and she calls it Yorkshire Pudding—she doesn't
specify which sorts of meat it should be eaten with, but she
does mention that marvellous northern habit of eating it alone
with the gravy.

Shepherd's Pie

For 6

Large onion, chopped	Salt, freshly ground black pepper
3 cloves garlic, chopped	2–3 lb potatoes
3 tablespoons oil	3 oz butter
1 lb beef, chuck or shin, minced	½ pt milk
Tablespoon tomato concentrate	1 oz grated cheese, preferably
¼ pt dry white wine	Cheddar
½ pt beef stock	1 tablespoon grated Parmesan
3 heaped teaspoons cornflour	

Stew onion and garlic in the oil until soft. Raise heat and add
minced beef, stirring it about until it is nicely browned. Mix in
tomato, wine and half the stock. Slake cornflour with remaining
stock, and pour into the pan. Season well, particularly with the
pepper, and simmer for 10 minutes, covered. Pour off any
surplus fat.

Meanwhile boil potatoes in their skins, peel them, and mash
them with butter and milk.

Put the minced meat into one large or a number of small
individual pots, and cover it with the mashed potato. Fork the
potato up and sprinkle it with cheese. Bake for 10 minutes at
mark 6, 400°, then reduce the heat to mark 4, 350°, and bake
for a further ¾ hour. If more convenient, shepherd's pie can be
baked for an even longer time at a lower temperature to suit

your convenience. The 10 minutes, though, at a high temperature, is a good idea to start the top browning.

'1885. *Pall Mall Gazette*. The Eastbourne board of Guardians
have ordered a mincing-machine . . . for the use of aged and
toothless paupers in their workhouse.' Originally mincing meant
chopping something with a knife. With meat, it helped to make
the less noble parts edible without prolonged cooking. Fair
enough. But with the first mincing-machines, prison, school and
seaside boarding house cooks acquired a new weapon to depress
their victims, with water mince, shepherd's pie with rubbery
granules of left-over meat, rissoles capable of being fired from a
gun.

If you use fresh meat and mince it or chop it yourself at
home, if you season the dish well, if you cook and mash the
potatoes especially for it, shepherd's pie—or cottage pie, as it's
sometimes called—can be well worth eating. Anyone can cook
steak. It takes a modest and generous skill to turn cheaper cuts
of meat into something good.

Cockie-Leekie

1 lb prunes   3 lb leeks, trimmed
2 lb piece of stewing beef Salt, pepper
Boiling fowl, capon or chicken

Soak the prunes overnight. Three to four hours before the meal,
put the beef into a pot large enough to hold the chicken as
well at a later stage. Cover it with plenty of water, and bring
it slowly to the boil. Skim off the grey foamy bubbles as they
rise. Simmer for one hour, then add seasoning, and the bird
if it is a boiling fowl. In any case, add half the leeks which
should be tied together in a bundle. If the bird is a capon or
roasting chicken, add it 1½ hours before the end of the cooking
time or a little less according to size. The prunes should go in
20 minutes before the cockie-leekie is ready. Meanwhile cut the

remaining leeks into slices; they should be added for the last 5 minutes of cooking time, so that they keep a little of their crispness. The big bundle of leeks should be discarded, as all the flavour will have gone into the stock.

The correct way of serving cockie-leekie is to put a slice of beef, a bit of chicken, some prunes, leeks and soup into each bowl. The convenient way is to drink the soup first, then to eat the other items as a main course afterwards.

Like haggis, cockie-leekie is now firmly tied to Scotland in most people's minds. However, in 1867, Lady Llanover gave an identical recipe in her *Good Cookery*, which has to do with Welsh food. And if one compares the basic ingredients with the recipe for Hindle Wakes (page 164), it becomes obvious that these are very old dishes, European dishes if you like, which have survived from many centuries back in those parts of the country which have not been too buffeted by new fashions.

Veal Rolls

Allow one large, thin escalope of veal for each person. Spread it with a thick layer of parsley and lemon stuffing, or herb stuffing (page 285), and roll it up starting with one of the long sides. Tie it with thread in three or four places, then cut it into three or four pieces. Brush each piece with beaten egg, dip it into flour and string it on to a skewer, one skewer for each person. Grill for 20–30 minutes, preferably on a spit, basting them from time to time with melted butter. Serve them with fried mushrooms and lemon quarters.

Veal (or Lamb) Cutlets

When preparing veal or lamb cutlets from the best end of neck, dip them into beaten egg, then into a mixture of breadcrumbs made piquant with chopped parsley, marjoram, thyme, winter savory and grated lemon peel. Press the breadcrumbs well into the meat, then fry it gently on both sides in clarified butter. When the cutlets are done, transfer them to a serving dish. Sprinkle the pan juices with a scant tablespoon of flour, then stir in about half a pint of veal or lamb or chicken stock to make a sauce. Off the heat, whisk in a good knob of butter, correct the seasoning and sharpen it with lemon juice. Strain into a sauceboat and serve with the cutlets.

Slices of boned veal or lamb loin may be cooked in the same way: they should not be cut too thick—about $\frac{1}{2}$ an inch is right. The method can also be used for reheating roast veal or lamb which has not been overcooked in the first instance.

Lemon quarters, mushrooms, watercress, a few boiled potatoes, are the right kind of setting for meat cooked in this way. The sauce should be well seasoned, and not too copious or thick.

Brine curing for pork, beef, etc

Basic	*Aromatics*
5 pts water	1 level teaspoon juniper berries
$\frac{3}{4}$ lb sea salt	Small piece of ungrated nutmeg
$\frac{3}{4}$ lb brown sugar (granulated will do)	1 bay leaf
	3 sprigs thyme
2 oz saltpetre	1 level teaspoon black peppercorns
	4 cloves

The basic ingredients are the essentials—saltpetre gives pickled meat an appetising rosy colour (without it the meat would taste all right, but it would have a greyish appearance). Sugar counteracts the hardening effect of saltpetre and gives an extra flavour. Sea salt should be used, and it should be unadulterated; again, it's a matter of flavour. Pure rock salt is all right, but it lacks character.

The aromatics are variable, or they can be left out altogether.

Put all these ingredients into a pan, bring them to boiling point, skim and remove from the heat. Leave to cool down.

Meanwhile prepare the brine crock or plastic bucket. Clean them out with soda and boiling water. Rinse them well, and leave them upside down to drain. This is more hygienic than drying them with a cloth. At the same time, clean a plate or flat stone in the same way: this you will need to rest on top of the meat so that it remains submerged in the brine. The crock or bucket will also need a scrupulously clean lid.

When the brine is cool, strain it into the bucket or crock. Put in the meat, weight it down and put the lid in place. Always remove the meat from the brine with tongs, not fingers. And have a separate crock for each type of meat—one for pork, another for beef and so on. A certain amount of sediment falls into the brine from the meat, which is why you do not want to mix the different kinds.

On account of this, brine needs to be cleaned, reboiled and fortified every so often. The alternative is to chuck it out the moment little spots of white mould appear on the surface, and start again (the meat underneath will be all right). Naturally the crock or bucket must be washed and cleaned with a soda solution. In pork factories, like Harris's at Calne, the brine is years old in the huge white-tiled baths; the strength is carefully measured and reinforced each time one of the baths is drained. In the uncertain hygiene of most private houses, I would recommend throwing the brine away and starting again. However, if you want to add a corrective dose, bring a pint and three-quarters of water to the boil with 7 oz of salt and 7 oz of sugar and 3 oz of juniper berries; leave it to cool after skimming, amalgamate with the old brine which has been poured off through a muslin-lined strainer into a newly-cleaned crock, then replace the meat. Remember that each time you remove a piece of meat from the brine, you are also removing salt—with small pieces not much, but with legs of pork quite a quantity.

The times for salting meat vary, as you might expect, with the thickness of the piece; and also with the purpose of the salting—for instance, a 5 lb joint of pork for roasting is much improved by an overnight sojourn in the brine tub. Next day it will be agreeably seasoned, without being too salty for roasting. Pigs, heads and trotters for making brawn (page 140) are also improved by 24 hours in brine. Small pigs' tongues, which weigh about 8 oz, can be cured in 36–48 hours, whereas large tongues such as ox tongues can do with five days. If you want to turn a shoulder or leg of pork into a ham, allow ten days. Never worry about over-salting. You can soak the meat in water overnight before cooking it. Alternatively, you can put it into a pan of cold water, plenty of cold water, and bring it slowly to the boil. After five minutes' simmering, taste the liquid and if it is on the salty side, throw it away and start again. This is why one should never add vegetables and so on to the water until it has been boiling for 5 minutes—by which time you will know whether it is all right to continue, or whether you have to throw it away.

You will soon find out how long or how short a time different parts and kinds of meat take. This is also a matter of individual preference. Some people like a very light cure, others a stronger, saltier cure. Here, though, is a guide to salting times which I find useful :—

Trotters, heads of pork halved : 24 hours
Duck (giblets removed) : 36–48 hours
Pork loin, leg, shoulder : 3–10 days
Beef silverside, brisket : 7–10 days
Lamb or mutton shoulder, leg, loin : 7–10 days

These times are for meat which is going to be boiled. For roasting joints, 6–8 hours is about right.

The interesting thing about old methods of preservation, like salting, is that they alter the character of the original substance —i.e. a loin of pork and a salted loin of pork are two quite different things from the eater's point of view. The trouble with freezing is that it doesn't transform the original substance (in many cases it diminishes its flavour and goodness). On the other hand, it is able to preserve food in perfect condition for much longer periods of time. One has only to think of the ever-increasing hardness of dried haricot beans, or split peas. Or the extremes of salt in the old-fashioned hard cures needed for keeping bacon from one pig-killing to the next.

An interesting but difficult situation used to arise on farms at harvest-time. There were many extra people to feed, and they had to eat well with such hard work. The ham and bacon from last autumn's pig was uneatable by that time—and it had probably been attacked by blow-flies. Yet if one killed a pig in the early summer, curing was made difficult and uncertain by the vagaries of the weather which is often humid at that time and hot one day, cold the next. There would be cheese and bread, and plum pudding to finish with, but that was not enough. There might be a few early apples, and plums for tarts, but meat was the thing. In the eighteenth century particularly, before the introduction of commercial refrigeration, farmers' wives expected to feed their families and workers from the resources of the farm itself, buying in the very minimum. A situation which we are quite unfamiliar with today, but one which still pertains in parts of France—and no doubt in a good deal of Europe.

When the time for grape-picking arrives, at the end of September and the beginning of October, the Touraine *vigneron*'s wife makes a review of her resources. From the hutches, she will pick out a couple of rabbits for a pâté for lunch around the wine-press. The hens will be especially well fed for the sake of their eggs. The chickens will be fattened, and eaten at the final party when all the grapes are in. There will be jars of potted pork, from the pig which was killed at Easter. And at that time of year, fruit is no problem. Neither is the wine. And when a farmer's wife does acquire a deep-freeze, she does not fill it from the bulk-suppliers, but from her own yard and sties and garden.

To Cook Salt Pork and Hams

Weigh the joint, after rinsing it rapidly under the cold tap.

Calculate the cooking times, which become progressively less as the ham becomes larger. For instance : —

> Salt pork and small hams up to 4 lb : 30 minutes to the lb, plus 30 minutes—but this is not always necessary, it depends on the thickness of the piece. From 5–10 lb : 20 minutes per lb plus 20 minutes.

Over 10 lb, use the graph below from Bulletin 127 of the Ministry of Agriculture and Fisheries, *Home Curing of Bacon and Hams*—for instance, a 12 lb ham needs 3½ hours.

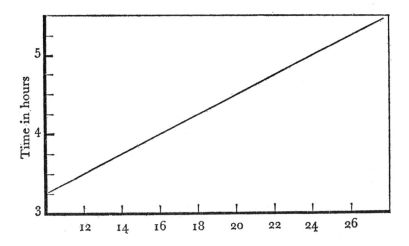

Put the joint into a ham kettle—or if it is very large, suspend it with string from the lid of an electric washing copper— cover it with water and bring slowly to the boil. After 5 minutes' simmering taste the water, as I mentioned on page 119. If it tastes salty, throw it away and start again. Add vegetables and aromatics after the first 5 minutes, and count your cooking time from then. A bouquet garni, onions, carrots, leeks and turnips will all help to improve the flavour of the ham—and of the stock, which can be used for soup (particularly pea soup, page 9) later on.

TO EAT COLD

When the time is up, remove the pan from the heat and leave it for a couple of hours. Then remove the joint of pork or ham to a dish: the best kind to use is a large meat plate with a strainer tray fitted into it. If you do not have the benefit of an old dinner service, look in second-hand shops. They are often to be bought quite cheaply. On other occasions, the strainer tray can be removed and the dish used for a large mixed salad, or for a hot joint surrounded by vegetables.

Remove the skin as soon as it is cool enough to handle. It should peel off easily. Toast plenty of white breadcrumbs to a pale brown and roll the meat in it while it's still tepid. Do not use those appalling bright yellow crumbs sold in some grocer's shops and supermarkets.

If you decided to bone the ham before cooking it, remember to remove the string, and to cool it under a weight so that it keeps its firmness. The crumb coating will have to come last of all—as the joint will be cold, see that the crumbs are still warm and press the pork well down into them.

In my opinion, a boned loin of pork makes the best flavoured and easiest kind of home-cured ham. But many people prefer to stick to the traditional leg, complete with bones. Certainly it looks more splendid for a party, and one can decorate the knuckle end with a ham frill (opposite).

TO EAT HOT

There are two traditional ways of doing this, or rather, three.

First, remove and skin the ham while hot, and serve it, as it is, with a Madeira sauce, or with an apple sauce or onion sauce, or surrounded by appropriate vegetables—broad beans, for instance, in which case you would supply a parsley sauce.

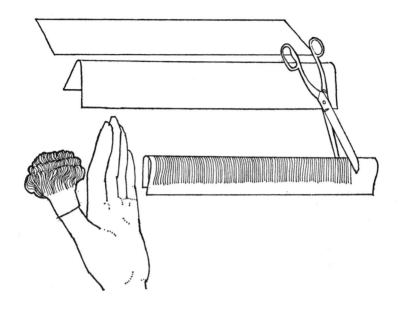

The second way is to remove the salt pork or ham half an hour before the cooking time is up. Peel off the skin, score it with a diamond pattern being careful not to go completely through the fat to the meat, and rub it over with a sweet, piquant glaze. The intersections of the lattice pattern can be studded with cloves. The pork or ham then goes into the oven at mark 5, 375°, so that the glaze can melt to a delicious crusty sheen—be careful that the sugar doesn't catch and burn. The addition of a few spoonfuls of the boiling liquor to the pan is a good idea : when the time is up, remove the meat to a serving dish, boil up the juices in the pan and turn them into a sauce by adding wine, or a fortified wine, or some cream.

Everyone can concoct their own glazes, but the thing is to have a basic mixture of mustard (either dry or French mustard) and sweetness (brown sugar, marmalade, redcurrant jelly and so on). If you do not intend to score the meat, add a couple of spoons of breadcrumbs to the glaze which will add a textured coating. Here is a basic glaze mixture :—

1 tablespoon French mustard
1 tablespoon brown sugar, or melted redcurrant jelly, marmalade, or apricot jam
1 tablespoon double cream

1 teaspoon ground cloves or cinnamon
2 heaped tablespoons breadcrumbs (optional)

Depending on the glaze you choose, prepare a garnish—this is instead of an apple or onion sauce. If you've used marmalade, slices of oranges reheated in the pan sauce would be a good idea. With apricot jam, a pilaff of rice with almonds, and dried apricots. With redcurrant jelly, or brown sugar, a few potatoes plus some glazed onions and carrots, or just potatoes with a green salad to follow. Spinach is another good vegetable for ham cooked in this way, particularly when fortified wines have been used in the pan sauce. Broad beans are not for baked ham, keep them for the plainly boiled kind.

The third way, rather a grand-looking way, is to encase the ham or pork in pastry. This is much simpler than you might suppose. Calculate the cooking time of the meat, then boil it gently for three-quarters of the time. Leave it to cool down for an hour in the cooking liquid. Meanwhile make the pastry, a shortcrust. For a 12 lb ham you will need 3 lb plain flour, $\frac{3}{4}$ lb butter and $\frac{3}{4}$ lb lard, and a little iced water for mixing. Roll it out on a large table. Take the ham from its pot, drain it well and peel off the skin. Lay it plump side down on the pastry and mould the coating round it, cutting off the surplus. Naturally the pastry should not have been too thinly rolled out. Turn the ham over on to the rack of a roasting pan, so that the 'seam' is concealed underneath. Decorate with leaves, flowers, and so on, or with abstract shapes : make a small hole for the steam to escape from, at the top of the crust. Brush over with a beaten egg mixed with a saltspoon of salt. Bake for an hour at mark 5, 375°. Take out of the oven, pour a small glass of Madeira or other fortified wine in through the steam-escape hole, and serve—spinach and potatoes and Madeira Sauce, are good accompanying items.

Smoking meat

This is something which few people care to undertake now, firstly because they don't have the right kind of chimneys and open hearths in their modern houses and flats, and secondly because they are afraid of losing an expensive piece of meat if something goes wrong. Particularly for this second reason, I would advise against smoking meat unless you have an experienced friend to guide your early steps. It is easier in one way nowadays, because smoke has been reduced to a cosmetic from its original status of preserving agent. We eat smoked food because we like the taste; we don't regard it as an essential part of winter stores. If you want to have your own smoked ham, cure it in brine yourself for a fortnight—then take it along to the bacon factory and see if you can persuade someone to complete the cure for you. Small concerns are more likely to be sympathetic to such requests. And of course it is sensible to make enquiries first.

'When there were plenty of *farm*-houses, there were plenty of places to smoke bacon in; since farmers have lived in gentlemen's houses, and the main part of farm-houses have been knocked down, these places are not so plenty.' This is William Cobbett, writing in 1821, about the cottager's life in Jane Austen's England; he might be talking about the Martin family in *Emma*, who were so genteel though not quite gentlemen. 'However, there is scarcely any neighbourhood without a chimney left to hang bacon up in. Two precautions are necessary: first, to hang the flitches where no *rain* comes down upon them: second, not to let them be so near the fire as to *melt*.' This is very important, the fat must not cook at all, the smoke must be cool, the fire well damped down with saw dust. And, of course, it must be a wood fire, not turf, peat or coal. 'Stubble or litter might do: but the trouble would be great. *Fir*, or *deal*, smoke is not fit for the purpose. I take it, that the absence of wood, as fuel, in the dairy countries, and in the North, has led to the making of pork and dried bacon'—by which he means salt pork, the kind that is eaten with pease pudding in the

North, and green bacon which has been salted, then dried in a good draught, and not smoked.

'As to the *time* that it requires to smoke a flitch, it must depend a good deal upon whether there be a *constant fire beneath*, and whether the fire be large or small. A month may do, if the fire be pretty constant, and such as a farmhouse fire usually is. But over-smoking, or, rather, too long hanging in the air, makes the bacon rust. . . . The flitch ought not to be dried up to the hardness of a board, and yet it ought to be perfectly dry.'

He then goes on to say that it is important to keep the bacon 'sweet and good, and free from nasty things that they call *hoppers*; that is to say, a sort of skipping maggots, engendered by a fly which has a great relish for bacon'. It's a good idea to adopt the American habit of sewing a ham into a coarse linen bag, then lime-washing it. The alternative is to store the ham, embedded in ashes, in a box or chest or in sand, which will keep the air out as well as the flies.

You can see from this description why I do not recommend the home-smoking of bacon.

I do recommend, though, William Cobbett's *Cottage Economy*, which he finished in 1821. It's a book written with passionate concern and an earthy sense of reality, which seem to us these days very sympathetic. He has prejudices against potatoes (even for pigs) and tea. He wants to convert everyone to the virtues of maize, which he had seen growing so successfully as a main crop in America. He understood, too, how flashiness and falsity were beginning to overwhelm the country outside London, encouraging farm and cottage families to a 'niceness in food and finery in dress', which reduced many of them to a 'quarter of a bellyful and rags'.

In *Cottage Economy*, one senses the beginning of Victorian London, the desire for niceness and finery which was to send farmers' and craftsmen's children crowding up to London, the Galsworthys and Hardys, all in search of a fortune and the good life. Some of them, many of them I suppose, succeeded, if not always as solidly as the Forsytes. Others, like my own great-grandfather, came to disaster : he drank his profits and time away, and overlooked debts with an amiability he could not afford (he was a naval tailor—his clients had the disconcerting habit of disappearing with the tide). He couldn't shake off his country habits of thought. He was incapable of realizing that people in big cities were not as reliable in their ways as the slower inhabitants of Old Bewick, Morpeth and Rochester at home in Northumberland.

Cottage Economy describes a whole way of life, the substructure on which the gentry and nobility floated in such elegant style, and which was ignored by contemporary novelists apart from a few picturesque details. It makes subsequent 'shilling' cookeries for the poor look thin and patronising. No wonder, as such things were written by grand chefs in London who had come a long way from their simple origins, who had 'risen above' such a life and found fame in the kitchens of royalty and fine London clubs. Incidentally, I wonder what Cobbett would think of today's school cookery teachers, who instruct their pupils to make Cottage or Shepherd's Pie from a tin of minced steak and a packet of instant potato. Or of women in supermarkets saying, to television interviewers, that they never eat meat nowadays as chops and steak are so expensive. 'A quarter of a bellyful and rags.' Cobbett could congratulate himself on his prescience and prophetic powers, but being the kind of generous man he was, he would be sad at such miserable ignorance. I can imagine his rage at the way such ignorance is encouraged by advertisers, and perpetuated by many of the home economists let loose in our schools.

Boiled Salt Beef and Dumplings

3 lb salted silverside or brisket	2 blades of mace
2 large onions, unpeeled	Small piece of nutmeg
8 cloves	Plenty of black pepper

To salt your own beef, see pages 117–20. Alternatively, buy a joint of salted beef from a reputable butcher. It should not need soaking, but it is always a good idea to ask.

Put the beef into a deep, fairly close-fitting pot. Add the onions, into which you have stuck cloves—the onion peel is not removed because it improves the colour of the stock. Add enough tepid water to cover the meat by $\frac{1}{4}''$, and put in the remaining spices. Don't stint the pepper. Bring to simmering point, and leave to cook for $3\frac{1}{2}$ hours (to calculate cooking times for different-sized joints, turn to page 121). Remove the scum as it rises and taste the cooking liquor after about 10 minutes: if it tastes very salty, drain it off and add fresh water and start again. During the cooking time, the water should never boil. A few bubbles should hiccough to the surface in a desultory kind of way. When you are satisfied that the pot is over a correct heat, cover it tightly.

Many recipes suggest adding various vegetables to salt beef, but it has so much flavour already that they can do little for it; and they end up sodden and uneatable, whatever the peasant school of cookery maintains. It is far better to cook them separately. Glazed carrots are a good accompaniment, lightly cooked leeks are good too, and some people cannot entertain the thought of salt beef or salt pork without pease pudding (page 40). I sympathize with this, but suggest too that dumplings should not be overlooked.

DUMPLINGS

4 oz plain flour
1 teaspoon baking powder
Good pinch salt
2 oz shredded suet
Water

Either
1 tablespoon chopped parsley and chives
Or Creamed or grated horseradish
Or 12 cubes of bread fried in butter

Sieve the flour, baking powder and salt together. Mix in the suet, herbs if used, and then enough water to form a slightly sticky dough. Flour your hands and roll the dough into little balls—remember that they will swell a good deal as they cook.

Into the centre of each ball, put a little horseradish or a cube of fried bread, and fasten the dough firmly over. Remove the meat from the cooking liquor when it is ready, and keep it warm : this will give you plenty of space to poach the dumplings for 10–20 minutes, depending on their size.

Just before putting the dumplings into the beef stock, it is a good idea to remove about ¾ pt of it and boil it down in a separate pan to concentrate the flavour. This can be served in a separate sauceboat.

Sweet-sour pickled cucumbers are an excellent, if not very English, addition to boiled salt beef, which makes wonderful sandwiches with rye bread and some *Moutarde de Meaux* or German mustard, particularly if it is still slightly warm. As a general principle, the larger the joint of salt meat, the better the flavour.

Boiled Silverside of Beef

Cook in the same way as the salt beef in the previous recipe, but in this case it is worth adding a parsnip, carrot and a small piece of turnip to the broth. Serve with horseradish sauce, carrots, potatoes. As in the previous recipe, the stock will make beautiful soup.

Pressed Beef

Salt or fresh beef cooked in the usual way (see page 127). Leave to cool in its broth for 2 hours, then put it into a tongue-press, or wrap it up in foil and place a board with some really heavy weights on top. Serve with horseradish sauce, and an avocado and potato salad dressed with an olive oil vinaigrette, pages

296 and 289, or with pickled vegetables (onions, cucumbers, etc.) and wholemeal or rye bread and butter.

Spiced Salt Beef

For 8–10

6 lb joint silverside or round of beef, cut and tied for salting

Spiced salt
3 oz dark brown sugar
¼ oz saltpetre

4 oz sea salt
1 oz black peppercorns
1 oz allspice berries
1 oz juniper berries

Rub the beef over with the sugar. Leave it for 2 days in a cool place in a deep, straight-sided pot, turning it over once or twice. Crush the remaining ingredients together and rub this mixture into the beef. Return it to its pot, and leave for a further nine days, turning it over every day and rubbing the salty mixture into it (the salt will become very moist as time goes on with the juices from the meat, but go on rubbing it in just the same).

To cook the beef, dab off all the bits of spice, or rinse it very quickly under the tap. Place it in a close-fitting pot with 8–10 oz water. Put a layer of shredded suet over the top of the meat (this helps to keep in the moisture during cooking). Cover the pot tightly, with two layers of foil jammed in place with the lid, so that no steam can escape. Bake in the oven at mark 1, 275°, for 45 minutes a pound (if you are spicing a small joint, allow 50 minutes per pound). Take out of the oven and leave undisturbed to cool down for 3 hours. Take off the lid and foil, drain the meat and place it on a board. Cover with greaseproof and put a 4 lb weight on top. Leave for 24 hours at least before carving into thin slices. The best accompanying dishes are avocado and potato salad, and horseradish sauce (page 296).

Wrap the beef up in greaseproof in between servings. It will keep in the refrigerator for three weeks. Useful for Christmas.

Brains with Curry and Grape Sauce

For 4

1½ lb brains
Salted water
Milk
1 oz butter
1 rounded tablespoon flour
1 teaspoon curry powder

¼ pt hot chicken stock
¼ pt double cream
½ lb grapes, preferably Muscat grapes, peeled and pipped
Triangles of fried bread

Rinse the brains under the cold tap, and remove the fine membrane which holds the blood vessels, easing it out of the convolutions. If this proves difficult, soak the brains in salted water for an hour and try again, rinsing them well.

Put the brains into a pan, cover them with milk and bring them to the boil. Simmer for five minutes, until the brains are firm. Strain off the milk, which will be needed for the sauce. Slice the brains, arrange them on a serving dish and keep them warm.

To make the sauce, melt the butter in a small pan, stir in the flour and curry powder and cook for two minutes. Add the hot chicken stock gradually, then ¼ pt of the milk the brains were cooked in. Simmer for about 20 minutes, stirring from time to time. Add the cream and correct the seasoning. Last of all, tip in the grapes and any juice, and leave for a few moments to heat in the sauce, which should be the consistency of double cream but not gluey. Extra stock can be added if necessary.

Pour the sauce over the brains and garnish them with triangles of bread fried in butter.

This sauce goes well with boiled chicken, or with sweetbreads which have been prepared in the usual way and then fried.

Skuets

For 4

1 lb lamb's or veal sweetbreads	16 mushrooms
Salt	Chopped parsley and thyme
Light veal or chicken stock	Freshly ground pepper
2 teaspoons lemon juice or wine vinegar	Browned breadcrumbs
	Bread sauce, page 290
8 thin rashers of smoked streaky bacon	

To prepare sweetbreads, place them in a bowl and cover them with water. Stir in a tablespoon of salt. Leave for an hour or longer if you like. If they are frozen, leave them for several hours. Drain them, rinse them with cold water and place them in a pan. Pour enough stock over them to cover them by about $\frac{1}{4}''$, and add the lemon or vinegar. Bring slowly to the boil, and simmer gently until they lose their raw pinkish white look and turn opaque. This takes a couple of minutes with lamb's sweetbreads; veal sweetbreads, being much larger, can take 20 minutes. Pour off the cooking liquor, which can be used in soups and sauces (some sweetbread recipes use the stock to make the appropriate sauce). Run the sweetbreads under the cold tap and pull off the gristly bits. Go carefully, though, if you pull off too much, sheep's sweetbreads will disintegrate into very small knobs. Put the sweetbreads on a plate, with another plate on top to press them. They can now be left for later use, or overnight.

To assemble the skuets, cut the sweetbreads into slices or chunks about an inch wide, and divide them into four even rows. Cut the bacon into enough small pieces to go between them, and put them in place. The mushrooms should be fitted in at appropriate intervals. Scatter with chopped parsley and thyme. Now take four skewers and run them through the four lines of sweetbreads and bacon, etc. Brush them over with melted butter and grill them under a medium heat for about 15 minutes.

Serve them on a long dish scattered over with the browned crumbs. The bread sauce should go in a separate bowl.

I first came across this recipe in French, in Carême's *L'art de la cuisine française au dix-neuvième siècle*, which first came out in 1833. He describes it as an English recipe, and praises it. I imagine he may have come across it in England while he was working for the Prince Regent. The odd thing is that it is not in the most popular cookery books of the eighteenth and early nineteenth century. I came across it eventually in *The Compleat Housewife*, by E. Smith, a reprint from the fifteenth and eighteenth editions, of 1753 and 1773 (the earliest edition now held is the third, of 1729). This early recipe lacks the bread sauce, and the crumbs are pressed into the skuets of meat before they are hung up to roast before the fire. Carême's refinements really make the dish.

Tongue and Mushroom Crumble

For 6

3 lb pickled, uncooked tongue (pig's, calf's, or ox tongue)	4 oz butter
1 medium carrot	4 oz mushrooms
2 medium onions	1 rounded dessertspoon flour
Bouquet garni	3 oz dry white wine
$\frac{1}{2}$ pt dry cider	1$\frac{1}{2}$ oz fresh white breadcrumbs
Water	Salt, pepper

Either buy the tongue(s) ready pickled, or leave in the brine on page 117 for a couple of days. Always be prepared to soak tongue overnight, if it comes from the butcher's brine tub.

To cook the tongue, put it into a large pan with the carrot, chopped, and one of the onions coarsely chopped. Add bouquet, cider and enough water to cover by $\frac{1}{2}''$. Bring slowly to the boil, skim and cover. Leave to simmer until tongues are cooked—from 1–3 hours depending on individual size or sizes. Remove to a dish, peel off the skin and cut out any tiny bones. Leave to cool. Strain stock into a jug.

To assemble the dish, slice tongue and place in the bottom of a shallow, butter-greased ovenproof dish. Cook sliced mushrooms in 1 oz of the butter, season them and distribute evenly over the tongue slices. Cook the second onion, finely chopped, in 2 oz of butter in a small heavy pan; cover it and see that the onion doesn't brown. Stir in the flour, cook for 2 minutes, then add wine and enough stock from the jug to make a thin sauce. Leave to cook down to a well-flavoured moderately thick sauce, then tip over the tongue slices which should be well moistened, but not swimming about. Melt the last ounce of butter, mix in the crumbs and spread on top of the dish. Bake at mark 5–6, 375–400°, until everything is well heated through and bubbling, and the top nicely browned. All the preparations can be done in advance, with only the reheating to be carried out before the meal.

Boiled Ox Tongue

For 6–10

2½–5 lb ox tongue, pickled	1 sliced carrot
Water or light stock	½ stalk celery
Bouquet garni	12 peppercorns, slightly crushed
Onion stuck with 2 cloves	

Soak the tongue for 6 hours, or as the butcher suggests. Put it into a deep pan and cover it with water or stock and bring to the boil. Remove the scum which will rise to the surface in a greyish foam. Add the vegetables, bouquet and pepper. Cover with a lid, and simmer for 3–4 hours until a larding needle or skewer goes in easily. Do not allow the liquid to boil, an occasional bubble is the best thing. It is prudent to taste the cooking liquid after half an hour: if it is unpleasantly salty, throw it away and start again, knocking half an hour off the cooking time.

When the tongue is cooked, remove it to a board and peel off the skin. See if there are any tiny bones and gristly bits at the throat end, and cut them away if there are.

To serve cold: place a 5″–6″ cake tin—with the removable base removed—on to a baking sheet. Push the tongue into it, curling it as you go. Put the base on top and weight it down with heavy tins. Leave to cool. Serve cut in thin slices across, with a simple salad or two and some horseradish sauce (page 296). The Victorians used to press the tongue into a slipper shape, and then decorate it with aspic jelly and bits and pieces. I think we have lost sympathy with over-presented food of this kind : it always arouses my suspicions—I wonder what the caterer is trying to conceal.

To serve hot : slice the tongue whilst still hot and arrange it decoratively on a large shallow serving dish. Cover with a suitable sauce, boiling hot; place in the oven to heat through for about 10 minutes. Do not allow the sauce to drown the tongue —serve any extra in a sauceboat. Madeira sauce is a favourite English choice, but the black cherry sauce on page 301 is more unusual.

Potted Tongue

Using an electric blender or chopper, reduce $\frac{1}{2}$ lb of cooked tongue to a paste with 4–5 oz of clarified butter. Season with salt, pepper and mace. Pack firmly into a pot. When chilled to firmness, the meat should be covered with a $\frac{1}{4}''$ layer of clarified butter, then with foil : if you intend to use the potted meat in a day or two, a thinner layer of butter—for appearance rather than preservation—will be enough. Serve with thin toast or baked bread. Beef, salt beef, venison, game may all be potted in the same way—sometimes a couple of anchovy fillets may be substituted for the mace.

To make a grander dish, cooked chicken can also be reduced to a paste as well. The two mixtures can then be layered into a pot, or placed together in uneven lumps for a marbled effect, before being pressed down and covered with clarified butter. When cut, the potted meat will have a most attractive appearance, and the milder flavour of the chicken will temper the stronger-tasting cured tongue.

A Fine Way to Pot a Tongue

5–7 lb dressed weight roasted chicken	$\frac{1}{4}$ nutmeg, grated
2$\frac{1}{2}$ lb tongue, boiled, skinned	A level dessertspoon sea salt
1 teaspoon each ground mace, ground cloves, black pepper	About 2 lb butter

Bone the chicken (or ask the butcher to do it for you). Lay it out on a board, skin side down. Trim the tongue, cutting away any tiny bones or gristle. Mix the spices with the salt, and rub the inside of the chicken with two-thirds of the mixture. Place the tongue on top, and wrap the chicken round it. Put the chicken cut side down, breast side up into as tightly fitting a deep casserole as possible (the better the fit, the less butter will be required). Scatter the remaining spices on the top. Melt just enough butter to cover. Put the lid on the pot. Bake at mark 6, 400°, until you can hear the butter bubbling hard when you open the oven door—reduce the heat to mark 4, 350°. After an hour's total cooking time, test the chicken with a larding needle to see if it is done. If the juices look a little pink, leave the bird for another 15 minutes.

When it is cooked, remove the chicken on to a rack to cool. Pour off the butter and juices into a basin. When the chicken is cold, replace it in the cleaned casserole. Bring butter, entirely freed of meat juices, to the boil and pour over the chicken. If you wish to keep it for longer than three days, add more clarified butter to cover the chicken by $\frac{1}{4}''$. It should not be eaten until 36 hours later in any case, so that all the flavours have time to develop.

To serve, leave the chicken in the pot and cut it down into slices like a pâté. Eat with wholemeal bread and some of the butter.

Toad-in-the-Hole

For 4

Yorkshire pudding batter made with 1 pt milk and other ingredients in proportion	1 lb pork sausages
	1 oz lard or pork fat

Make the batter in the usual way. Separate the pork sausages and cook them for 5 minutes quickly in the lard or pork fat in a frying pan. Strain off the fat into a large roasting pan, pour in a thin layer of batter and bake in the oven for 5 minutes at mark 7, 425°, so that it sets. Place the sausages on top and pour over the rest of the batter. Bake for a further 30–35 minutes until the batter has puffed up and browned. Serve straightaway.

Originally toad-in-the-hole was made with pieces of meat, rather than sausages. They could be freshly browned chops or steak, but were more often the left-overs of an earlier meal which gave Toad-in-the-Hole a bad name as one of the meaner English dishes—like shepherd's pie. In fact if you are able to buy really first-class sausages, Toad-in-the-Hole makes an excellent family dish which no one has any call to feel ashamed of.

White Puddings

Pork butchers in the Midlands and Wiltshire and Oxfordshire often sell large white sausages tied together in a horseshoe shape at the ends. They are filled with minced lean and fat pork, chopped parsley and a cereal filler.

They make a good family lunch dish, particularly when they are fried with plenty of streaky bacon. Such things are not at all to be despised. When the puddings burst, and the sausage part browns in the bacon fat, they taste even better.

Black Puddings

Black puddings have to be chosen carefully. Many manufacturers put far too much barley and oatmeal with the blood and pork fat, which makes them stodgy by comparison, say, with the delicious black puddings of France. To my way of thinking, the inside should remain soft and spicey when cooked; it should never be dry or hard.

The usual way is to slice black puddings and fry or grill them with bacon. I think they taste better when cut into lengths, and fried with chopped bacon and chopped apple. Serve with mashed potato and mustard. Then they are really delicious.

Cumberland Sausage

Do you agree with me that most national brands of sausage are a bland, pink disgrace? If so, it is worth looking out for Cumberland sausage even if you do not live in Cumberland. Ignore the packages of small sausages, and go for the great coil that lies on the counter fresh and speckled and glistening. Buy it according to the length you think you are going to need, rather than by weight. Fry it still in the piece, and present it on a dish of boiled, buttered potatoes, and apple rings which have been lightly fried in butter and sprinkled with pepper and nutmeg. Or use a spiced apple sauce, page 293, instead of the rings. Many people like it with red cabbage and apple cooked together in the German style.

Discard the skin and you have the perfect unstodgy basis for pâtés and pies and stuffings.

If you want to buy the real thing, in its most superior form, you will have to visit Keswick or Carlisle. I bought some in the triangular central square of Carlisle, from a butcher tucked away under an arched snicket. He told me that it contained ninety-eight per cent pork (including plenty of fat, which sausages should have), coarsely chopped, seasoned with salt and pepper only. Nothing else, no secret. But once minced, the meat and seasoning are mixed together by hand. It seems that only butchers in the north-west have the right *tour de main*. Perhaps they know the pigs better than many large sausage makers seem to.

Faggots and Peas

1 lb pig's liver, minced	½ teaspoon mace
10 oz belly of pork, minced	2 medium eggs
2 large onions, chopped	Up to 4 oz breadcrumbs
1 clove garlic, chopped	Salt, pepper
4 sage leaves, chopped, or 1 tea- spoon dried sage	Piece of caul fat ¼ pt stock beef or veal or pork

Put liver, pork, onion, garlic and sage into a frying pan, and cook gently for 30 minutes without allowing the mixture to brown. Stir occasionally.

Strain off the juices and set aside. Mix the meat, etc., with the mace, eggs and enough breadcrumbs to make a firm, easy-to-handle mixture. Taste and season. Soften the caul fat in a bowl of tepid water and cut it into roughly 5″ squares. Divide the meat into 2 oz knobs, and wrap each one in a square of caul fat. Place side by side close together in an ovenproof dish, which is not too deep : the faggots should stick up slightly above the rim. Pour in the stock. Bake for 40–60 minutes in a moderate oven, mark 3–4, 325–350°, until the tops are nicely browned. About 20 minutes after the start of cooking time, strain off the juices into the liquor which was left from the first cooking. Stand the bowl in a bowl of ice cubes, so that the fat rises quickly to the surface and can be skimmed off. Pour the stock over the faggots about 5 minutes before the end of cooking time. Serve with garden peas in the summer time, or with a purée of dried peas (page 41) in the winter.

Faggots are a good-tempered dish. They can be reheated. They can be cooked at an even lower temperature, if this suits your convenience. Should they not be nicely browned, a few minutes under the grill should do the trick.

Faggots were popular in the past as a way of using up odd bits and pieces left over after a pig was killed. They often included the lights, heart and melt—and indeed many butchers who sell their own faggots use these parts still, rather than the belly of pork in this recipe, as well as the liver. Recipes vary in different parts of the country, just as pâté recipes do in France.

Welsh faggots, for instance, may include a chopped cooking apple, and omit the egg. The rich savoury pleasure of faggots—one name given to them is savoury ducks—is very largely due to the enclosing grace of caul fat which keeps the dark lean meat well basted. For this you will need to go to a small family butcher, preferably an older man, who really understands meat.

The word faggot means a bundle, like a faggot of kindling for a fire, so do not be afraid to vary the recipe with additions and alterations of flavouring.

Brawn or Head Cheese

½ pig's head, including the tongue but not the brains
2 pig's trotters
1 lb shin of beef
Piece of shin bone

2 cloves garlic, chopped
Large bouquet garni
10 black peppercorns
2 tablespoons wine vinegar
Salt to taste

Aromatics
2 onions, each stuck with 2 cloves
2 carrots, quartered
2 leeks, split

To finish
Hard-boiled eggs
Toasted breadcrumbs
Chopped parsley, chives, chervil

Ask the butcher to chop the head into two or three convenient pieces. Try and buy good long trotters, ending in a meaty piece of hock : they should be chopped in two. Submerge the pork in brine for 24 hours, if you can (see page 117). This isn't essential but it does improve the flavour. Ask the butcher if he can let you have the shin of beef on the bone, allowing extra weight (make sure that he reduces the price per pound accordingly). He may at first be startled, but even in a supermarket meat does have bones. Don't salt the shin.

Put all the meat into a large pan. Cover it with water and add the aromatics. Bring to the boil, skim, and then cover the pot closely, using foil to wedge the lid so that as little steam as possible escapes. Incidentally, don't add salt until the pot has come to the boil, then use sparingly.

Leave the pot to simmer for 2 hours and then try the smaller pieces of meat. If they are ready, they should part easily and cleanly from their bones. Remove them as they are cooked, and start the business of picking off the meat and chopping it. The bones can go back into the pot, or be thrown away.

As you chop the meat, pull away the few odd hairs and look out for tiny bits of bone. Neither improves the finished brawn. And whatever you do, *don't mince the meat*. If you are in a hurry, put the whole thing into the refrigerator until you can spare the time to finish the brawn properly. Mincing is the ruin of dishes like this. It reduces meat to a mush.

Having dealt with the meat, put it all into a commodious basin and set it aside. Strain off the stock into a clean pan (discard vegetables, herbs, spices, etc.) and boil it down to a concentrated flavour. This will partly depend on how much salt you added at the beginning: if you were sensible, you didn't add too much because the stock is greatly improved by reduction.

The next decision is how much of the reduced stock to add to the chopped meat. You do not want the brawn to look thin and mean. On the other hand, if the meat is too solidly packed, the brawn becomes too heavy to be enjoyable. This is something that can easily be judged by eye, and from the experience of brawn bought in shops.

When meat and stock have been mixed, put them in a pan and simmer for 20 minutes. Taste and adjust the seasonings— sometimes a little lemon juice is a great improver; and continue to taste as the brown cools.

To finish, pour a layer of meat and stock into a loaf tin. Leave it to set in the coldest part of the fridge. Sprinkle with chopped herbs, lay hard-boiled eggs along the centre, and cover with more meat and stock. Leave to set. Turn out of the tin and press the brawn into warm, toasted breadcrumbs. Eat cold with salad, mustard and potatoes—mashed potatoes, for instance. Or else with wholemeal or rye bread and butter.

Although shin of beef is not an essential ingredient of brawn, it does make a big improvement in flavour and texture. And the gelatine in the meat and bone helps to make an even better jelly.

The idea of cooking two meats together may seem odd at first. True, we eat veal and ham pies, chicken or turkey and ham pies, but there the partnership is so obviously complementary that we never question it, or even think about it.

Boiling two kinds of meat together of less pronounced harmony is another matter. The Scots do it when they make a proper cockie-leekie, which consists of an old boiling fowl and a piece of boiling beef cooked together with leeks, and finished with prunes. So do the Italians, who produce a splendid *bollito misto* in Piedmont, a 'mixed boiling' of beef or veal, chicken, and a gelatinous item such as calf's or pig's head and trotters to improve the smoothness of the dish.

Such dishes as these are the surviving elegancies of iron-pot cooking over the fire. I am sure they often lacked the contrived balance of a modern 'bollito misto'. It was a case of cooking what you happened to have, with as little firing as possible—meats, vegetables, a suet pudding or dumplings all in together.

Cornish Pasty

Shortcrust pastry	*Filling*
12 oz plain flour	1 lb skirt or chuck steak
¼ teaspoon salt	4–5 oz chopped onion
6 oz lard	3 oz chopped turnip
Water	8 oz thinly-sliced potato
	Salt, pepper
Glaze	Pinch of thyme
Beaten egg	

Make the shortcrust pastry in the usual way. Do not be tempted to use butter or any other kind of fat, because lard gives the right flavour and texture to the crust. Leave the pastry in a cool place for an hour to rest.

Meanwhile remove the lean meat from the skin, gristle, etc., and chop it with a sharp, heavy knife. There should be a generous half pound (the trimmings can be kept for stock-making). Mix the meat with the vegetables and seasoning.

Roll out the pastry and cut it into two large dinner-plate circles. Divide the steak mixture between the two, putting it down the middle. Brush the rim of the pastry with beaten egg. Bring up the two sides of pastry to meet over the top of the filling, and pinch them together into a scalloped crest going right over the top of the pasty. Make two holes on top, either side of the crest so that steam can escape. Place the pasties on a baking sheet and brush them over with beaten egg. Bake at mark 6, 400°, for 20 minutes, then lower the heat to 350°, for a further 40 minutes. Serve hot or cold.

When a friend was a little boy in Cornwall, in the village of Pelynt near Looe, everyone made family-sized pasties like these (except for 'foreigners' like his mother, the vicar's wife, who was given to the sort of ladylike pasties that are sold in England today). When he needed comforting and a friendly lap, he would go to see his special friend Bessie, who worked for his mother, and she would get a large pasty out of the meat-safe and cut him off a slice. On a really good day, she might bring out an apple pasty, flavoured with cloves. He would watch her cut off the end, and pour in brown sugar and clotted cream, before handing it to him. The pasty is a good shape for holding in both hands. No need to bother with a plate or cutlery.

Individual pasties, in appropriate sizes, were baked for the men who had to go out into the fields all day, or down the mines, or for children to take to school. Different members of a family might have different ideas on the seasonings, so these pasties would be marked with initials at one corner. This had the added advantage that a half-eaten pasty could be reclaimed by its rightful owner.

In hard times, the proportion of steak to vegetables would be reduced—sometimes to nothing. Potato, onion and turnip, flavoured with herbs, would have to do, or quite a different mixture of leek, bacon and hard-boiled egg. Remember that a pasty should always be firm and full, never wet or too juicy to eat comfortably in the hands, never dry. Always chop or slice meat and vegetables—never mince them.

Cornish pasties are pronounced with a long 'a'.

Raised Pies

Hot-water crust	*Jellied stock*
7 oz water	See below
6 oz lard	
1 lb plain flour	*Filling*
½ teaspoon salt	See below
1 egg (optional)	

Glaze
Beaten egg

To make the crust, bring water and lard to the boil, then tip it quickly into the middle of the flour and salt, mixing everything rapidly together to a dough with a wooden spoon or electric beater. Add the egg if you like; it gives extra colour and richness, but is not essential—some people use a scant tablespoon of icing sugar instead which increases the crispness of the pastry. Leave the dough until it can be handled without too much discomfort, but do not allow it to cool. Cut off about a quarter for the lid, and put the rest into a hinged raised pie mould, or a cake tin with a removable base. Quickly and lightly push the pastry up the sides of the tin, being careful to leave no cracks. If the pastry collapses down into a dismal heap, it is a little too hot, so wait and try again.

Many butchers making their own pies used wooden pie moulds and 'raised' the dough round them. Jam jars can be used instead, but they need to be well-floured, or you will find it difficult to remove the jar without spoiling the raised pastry. Before putting the filling in, a band of brown paper was tied round the pies to help them keep their shape, and this remained in place during baking. Unless you are very skilful with your hands, and have plenty of time, the first method is much quicker and more successful—particularly if you invest in one of the attractively-decorated hinged pie moulds.

Having raised the crust, make the jellied stock and choose a filling from the recipes below. Pack the filling into the pastry, roll out the lid and fix it in place with beaten egg. Make a central hole and decorate the pie with leaves and roses made from the trimming (sweet pies are not decorated in English cookery, but the meat ones often end up looking very decorative). Brush it over with beaten egg, and put into the oven at mark 6, 400°, for half an hour to firm the pastry and give it a little colour. Then lower the heat to mark 3, 325°, and leave for 1 hour (small pies) to 2 hours (large pork and chicken pies) so that the meat can cook. Keep an eye on the lid and protect it with brown paper if it colours too quickly.

Remove the pie from the oven, and take it out of the mould (or untie the brown paper bands). Brush the sides with beaten egg and return to the oven for 10 minutes to colour them. When they look appetisingly brown, take them out and pour in jellied stock through the central hole using a tiny kitchen funnel or a cone of cardboard. This stock will fill the gaps left by the shrinking meat : it is important to have it nicely flavoured.

Leave the pies for 24 hours before eating, or even longer.

The importance of using a hot-water crust is that it absorbs the meat juices inside, and the rich fat, while remaining crisp outside. A short-crust pastry has too high a proportion of butter to do this as successfully.

Jellied Stock

Bones from the meat used to make the fillings
2 pig's trotters, or 1 veal knuckle
Large carrot, sliced

Medium onion stuck with 3 cloves
Bouquet garni
12 peppercorns
4–5 pints water

Put all ingredients into a pan and simmer for 3–4 hours steadily (cover the pan). Strain off the stock into a clean pan and boil down until you have about ¾ pt of stock. Season with salt, and add more pepper if you like. This liquid will set to a firm jelly, and is much better than the stock plus gelatine recommended in some pie recipes.

Fillings

For 4–6

PORK PIE FILLING

2 lb boned shoulder of pork or spareribs, with approximately ¼ fat to ¾ lean meat
½ lb thinly cut unsmoked bacon
1 teaspoon chopped sage

½ teaspoon each cinnamon, nutmeg, allspice
1 teaspoon anchovy essence
Salt, freshly ground black pepper

The characteristic note of pork pies from Melton Mowbray, the great pie centre of England—at least in times past—is the anchovy essence. It makes an excellent piquancy without the least fishiness, rather as oysters do in a steak and kidney pudding.

Chop some of the best bits of pork into ¼″ dice. Mince the rest finely with 2 or 3 rashers of the bacon (the bacon cure improves the colour of the pie on account of the saltpetre: without it the filling would look rather grey when the pie is cut). Add the seasonings. Fry a small amount and taste to see if adjustments are needed. Mix in the diced meat. Line the base of the pastry with remaining bacon, and fill with the pork mixture. You will always get a better texture if the meat is finely chopped rather than minced.

CHESHIRE PORK AND APPLE FILLING

2 lb sparerib or shoulder pork, boned
3 thin rashers unsmoked bacon
8 oz onion
Salt, pepper, nutmeg
4 oz white wine, cider or light ale

1½ oz Cox's Orange Pippins or other crisp dessert apple
Brown sugar
Butter

Mince pork, bacon and onion together rather coarsely. Flavour with salt, pepper and nutmeg, and beat in the wine, cider or light ale. Peel, core and slice the apples.

To fill the pie, put in a layer of pork, then apple, and scatter it very lightly with sugar (cooking apples can be used—they will need a little more sugar : on the whole dessert apples are to be preferred as they keep a crisper texture—originally windfall pippins were used). Repeat the layers, ending with pork.

GAME, CHICKEN OR RABBIT PIE

½ lb hard back pork fat
¾ lb lean pork
½ lb lean veal
½ lb thin rashers of bacon
3 tablespoons brandy or Madeira or 5 tablespoons dry white wine

Salt, pepper, nutmeg, cinnamon, cloves
Heaped tablespoon chopped parsley
1 lb game, chicken or rabbit cut from the bone

Mince fat and lean pork, veal and 3 rashers of bacon together, as well as any trimmings left from removing the game, chicken or rabbit from their bones. Season with wine, salt, pepper, spices and parsley. Cut the game, chicken or rabbit into nice pieces and season them. Put remaining bacon into the pastry case to form a lining, and layer in the minced meat and game.

VEAL, HAM AND EGG PIE

1½ lb pie veal
¾ lb unsmoked bacon, ham or gammon in a piece (ham must be uncooked like the gammon or bacon)

Salt, pepper
Grated rind of ½ a lemon
1 tablespooon chopped parsley
1 teaspoonful dried thyme
3 eggs, hardboiled and shelled

Dice veal and bacon, ham or gammon into ¼″ pieces—do not mince them. Season with salt, pepper, lemon rind and herbs. Put half into the pastry, arrange the eggs on top and cover with remaining meat mixture.

RAISED MUTTON PIES

1 best end of neck, or 1 lb fillet from the best end if sold off the bone
3 shallots, chopped, or 4 oz chopped onion
4 oz mushrooms, chopped

1 tablespoon chopped parsley
1 teaspoon dried thyme
Salt, pepper
Brown gravy made from the lamb bones, slightly thickened

Make the hot-water crust into small pies. For the filling, chop the meat finely after removing the skin, and include about a quarter of the fat. Discard the rest (with fillet bought off the bone, there will be very little fat so include it all). Mix with shallot or onion, mushrooms, herbs and seasoning. Put into a saucepan with 4 oz of water, bring to the boil and simmer for 5 minutes. Cool, then fill the pastry cases. Bake the pies for 45 minutes at mark 6, 400°. When they are ready, pour in the gravy made from the bones, instead of jellied stock. Eat very hot, or cold.

Devonshire Squab Pie

For 6

Shortcrust pastry made with 8 oz flour, and 2 oz each of butter and mutton fat or lard
1 best-end of neck of lamb, or 1½ lb lamb fillet off the bone
2 lb Cox's orange pippins or other good dessert apple

2 medium onions, finely sliced
16 unsoaked prunes
½ nutmeg, grated
Level teaspoon each mace, cinnamon
Salt, pepper
¼ pt lamb stock
Clotted cream

This pie is made in a deep dish and only covered with pastry, so make pastry and set aside to chill while you deal with the filling.

Slice the meat, including a small proportion of the fat, but discarding the bones which can be used to make the stock. Peel, core and slice the apples. Cut the prunes into pieces and throw away the stones.

Grease a deep pie dish. Arrange meat, apple and onion in layers, sprinkling them with spices and seasoning and chopped prunes. If the apples are on the tart side, sprinkle them with a little brown sugar: if you are using windfalls, this may well be necessary, but do not over-sweeten the pie. Pour in the stock and cover with a pastry lid in the usual way. Bake at mark 6, 400°, for 20–30 minutes to set and colour the pastry. Protect it with some brown paper and lower the heat to mark 3, 325°— leave for a further 45 minutes. Eat hot with clotted cream.

The name of this pie has puzzled people so much that some very odd stories have been invented to account for it. The recipe goes back at least as far as the first part of the eighteenth century—in those days squabs from the dovecot were a manorial perquisite; perhaps cottagers imitated the aristocratic pigeon pies with cheaper mutton and lamb, but kept the name of the original meat.

Steak, Kidney and Oyster Pie

For 6

Filling ingredients, page 151, as for   Beaten egg to glaze
    Steak, Kidney and Oyster Pudding
12 oz weight puff or shortcrust
    pastry

Make the filling, and leave it to cool as described in the next recipe. Check the liquid and add the oysters, if used.

Roll out the pastry. Cut off strips wide enough to cover the rim of the pie dish, and hang down a little inside it. Before putting them in place, brush the rim with water. Next put the cold filling into the dish. Brush water lightly over the pastry rim, and cover the pie over with the remaining pastry. Some people use a pie funnel which should be set in the middle of the filling : it's a good idea though not strictly necessary.

Press the edges of the pastry firmly together, nicking the pie at intervals if you are using puff pastry, or pressing it up in a scalloped shape if you are using shortcrust. With the trimmings make a simple leaf decoration, with a rose. Make a hole in the centre through which the steam can escape, and place the decorations round it. If you make a stem to the rose, it can be placed loosely in the centre hole and will not impede the steam escaping. Brush everything over with beaten egg. Bake at mark 7–8, 425–450° (lower temperature for shortcrust, higher for puff pastry), for 15–20 minutes, then lower the heat to mark 3, 325°, and leave for another $\frac{3}{4}$ of an hour, or a little less if the filling was adequately cooked before the pie was assembled.

Steak, Kidney and Oyster Pudding

For 6

Filling	*Suet crust*
2 lb rump steak	10 oz self-raising flour
1 lb veal or ox kidney	1 level teaspoon baking powder
2 tablespoons seasoned flour	$\frac{1}{4}$ teaspoon salt
1 large onion, chopped	Freshly ground white pepper
3 oz butter	$\frac{1}{4}$ teaspoon thyme
1 pt beef stock, or $\frac{1}{2}$ pt each stock and red wine	4 oz chopped suet
	Cold water
8 oz mushrooms, sliced	
Bouquet garni	
18–24 oysters (optional)	

The traditional method of making a steak and kidney pudding is to put the meat raw into the pastry-lined pudding basin. I think that one gets a better, less sodden crust if the filling is cooked first, a day, two if you like, in advance. This reduces the steaming time to $1\frac{1}{2}$ or 2 hours from 4 or 5, and the pastry remains slightly crisp outside which makes the whole thing less heavy.

To make the filling, cut the steak into neat 1″ pieces and slice the kidney. Discard all the fat and skin from both meats. Sprinkle them with seasoned flour. Cook the onion until lightly browned in two-thirds of the butter, put it to one side and add the meat, in batches, to colour rapidly. Transfer the meat as it is browned, to an ovenproof casserole. Pour the stock, or stock and wine into the frying pan and allow it to boil hard for a few moments, while you scrape in all the nice brown bits and pieces. Pour this over the meat. Fry the mushrooms in the remaining butter and add them with the bouquet to the casserole. Cover it with a lid and simmer in the oven at mark 1–2, 275–300°, until the steak and kidney are almost cooked—about $1\frac{1}{2}$ hours. Remove the casserole to a cool place, and leave for several hours or overnight. When you wish to make up the pudding, take a critical look at the liquid part of the filling. If it is on the copious and watery side, strain it off into a pan and boil it down to a more acceptable flavour and consistency. This is particularly important if you are using oysters, as they will contribute their own delicious liquor to the sauce. When you are satisfied on this point, open the oysters and add them, liquor and all, to the filling ingredients. Taste and correct the seasoning.

To make the crust, mix all the dry ingredients in a large bowl. Use your hands and slide them under the flour, etc., and up through it, so that the suet is thoroughly mixed in and evenly distributed. Stir in cold water with a wooden spoon to make a firm dough (use as little water as possible). Roll out on a floured surface to a large circle, cut away a quarter and put to one side for the lid. Butter a 3-pint pudding basin generously, and drop the three-quarter circle of pastry into it. Press it gently to fit the basin, allowing an inch overhanging at the rim. Put the filling into the basin : it should not come higher than an inch below the rim. Roll out the remaining suet crust and cut a circle to make the lid. Brush the pastry overhanging the rim of the basin with water. Put the lid in place and press the edges together to make a firm seal. Cut some foil to make a circle 2″ larger all round than the top of the pudding basin. Fix it in place with your fingers so that it balloons above the pudding, leaving it room to rise. Tie a string twice round the rim of the basin, and make a handle of string over the top so that it can easily be lifted in and out of the steamer.

When the water is boiling in the lower part of the steamer, put the pudding in and leave for $1\frac{1}{2}$ to 2 hours. One of the advantages of this kind of recipe is that exact timing is not important; so long as one allows enough time for the meat to be cooked, an hour longer will not spoil the pudding. With the short steaming time of this recipe, it is unlikely that the water will boil away. All the same, it is wise to keep an eye on it, and top it up if necessary with more *boiling* water, and keep everything well covered.

If you do not have a steamer, put a trivet on the base of a large saucepan and put about 4″ of water into it. When this water is boiling steadily but not fiercely, lower the basin into it. The water should come about two-thirds of the way up the sides, so add some more if it doesn't. Put the lid on the large saucepan and leave to boil for 1½ to 2 hours. Keep an eye on the water, and top it up if necessary with boiling water.

When the pudding is cooked, remove the basin from the pan and take off the foil cover, cutting away the string. Tie a cloth napkin round the basin and serve immediately. Brussels sprouts go well with steak and kidney pudding or pie.

This favourite English dish does not, it seems, go back more than 120 years. Eliza Acton, in *Modern Cookery* of 1845, calls a steak pudding John Bull's pudding, which suggests a certain national fame which had spread to other countries. Mrs Beeton's recipe in *Household Management* of 1859 is the first to add the essential kidney.

Young Mrs Beeton started by writing the cookery section of her husband's magazine for women, *The Englishwoman's Domestic Magazine*. Then with the aid of contributions from her readers, she compiled *Household Management*, which appeared in monthly parts with the magazine, beginning in 1859. It first came out in book form in 1861. As she makes particular mention of the source of this recipe, one may presume that it was a little unusual and would not be taken for granted by the majority of her readers, at any rate. It was sent to her by a reader in Sussex, a county which had been famous for its puddings of all kinds for at least a century, so it is fitting that such a well-liked national dish should have had its roots there.

Oysters or mushrooms were the extra flavouring ingredient. In those days oysters were the cheaper of the two as mushroom cultivation in Europe was a spasmodic and ill-understood business, except around Paris, until the end of the century, when two French mycologists at the Pasteur Institute established a service of sterilized mushroom spawn for growers. Even so, the great boom in mushroom production in England didn't occur until after World War Two. Up to then, they were a luxury and priced accordingly. Though by that time, of course, oysters had far outpriced them. Which would have surprised Mrs Beeton, because for her and her readers, oysters were still a

Mrs Beeton's Sussex pudding basin

commonplace, though becoming scarcer with the increase in population and the pollution of estuaries.

Chicken and Leek Pie from Wales

For 6

1 boiling fowl, or roasting fowl	4 oz cooked, sliced tongue
1 onion, unpeeled	6 fine leeks, trimmed
2 tablespoons chopped celery	2 tablespoons chopped parsley
Bouquet garni	8 oz weight shortcrust pastry
Salt, pepper	Beaten egg to glaze

Put the chicken into a deep pot, with the onion, celery, herbs and seasoning. Add enough water barely to cover. Simmer until the chicken is cooked. Remove the pot and leave it to cool down. Cut the chicken into convenient pieces. Skim the fat from the cooking stock.

Take a pie dish and arrange the chicken in it, with the tongue which should also be cut into neat pieces. Slice the leeks, cook them for 2 minutes in boiling salted water. Drain them well and add them to the chicken and tongue with the parsley. Season and pour over just enough of the chicken stock barely to cover the contents of the pie. Roll out the pastry. Cut a strip from it and place round the rim of the pie dish. Brush it with beaten egg, and lay the main part of the pastry over the pie to make a lid. Press down the edges, trim off the surplus pastry and decorate the pie with a few pastry leaves. Make a central hole so that the steam can escape. Brush the whole thing over with beaten egg and put into the oven at mark 8, 450°, for 20–25 minutes until the pastry is a nice colour—then lower the heat to mark 4–5, 350–375°, and leave for another 20 minutes or so.

Cornish Charter Pie

For 6–8

12 oz weight rich shortcrust pastry	3–4 oz bunch of parsley
Beaten egg to glaze	1 leek, or 6 spring onions
	$\frac{1}{4}$ pt milk
Filling	$\frac{1}{4}$ pt single cream
Two 3-lb chickens, jointed	$\frac{1}{2}$ pt double cream
Seasoned flour	Salt, pepper
1 large onion, chopped	
4 oz butter	

Roll the chicken pieces in seasoned flour. Cook the onion gently in half the butter in a frying pan, then remove it to a large shallow pie dish. Add the rest of the butter to the pan and when it is really hot, put in the chicken and brown it slightly— a golden colour is right, not a very crusty brown. Fit the chicken into the pie dish on top of the onions, in a close, single layer. Chop the parsley leaves, and the leek or spring onions, and simmer them for 2 or 3 minutes in the milk and single cream. Pour the whole thing over the chicken, and add about a third of the double cream. Season everything well.

Roll out the pastry and cover the pie in the usual way. Make a central hole large enough to accommodate a small kitchen funnel, and put a pastry rose with a $\frac{1}{2}''$ stem down through the middle. Surround it with some leaves. Brush over with beaten egg. Bake at mark 7–8, 425–450°, for about 20 minutes, until the pastry is golden. Lower the heat to mark 4, 350°, and leave until the chicken is cooked—about an hour. Just before serving ease out the rose from the centre, and pour in the remaining cream which should be at boiling point. Replace the rose, and serve hot, very hot, or cold (the juices set to a delicious jelly).

When I came across this recipe a year or two ago in Lady Sarah Lindsay's *Choice Recipes*, of 1883, I thought it explained something which had puzzled me for a long time. Now I am not so sure.

The puzzling thing was a couple of references in Parson Woodforde's diary, to the Charter. It occurred in the middle of a list of dishes he had had at a dinner party on July 13th, 1775, without any explanation. Obviously it was something to eat, because on another occasion the Parson helped his niece Nancy to make the Charter, this time for a party at his brother's house in Somerset. They put the Charter into the cellar to cool, the dog got into the cellar, and the dog ate the Charter. This suggests something meaty, unless it was an especially greedy dog which guzzled anything it could get hold of. And this is why I was delighted to find the recipe above. It seemed to explain everything.

Or does it? Why should the Parson have helped to make a chicken pie? Although he was always concerned with food—in particular when guests were arriving at short notice—he does not give the impression that he helped in the kitchen, even in an emergency.

English Game Pie

2–4 game birds, according to size (pheasant, grouse, partridge, woodpigeon)	2 oz butter
	1 rounded tablespoon flour
	6–8 rashers bacon (optional)
Bouquet garni	3–4 hard-boiled eggs, quartered
Stock or water	Salt, pepper, parsley
1 large onion, chopped	8 oz puff or shortcrust pastry
8 oz mushrooms, sliced	Beaten egg for glazing

For this recipe choose older birds or wood pigeons, rather than young roasting game. Put them into a pan with the bouquet and cover with stock or water plus salt and pepper. Simmer, covered, until the meat begins to part from the bone, and can be cut away from the carcase in good-sized pieces. Arrange them in a pie dish. Brown the onions and mushrooms lightly in the butter—they should be golden rather than deep brown. Stir in the flour, and enough stock to make a rich, fairly thick but not gluey sauce. Simmer while you cut the rashers into convenient-sized pieces for small rolls: these should be lightly grilled, then arranged round the meat, along with the pieces of hard-boiled egg. Season with salt, pepper and chopped parsley. Pour over the onion and mushroom sauce which should come to within half an inch of the top of the pie dish. Cover with puff or shortcrust pastry in the usual way (puff pastry is traditionally used, but many people prefer a good shortcrust with meat). Brush over with beaten egg and bake for 30 minutes at mark 7, 425°. The heat may be lowered once the pastry has risen well (puff) and is nicely browned (puff and shortcrust).

If the game has been cooked in advance, and is put into the pie when cold, allow slightly longer cooking time. The filling must be thoroughly heated through at boiling point. If you are uncertain about this, use a glass pie dish so that you can see what is happening.

To make a Yorkshire Christmas Pye

'First make a good standing Crust, let the Wall and Bottom

be very thick; bone a Turkey, a Goose, a Fowl, a Partridge and a Pigeon. Season them all very well, take half an ounce of mace, half an ounce of nutmegs, a quarter of an ounce of cloves, and half an ounce of black pepper, all beat fine together, two large spoonfuls of salt, and then mix them together. Open the fowls all down the back, and bone them; first the pigeon, then the partridge, cover them; then the fowl, then the goose, and then the turkey, which must be large; season them all well first, and lay them in the crust, so as it will look only like a whole turkey; then have a hare ready cased [skinned] and wiped with a clean cloth. Cut it to pieces; that is, jointed; season it, and lay it as close as you can on one side; on the other side woodcocks, moor game, and what sort of wild fowl you can get. Season them well, and lay them close; put at least four pounds of butter into the pye, then lay on your lid, which must be a very thick one, and let it be well baked. It must have a very hot oven, and will take at least four hours.

This crust will take a bushel of flour. . . . These pies are often sent to London in a box as presents; therefore the walls must be well built.'

This remarkable recipe from Hannah Glasse's *Art of Cookery* is not so eccentric as it sounds, nor so archaic. In Burgundy, at Saulieu, one may eat a similar dish, described on the menu as the 'Oreiller de la Belle Aurore'. It is one of the great specialities of the restaurant—inside the pastry crust, there is a good mixture of game, though it is not arranged in the Russian doll style of Hannah Glasse's recipe.

Certainly in England, the habit continued for nearly another century. Yorkshire Pies were being made and sent down to friends at Christmas time in the 1840s. I imagine that the crust was not quite so thick, now that goods came down by train, but the contents were unchanged. In 1845, Hawksworth Fawkes of Farnley Hall, near Otley in Yorkshire, sent one down to his friend, the painter J. M. W. Turner. Turner wrote back to say thank-you for the kindness 'in remembrance of me by the Yorkshire Pie equal good to the Olden-time of Hannah's . . .

culinary exploits'. He is referring sadly to the years between 1810 and 1823, when he visited his great patron, Walter Fawkes, Hawksworth's father, at Farnley Hall, where so many of his paintings still are.

Such presents—pies, game, puddings—arrived every year. In 1849, a goose pie turned up very punctually—'Mother Goose came to a rehearsal before Christmas day, having arrived on Saturday for the Knife, and could not be resisted in drinking your good health in a glass of wine to all friends at Farnley Hall . . . The pie is in most excellent taste, and shall drink the same thanks on Christmas day.'

If you feel like a similar 'culinary exploit' at Christmas time, I suggest you try the goose pie rather than the Yorkshire pie :—

To make a Goose Pye

'Half a peck of flour [5 lb] will make the walls of a goose-pie. . . . Raise your crust just big enough to hold a large goose; first have a pickled dried tongue boiled tender enough to peel [page 134], cut off the root, bone a goose and a large fowl; take half a quarter of an ounce of mace beat fine, a large teaspoonful of beaten pepper, three teaspoonfuls of salt; mix all together, season your fowl and goose with it, then lay the fowl in the goose, and the tongue in the fowl, and the goose in the same form as if whole. Put half a pound of butter on the top, and lay on the lid. This pie is delicious, either hot or cold, and will keep a great while. A slice of this pye cut down across makes a pretty little side-dish for supper.'

A splendid centre-piece for a party. Unless your pie has to go by train to London, like Mr Turner's, there is no need to make such a thick crust. However, it must be thick enough to keep in the juices as far as possible. I recommend a hot-water pastry made with 3 lb of flour, and a roasting pan $11\frac{1}{2}'' \times 9'' \times 2''$ deep as a mould (unless you have something of a comparable size which is deeper). It seems that the varieties of poultry in Hannah Glasse's day were not so large as they are now, because you need to increase the seasonings. My ingredients worked out like this :—

For 20–25

Hot-water crust made with 3 lb flour
1 10-lb goose, boned
1 5-lb farm chicken, boned
1 2½-lb pickled tongue, soaked, boiled, trimmed and skinned

¼ oz mace
2 heaped teaspoons freshly ground black pepper
5 rounded teaspoons sea salt
2 oz butter

To bake the pie, put it into a hot oven, mark 7, 425°, for 20 minutes. Then lower the heat to mark 4, 350°, and cover the top with brown paper to protect it from becoming too brown too soon. Leave for 3 hours.

It is only prudent to check the pie from time to time. Lower the heat, if it is bubbling away too fast, to mark 3, 325°. Towards the end of this time, push a larding needle or skewer into the pie through the top central hole; if the juices come out very red, leave the pie a little longer. On the other hand, if they come out a pale pink, that is all right—the pie continues to cook as it cools down (I took mine out of the oven at 1 a.m., and it was still not quite cold by lunchtime next day, with the juices still liquid : it should have been left until the evening, with an hour or two in the refrigerator to set it properly).

Salmi of Game (or duck, or fish)

Game birds roasted rare
3 shallots, chopped
2 oz butter
1 heaped tablespoon flour
Bouquet garni
Thinly cut peel of an orange, preferably a Seville

Pepper, salt, lemon juice
¼ pt red or white wine
¼ lb mushrooms fried in butter
Croûtons of bread fried in butter
Orange quarters

Remove the meat in nice neat pieces from the carcase. Use the bones and trimmings to make ¾ pt stock. Melt the butter and cook the shallots in it until they are a rich golden colour, then stir in the flour, and moisten with the stock. Simmer steadily for at least 20 minutes, with the bouquet and orange peel, until you have a rich, concentrated sauce almost of a coating consistency. Strain into a clean pan. Season to taste and add the wine and mushrooms. Simmer for 5 minutes, then put in the game, cover and leave for 10 minutes. The sauce should never boil properly once the game is added—it should barely simmer.

Place the pieces of game with a little sauce on top of the croûtons, and serve the sauce in a separate jug. Or else put the game and sauce into a serving dish, with the croûtons tucked round the edge. Garnish with orange quarters.

A salmi should really be made with game which has been roasted rare specially for the dish. In an imperfect world, it is more likely that a salmi contains the left-overs of yesterday's feast. Seen on a restaurant menu—at a restaurant price—it looks recherché, a dish of high-class French cookery. Don't be deceived. It is exactly what would have been eaten by Chaucer, or his son, at the court of Henry IV, or by that grand-daughter of his, Alice, Duchess of Suffolk, at her manor of Ewelme (where her husband built the church, and where she lies in such a splendour of alabaster). Only they would have called it salomene or salome. English court cooks had taken both name and recipe from medieval France, perhaps even from the *Menagier of Paris* of 1393, where the word *salemine* occurs, meaning something salted or highly seasoned (from the Latin *sal*, *salis*, salt).

Rabelais a century and a half later jazzed the word up with an extra syllable into *salmagonde*, and it soon came to have an extra meaning of a wild muddle or mixture of things, like another cookery word gallimaufry. You will see why if you turn to salmagundi on page 162. It is a highly seasoned recipe, but has no other similarity to salmi. Salmagundi gradually slipped out of favour towards the end of the last century—in England at least—but both the French and ourselves have most wisely clung to salmi. So good is the dish that the recipe has remained

in principle the same for five and a half centuries: the main
ingredient is roasted, then cut up and reheated in a highly
seasoned wine sauce. Here is the 1430 version of salmi, using
fish (in the same manuscript there is another, less well explained
salome for capon):—

SALOMENE

Take good wine, and good powder, and bread crumpled, and
sugar and boil it together; then take trout, roach, perch, or
carp, or all these together, and make them clean, and after
roast them on a griddle; then hew them in gobbets; when
they be cooked, fry them in oil a little, then cast them in the
bruet and when you dress it, take mace, cloves, cubebs, gilli-
flowers; and cast them on top, and serve forth.

Powder means ground spices, Cubebs are the berries of *Piper
cubeba*, one of the pepper family, with a spicy pungent flavour.
Bruet means a thick sauce.

Salmangundi for a Middle Dish at Supper

'In the top plate in the middle, which should stand higher
than the rest, take a fine pickled herring, bone it, take off the
head, and mince the rest fine. In the other plates round, put
the following things: in one, pare a cucumber and cut it very
thin; in another, apples pared and cut small; in another, an
onion peeled and cut small; in another, two hard eggs
chopped small, the whites in one, and the yolks in another;
pickled gherkins in another cut small; in another, celery cut
small; in another, pickled red cabbage chopped fine; take
some watercresses clean washed and picked, stick them all
about and between every plate or saucer, and throw nasturtium flowers about the cresses. You must have oil and vinegar,
and lemon to eat with it. If it is prettily set out, it will make
a pretty figure in the centre of the table, or you may lay them
in heaps in a dish. If you have not all these ingredients, set
out your plates or saucers with just what you fancy, and in
the room of a pickled herring you may mince anchovies.'

Hannah Glasse probably made use of those sets of glass or china, with a raised central bowl, surrounded by small ones at table level; but, as she says, you can lay it out in heaps on a large dish. This arrangement is more appealing than the more usual method of arranging the ingredients in layers, in a sugar cone shape, topped with the pickled herring.

Here are some of the other ingredients she suggests in the three other recipes she gives :—

Veal	Lettuce, cut in strips
Chicken (one of the most popular salmagundi ingredients)	Sorrel, cut in strips
	Spinach, cut in strips
Pork	Shallots, chopped
Duck	Lemons, chopped small
Pigeon	Pickles

Other garnishes suggested are peeled grapes, or blanched French beans, or grated horseradish, or barberries, or lemon slices, or a whole lemon or orange set on top at the apex of the sugar-loaf.

The tastes of salmagundi are built up of piquancy such as salt herrings, anchovy and pickled vegetables, set off by bland and crisp things such as chicken, eggs, celery and fresh salad vegetables. Made with care, it becomes a splendid hors d'oeuvre, for a cold table if you like (the Danes still eat a salmagundi, with everything chopped up together, herring, chicken, apple, beetroot, onion and so on, called *sildsalat*, herring salad). It can be elegant. Disaster, though, is inherent, and may be sensed from Hannah Glasse's remark that 'you may always make Salamongundi of such things as you have, according to your fancy.'

The fancy of frugal housewives has not always been successful in this country, one must admit. Salmagundi made a perfect excuse for clearing out the larder, which probably accounts for its gradual fall from grace towards the end of the nineteenth century. 'Such things as you have' is the knell for many English dishes. The staples of our larder do not include wine, cream, mushrooms, shallots, garlic, olive oil, and a number of green herbs, so perhaps we should be forgiven.

Hindle Wakes

5–6 lb roasting chicken or capon, or a really good boiling fowl
1 lb large prunes
8 oz breadcrumbs, made from slightly stale bread
4 oz chopped beef suet
½ teaspoon each sage, parsley, marjoram and thyme
Salt, pepper
1–2 tablespoons malt vinegar
1 tablespoon soft brown sugar

Stock
2 level tablespoons salt
1 stick celery
1 large onion, unpeeled, stuck with 3 cloves
1 bay leaf
4 sprigs parsley

4 sprigs thyme
About 6 pints water
4 oz malt vinegar
1 tablespoon soft brown sugar

Sauce
4 oz double cream
Juice of 1 lemon
Grated rind of 1 lemon
White pepper
1 tablespoon butter
1 tablespoon flour
4 oz milk

Plus
1 lemon
Good bunch of parsley
½ lb thinly cut slices of ham
Chive stalks

Remove the giblets from the bird. (Apart from the liver, which can be used for another dish, they will be needed for the stock.)

Soak the prunes for several hours or overnight, then simmer them for 5 to 10 minutes in the soaking water, so that they can be easily and neatly stoned. Set aside the neatest prunes for the final decoration, and chop the rest—just over half the total amount—for the stuffing. Crack the prune stones and remove the kernels.

To make the stuffing, mix the chopped prunes and kernels with the breadcrumbs, suet, herbs and seasoning. Add vinegar to taste, then the sugar. At this stage the flavour may seem odd, on account of the malt vinegar, but everything works out well in the end. Put this mixture into cavity and crop of the chicken, and retruss or sew it up.

Put the chicken into a deep pot, which fits it fairly closely. Add the giblets and all the stock ingredients, scaling the amount of vinegar down a little if less than 6 pints of water is needed. Be particularly sure to cover a boiling fowl by about an inch. The roasting birds should barely be covered. One wants to get as much flavour into the stock as possible, without the chicken becoming dry.

Bring the pot slowly to the boil, and simmer gently—a bubble or two should gurgle to the surface every few seconds—until the chicken is cooked. This will take from $1\frac{1}{2}$ to $3\frac{1}{2}$ hours, according to its antiquity. When the bird is done, remove the whole thing to a cool place. I cannot claim that the stock at this stage is particularly delicious, it takes getting used to (like the stuffing) but when it's cooked with the lemon and cream of the sauce it does have a delicious result. And as a cold dish, this is one of the best-flavoured I know.

Make the sauce while the bird is cooking, and almost ready. Bring the cream, lemon juice and rind with a little pepper very slowly to simmering point: let it simmer for 4 or 5 minutes, while you make a roux with the butter and flour. Pour half a pint of the stock from the chicken on to the roux, then the milk. Simmer for 20 minutes until the sauce is really thick. Finally strain in the lemon-flavoured cream, and cook for a little while longer so that everything is well blended. Correct the seasoning and allow it to cool.

When the bird is really cold, place it on a wire rack over some greaseproof paper. Reheat the sauce slightly—it will be solid when cold—so that you can spread it right over the chicken smoothly and evenly. Use a palette knife, and dip it in hot water, if need be, to enable it to run smoothly over the sauce. Scrape up the drips from the greaseproof and use them to patch up the odd corners. Slice the lemon thinly, nick out the peel to form a zigzag edging to each slice, and cut them all in half. Cut the prunes in half too, the ones you kept aside when making the stuffing. Divide the ham into a number of scallop-edged pieces and use them to make an edging on the serving dish. Put the chicken on top carefully. With the lemon slices, prunes, tufts of parsley and chive stalks, make a fairly exuberant design on the bird : a bunch of parsley makes a good backing if stuck in at the neck end. Use the remaining prunes and lemon slices to tuck round the base of the chicken, on top of the ham.

When you carve and eat the bird, you will be surprised to see how deliciously the malt vinegar has melted into the general flavours, and how good a mixture such a collection of ingredients can make. A superb buffet dish.

This recipe—as far as I have been able to find out—was first given, in a simple form, by Florence White in *Good Things in England*, published in 1932 by Jonathan Cape. She had the recipe from Mrs Kate A. Earp of Brighton, who wrote that 'We as a family in Lancashire called these fowls Hindle Wakes— why I do not know, unless it was because old hens were sold at the "wakes" [fairs]'. Her recipe was for an old hen, which was stuffed with prunes soaked in water and lemon juice, and then steamed for six or more hours until it was tender : the bird was then wrapped in bacon and roasted for an hour.

In 1954, Dorothy Hartley described a far more elaborate dish in *Food in England*. The stuffing was embellished with suet, breadcrumbs and vinegar. The fowl was then boiled in vinegar and water, and coated when cold with lemon sauce. Prunes and slices of lemon were used to decorate a rather more magnificent dish than Mrs Earp's. Moreover, it was eaten cold.

Miss Hartley says that her recipe was collected from a Lancashire family in 1900, but that it was centuries old and brought over by Flemish weavers who came to Lancashire in the fourteenth century, and settled at Bolton-le-Moor in 1337. However, the only things that they are recorded as having brought with them are wooden shoes—perhaps the origin of Lancashire clogs?—and jannock (oatmeal bread). I should have thought that it seems unnecessary to look any further than the medieval tradition of English cookery, which was influenced by France and the trade in spices and dried fruit from the Middle East.

What troubles me is the name. Miss Hartley says that it means Hen de la Wake, and Mrs Earp hints at a similar explanation. No etymologist would support a folk explanation of this kind (*hend* normally refers to hind, i.e. a young deer, as in Hindley, near Wigan, where the *ley* means place, so place of young deer).

It would seem that the name could have been taken from *Hindle Wakes*, a play written in 1912 by Stanley Houghton. It had much success, and is about the goings-on in an imaginary Lancashire town called Hindle during the annual holiday or 'wakes'. Wakes, the plural for a singular noun, came from the habit of keeping watch on the eve of the patronal festival of a parish church, a time which was celebrated as a holiday for everyone. The word continued in Lancashire when other parts of the country had given it up, and came to mean the annual closure of the factories in a town.

Lisanne's Chicken with Mussels

For 6

4–5 lb (dressed weight) roasting chicken	Bouquet garni
Large onion, chopped	½ pt dry white wine
Large carrot, chopped	4–5 lb mussels, scrubbed and scraped
2–3 tablespoons olive oil	Salt, pepper, parsley

Brown the chicken and vegetables in the oil. Transfer them to a deep, flame-proof pot. Add the bouquet and half the wine. Season, cover and cook gently but steadily for 45 minutes.

Meanwhile open 1½ lb of the mussels in a large pan, over a high heat, with the remaining wine. Discard the shells (and any mussels which remain firmly shut) and put the mussels into the cavity of the chicken which, after its 45 minutes' cooking, should be half-cooked. Strain the liquor into the pot and tuck the remaining mussels all round. Replace the lid on the pot, and finish cooking the bird—this will take from 30–45 minutes longer. Place the chicken on a serving dish and put the mussels in their shells all round it. Sprinkle with parsley and keep warm. Skim any fat from the chicken cooking juices, correct the seasoning and bring back to the boil. Strain into a hot sauce-boat. Serve with plenty of good bread to mop up the sauce. No vegetables, but a green salad afterwards.

This excellent dish was invented by a friend when she was staying in a remote hamlet in southern France. Suddenly she had to produce a special birthday dinner. All she had in the house—apart from basic supplies—was some mussels bought that morning for the family supper. Luckily a neighbour with a poultry yard always had a chicken, but that was all she could find. This recipe is very close to much older dishes of chicken with oysters, once very popular in England, which is why I include it in this book.

Roast Turkey with Parsley & Lemon Stuffing

For 8–10

12–14 lb turkey, drawn weight	Parsley and lemon stuffing, page 285
6 oz lightly-salted butter	4 oz dry white wine, or dry white
Salt, pepper	vermouth

Remove the giblets from the turkey, and use to make stock—see over the page. Soften the butter and add a teaspoonful of salt and plenty of black pepper, mashing it together. Make the stuffing and put it in the central cavity of the bird, then weigh the bird. Remove the bird's neck close to the breast to make the neck pudding described on page 171. Put the bird on its side on a rack in a roasting pan. Smear it all over with the seasoned butter. Put a double layer of foil over the top, fastening it tightly round the edges of the roasting pan to seal the turkey in.

Calculate the cooking time—up to 14 lb the turkey will need 15 minutes per pound. Over 14 lb, allow an extra 10 minutes per pound. So a 14 lb bird will take $3\frac{1}{2}$ hours : and a 20 lb bird, $4\frac{1}{2}$ hours. Preheat the oven to mark 5, 375°. At just under half time, turn the bird on to its other side. For the last 20–30 minutes, put the bird breast up and remove the foil; sprinkle the breast with salt and pepper.

Transfer the cooked bird to a warm serving dish. Boil up the pan juices and add the wine or vermouth. This can be served as a separate thin gravy, or it can be added to the thickened gravy made with the giblet stock.

At home in the north we always used to have a piece of boiled salt pork served with the turkey. I think this is better than bacon rolls—the delicate flavour of the pork, and its fatness, set off turkey meat better than anything else. Instead of cranberry sauce, we usually have a jelly made from the Cornell cherry bush in our garden which has a tart rich flavour. A few roast potatoes are essential, at least for the younger members of the family, and everyone likes sprouts and chestnuts.

Giblet Gravy

1 set turkey giblets, minus liver or 2 sets chicken giblets, minus liver	Bouquet garni
2 carrots, quartered	$\frac{1}{2}$ lb stewing veal, cut in pieces
1 onion, halved	2 tomatoes, halved and grilled
3 oz dry white vermouth, or 4 oz dry white wine	Salt, pepper
	$1\frac{1}{2}$ oz butter
	1 level tablespoon flour

Put the giblets, carrots, onion, wine, herbs and veal into a large pan over a high heat. Stir everything about and when it begins to change colour, add the tomatoes and enough water to cover by about an inch. Season with pepper and a little salt. Cover tightly and leave to simmer for 2 hours. **Strain carefully.**

In a small saucepan melt the butter and continue to cook it until it turns a golden noisette brown (it will also smell delicious). Stir in the flour, and when it is well mixed in, moisten the sauce with the hot stock. Allow to cook gently for about half an hour, so that the flavour is thoroughly mellow, then correct the seasoning.

If the sauce is to be served with chicken, add the rich brown juices from the roasting pan. In the case of turkey, the juices are likely to be more abundant, so pour off the fat and add a glass of port or Madeira to them and boil up together. Serve separately from the thickened gravy.

Boiled Turkey and Celery Sauce

For 8–10

14-lb turkey
Parsley and lemon stuffing, page 285

Stock
4 medium carrots, sliced
1 turnip, peeled, sliced
1 stick celery, sliced
3 onions, unpeeled, stuck with 3 cloves each
15 black peppercorns, slightly crushed
1 heaped tablespoon salt

2 bay leaves
4 sprigs thyme
Bunch of parsley stalks, left from the stuffing

Sauce
Head of celery
3 oz butter
¾ pt béchamel sauce
¼ pt double cream
Salt, pepper

Stuff the turkey, and put it breast down into a ham kettle or equally large pan (a kettle is best, because it has a strainer tray which helps you to lift out the cooked bird and drain it). Add the stock ingredients, and enough cold water barely to cover the bird. More salt may be needed. Bring to the boil and simmer for two hours, or until the turkey is cooked—the simplest way of judging this is to pull the bone end of the drumstick. If the leg parts easily, begins to part, that is, from the body, the bird is done. Keep the stock for soup. Place the bird on its dish.

Meanwhile make the sauce—wash, trim and string the celery. Cut it into strips and blanch them in boiling salted water for 10–15 minutes. The celery should be almost but not quite cooked. Drain it well, and return to the pan with the butter and simmer for a further 5-10 minutes, until it is cooked but not mushy. Add the béchamel sauce, stir it all well together and bring to boiling point. Liquidize it if you like a smooth sauce. Stir in the cream, adjust the seasoning and pour into a sauceboat.

A favourite dish of the Victorians and quite rightly so, because it is delicious—mild without insipidity.

Capon, Goose or Turkey Neck Pudding
Poddyng of Capoun necke (1430)

Take Percely, gysour—the gizzard—and the lever of the hearte, and perboyle in fayre water; than choppe hem smal, and put raw yokys of Eyroun ii or iii ther-to, and choppe for-with. Take Maces and Clowes, and put ther-to, and Safroun, and a lytil pouder Pepir, and Salt; and fille hym yppe and sew hym, and lay him a-long on the capon Bakke, and prycke hym ther-on, and roste hym and serve forth.

For 4

1 capon, goose or turkey neck (see recipe)	Mace, cloves and pepper to taste
½ lb high-quality sausage	Pinch of saffron (optional)
1 heaped tablespoon parsley	Salt
2 egg yolks	The liver of the bird

I always buy poultry with the head still on in order to make this delicious pudding. As the giblets are needed for the stock for the gravy, sausage meat provides the main filling.

With a pair of scissors, cut the skin of the neck as close to the breast of the bird as possible, right round. Then do the same as close to the beak as you can manage. Cut the skin straight up the middle, so that it can now be removed from the neck in an irregularly shaped oblong piece. Lay it out on a chopping board, skin side down.

Mix the sausage meat (discard the skins), with the parsley, egg, and spices. Steep the saffron in a very little hot water, and strain the liquid into the mixture when it is a good yellow. Season with salt. Spread this mixture out on the skin of the neck. Trim gristly or greenish bits from the liver, cut it into two or three large pieces and lay them down the centre of the sausage stuffing. Moisten your hands and bring the sausage up round the liver to enclose it completely. Fold the skin over and tuck the whole thing, cut side down, into a small loaf tin—I use one made of foil about 6″ long. Bake in the oven when roasting the bird, or if more convenient bake with other things at a temperature of mark 4, 350°, for 45 minutes. The top will brown lightly. If possible, leave for a couple of days in a cool place for the flavours to mature. Serve cut down in slices like any other pâté.

I had this recipe originally from a French friend, a superb cook who never wastes a thing. She was spending Christmas with us, and showed me how to stuff the turkey neck skin to make a dish for Christmas Eve supper. She simmered the neck for 20 minutes in the giblet stock which we were making for the gravy next day, but I think the flavour is better when it is baked. Every year since then the turkey, and any other large bird, comes complete with head. It amuses our supplier, but I feel cross about the waste of all those other necks.

Apart from the exquisite flavour, I have always admired this dish as an example of the French skill in turning every scrap to good account. The recipe is most popular in the foie gras districts of south-west France, where the left-over carcase of the fattened goose is salted and cooked gently in its own fat, and potted—again in its own fat.

Then I came across *Poddyng of Capoun necke*, and realized that fifteenth-century court cooks in England had done exactly the same thing as farmers' wives in Périgord. In fact their recipe, using the giblets of the bird as stuffing, is closer to the modern

French recipe than mine. I like to keep the gizzard, heart and neck inside the skin for the gravy stock, so substitute good sausage-meat for the giblets.

Pulled and Devilled Turkey, Chicken or Pheasant

For 6

Either
About 1 lb cooked turkey breast
One leg and thigh of the turkey, preferably undercooked and pink
Or
1 boiled or roasted chicken, with the brown meat a little underdone
Or
A brace of stewed or roasted pheasants

Devil sauce
1 rounded tablespoon Dijon mustard

1 rounded tablespoon mango or peach chutney
1 tablespoon Worcester sauce, or ½ tablespoon anchovy essence
¼ teaspoon Cayenne pepper
Salt
2 tablespoons corn oil

Pulled sauce
3 oz butter
6 oz double cream
Lemon juice
Salt, pepper
Chopped parsley

First pull the breast meat apart with your fingers into pieces about 1½″ long and the 'thickness of a large quill'. Follow the grain of the meat, so that you end up with somewhat thready looking pieces. Take the brown meat off the bones, and divide it into rather larger pieces than the breast meat. Slash each one two or three times.

Mix the devil sauce ingredients together, chopping up any large pieces of fruit in the chutney. Dip the pieces of brown meat into it, and spoon the devil into the slashes as best you can. Arrange in a single layer on the rack of a foil-lined grill pan, and grill under a high heat until the pieces develop an appetising brown crust. Keep them warm.

For the pulled sauce, melt the butter in a wide frying pan, and stir in the cream. Let it boil for a couple of minutes, and keep stirring so that you end up with a thick rich sauce. Put in the pulled breast, with any odd scraps of jelly, and stir about until the pieces are very hot indeed. Season with lemon, salt and pepper. Put in the centre of a serving dish, and surround it with the devilled bits. Serve with good bread or toast. Not a dish to be eaten with two vegetables. Keep them for afterwards, or simply serve a salad.

One of the most delicious dishes of eighteenth-century cooking, indeed one of the best of all English dishes. There is no better way of using up the Christmas turkey with the glory it deserves. It is also an ideal dish for a dinner party, as the bird or birds can be cooked in advance, the day before: spread the leg and thigh meat with the devil sauce several hours before grilling them, if you can. The flavours will then penetrate the meat even more thoroughly. Adjust the quantities of mustard and Cayenne pepper to suit your taste.

Duck stewed with Green Peas

For 4–5

4–5 lb duck	1 lb shelled peas
Bouquet garni (bay leaf, parsley, thyme, rosemary)	2 egg yolks
	4 tablespoons double cream
$\frac{1}{2}$ pt giblet stock	Salt, pepper, lemon juice
1 large lettuce, shredded	

Use the duck giblets to make the stock in advance. Boil it down to $\frac{1}{2}$ pt or a little more.

Prick the duck all over with a fork, and tuck the bouquet garni into the cavity. Brown it all over in a little oil—do this slowly so that the fat has a chance to run out. When it is a nice colour, a rich golden brown, place it in a deep pot, breast down, with the stock. Cover and simmer for $1\frac{1}{4}$ hours.

Turn the duck over. Add lettuce and peas, and some seasoning. Replace the cover and complete the cooking—another 45 minutes approximately. Take out the duck, and cut it into four pieces or carve it. Put the drained peas and lettuce on to a warm serving dish and arrange the duck on top. Keep it warm while the sauce is finished. Taste the cooking liquid. If necessary boil it down hard for 5 minutes to concentrate the flavour. Mix yolks and cream in a basin, pour on about half the stock, whisking it in well. Return this mixture to the cooking pot and stir the sauce together over a low heat without allowing it to boil. Finish with lemon juice, and correct the seasoning. Pour over the duck and peas and serve at once.

The sauce can also be thickened with beurre manié, but the yolks and cream are best. The dish has a remarkably fresh flavour, agreeably sweet but light and sharp at the same time. An ideal summer dish.

Duck with Mint

1 large duck	1 tablespoon chopped chervil
1 large bunch of mint	1 sprig thyme
1 large carrot, quartered	¼ bay leaf
1 large onion, stuck with 3 cloves	2 oz white wine vinegar
1 stick celery	2 oz dry white wine
Salt, pepper	Salt, pepper
	3 large egg yolks
Sauce paloise	6 oz butter, cut in pieces
1 tablespoon chopped shallot	Lemon juice
2 tablespoons chopped mint	Extra chopped mint

Season the duck inside and put into it the bunch of mint. Secure the opening, and wrap the duck in a large white napkin, tying it at each end like a Christmas cracker. Half-fill a large pan with tepid water, put in the carrot, onion, celery and seasoning and bring to the boil. Place the duck in this liquid, which should just cover it, and leave to simmer, covered, for 2½ hours.

Meanwhile make the sauce, about an hour before the end of cooking time. Place the shallot, herbs, vinegar and wine in a small pan. Add a pinch of salt and a good grinding of pepper. Bring to the boil and reduce the liquid by two-thirds or a little more. Allow it to cool, then whisk in the egg yolks and set over a low heat (or over another pan of simmering water, if you are not used to making egg-yolk sauces). Whisk in the butter bit by bit, never allowing the sauce to boil. When it is thick, season the sauce with lemon juice, and more salt and pepper. Strain it into a warm sauceboat, and stir in extra chopped mint. If the sauce has to wait, suspend the sauceboat over a pan of hot water.

To serve the duck, remove it from the napkin and drain it well. Put it on a serving dish, and surround it, if you like, with sprigs of fresh mint. Serve the sauce with it, also a purée of young turnips or broad beans.

Sauce paloise means sauce from Pau, which is the capital of the Béarn district of France. It is really a *sauce béarnaise* flavoured with mint instead of tarragon, a fact the French often forget when they sneer at our habit of serving mint sauce with lamb. This recipe, which is a marriage of English and Béarnaise sympathies, was invented by Guy Mouilleron. Coming from the Béarn, with its *sauce paloise*, he has experimented a great deal with mint, carrying its use further than most English cooks would have thought possible. See his other recipes on page 61 and page 99.

Guineafowl Braised with Mushrooms

For 4

1 fat guineafowl (1½–2 lb)	¾ lb mushrooms, sliced
4 oz butter	Salt, pepper, lemon juice
1 medium onion, chopped finely	

Brown the guineafowl all over in half the butter. Place it breast down in a deep, closely fitting pot and dab it all over with the remaining butter. Add the onion and some salt and pepper. Cover the pot with kitchen foil to seal it in tightly. Place in the oven at mark 5, 375°F, for 30 minutes.

Meanwhile season the mushrooms with salt, pepper and lemon juice. When the 30 minutes comes to an end, remove the bird in its pot from the oven and take off the lid. Turn it breast-side up and tuck the mushrooms in all round it. Season the breast and replace the foil. Return to the oven for a further half an hour. Discard the foil lid and leave the bird for another 10 minutes or so until it is cooked and lightly browned on top.

Carve the bird into eight—four slices of breast, two drumsticks and two thigh pieces. Arrange them on a hot dish with the mushrooms, which should be removed from the cooking pot with a perforated spoon. Taste the gravy and correct the seasoning, before pouring it over the bird. Serve immediately with good bread, or a few boiled potatoes to mop up the delicious juices.

This recipe is also good for pheasant. Indeed pheasant and guineafowl recipes are interchangeable.

Roast Guineafowl

For 6–8

2 fine guineafowl, 1½–2 lb each
6 rashers unsmoked streaky bacon, or 6 strips of pork back fat
Seasoned flour
1 glass port
½ pt stock made from the giblets, or from chicken giblets
1 bunch watercress

Stuffing
4 oz good sausages
1 heaped tablespoon breadcrumbs
1 tablespoon brandy
1 tablespoon port
1 heaped tablespoon chopped parsley
1 clove garlic, crushed
Salt, pepper to taste

First make the stuffing—remove the skins from the sausages and discard them (it is important to use a high-quality, meaty sausage, for instance, genuine Cumberland sausages, see page 138). Mix with the remaining stuffing ingredients and divide between the two birds—if the birds are sold complete with their livers, chop them up and add them to the mixture, but be sure to remove any bitter greenish parts first.

Put the bacon or pork fat across the breasts of the birds—or, better still, lard them with fat strips of pork and protect them

with butter papers. Place them on the rack of a roasting pan
and put them into a hot oven, at mark 7, 425°. After 15
minutes, lower the heat to mark 6, 400°, and leave them for 45
minutes. Take the guineafowl from the oven, remove bacon or
paper and sprinkle them with seasoned flour. Return to the oven
for 10–15 minutes until cooked and browned. Place the birds
on a serving dish and keep them warm. Pour the port into the
roasting pan juices, boil them up for a couple of minutes,
scraping in all the nice brown bits that have stuck to the pan.
Add the stock and boil down until you have a small amount of
strongly flavoured gravy. Pour round the birds, and garnish the
dish with watercress. Serve with bread sauce, and with celeriac,
or celery, or the chestnut and apple mixture on page 9.

The first time I saw guineafowl, they were humped along the
roof ridge of a French farmhouse, like a row of black and white
chequered tea cosies. Occasionally one of them would get up
and carefully pick its way along the row, or squawk down into
the farmyard. They look so decorative, and—which is more
important—taste so good, that I do not understand why they
have become so much less common than they once were. It's
true that the flesh can be a little dry, but larding or a jacket of
bacon or pork fat easily counteracts this slight disadvantage.
Even when frozen, they taste far better than frozen chicken or
turkey, having a slightly gamey flavour. (A friend suggested to
me recently that such birds, turkeys in particular, are best when
allowed to thaw out to *warm room temperature* before being
cooked : this is true, though nothing can ever take the place of
proper hanging in the matter of flavour.)

In some parts of this country, guineafowl are called gleenies,
a corruption and abbreviation of the Latin '*gallina africana*', the
African hen. Certainly the Romans were the first to appreciate
their delicious gamey flavour. They even appear as symbols of
the soul in bliss, along with the more usual peacock, on a mosaic
pavement in Justinian's church at Sabratha in Libya. 'The effect
is that of a couple of dazzling check sports-suits,' wrote J. M. C.
Toynbee in *Animals in Roman Life and Art*.

Game

All game needs to be hung, or it will be tough and thin of flavour. The general principle is to hang it until the tail feathers may easily be pulled out. In practice, this works out at 2–3 days for wild duck, mallard, teal, widgeon, etc., and about 7 days for pheasant, though in cold weather it may need 10. Venison, hare and wild rabbit should also be hung : from 3 to 10 days.

Game of all kinds is hung without being plucked, or skinned, and complete with innards. Birds are suspended by their necks; deer, hare and rabbit by the hind legs—this is particularly important when the blood of a hare or rabbit is needed for thickening the sauce.

The thing to watch when hanging game is the humidity of the weather. A warm muggy day, the kind that makes the stone floor of the cellar or back kitchen sweat with moisture, will increase the rate at which game matures in flavour. On the other hand, really cold weather will slow it down, acting like a refrigerator. One thing—always hang game before freezing it.

Plucking game birds is simple, if laborious. Hold the bird inside the mouth of a plastic sack (the plastic kind remain fairly rigid and remain open so that you can see what you are doing). Pull the feathers into the sack. Have a bowl of water to hand, so that you can rinse off the feathers that stick to the fingers. Pull the feathers the way they lie, so that the skin does not tear. Cut off the wing feathers, feet and other tricky bits. Some birds, the snipe for instance, should be skinned and not plucked : to do this chop off the wings and head, and ease off the skin and feathers. Snipe and woodcock should not be drawn as their entrails—usually referred to as the trail—are a delicacy.

Larger birds need to be drawn in the same way as poultry. This is not in the least unpleasant, and can be done quite neatly. Put the plucked bird on a large sheet of newspaper on the table; have a bowl of water handy, or do it by the sink. Make a small hole by the vent, and run your finger round the breast bone, easing the insides which are held together by membranes. Gradually they will come out, as you feel your way around and hook them towards you. When they are on the table, rinse the bird and set it aside. Remove the liver, heart and gizzard from the guts, as they can be used to make stock in some instances when a little gravy is required : the liver should have the greenish part removed, as this will taste bitter from the gall sac which stained it; the gizzard should be slit from top to bottom, to display the inside which is usually full of grain or greens— this can be removed by peeling away the wrinkled tough skin which lies next to the grain.

Cooking Game

With the game birds, only roast the young ones. The older creatures, or any you are doubtful about, should be braised or casseroled.

The test for youth varies slightly with different animals, but in general the feet will be soft and pliable, the ears in the case of rabbits and hares soft and easily torn. With rabbits and hares, creatures that one is used to, size will help you to form an opinion, and the young look of the skinned carcase.

The temperature for roasting these birds should be high, mark 7–8, 425–450°. The lower temperature for the larger pheasant, the higher for snipe and woodcock. It is wise to tie a jacket of pork fat round all but snipe and woodcock, which only need to be spread with softened butter. Another way of counteracting the dryness is to put a variety of things into the carcase to provide moisture : this ranges from seasoned butter to fruit. One of the nicest ways of all of serving game is to cut a piece of bread the size of each bird before it goes into the oven. As the bird roasts, fry the bread lightly in butter, then slip it under the bird about 5–10 minutes before the end of cooking time. This will soak up the delicious juices. The bird is put on to the serving dish, on top of the bread, and needs little more than watercress to go with it, though many other delicious things are often put on the table as well to prolong the pleasure and enhance the glory of the bird.

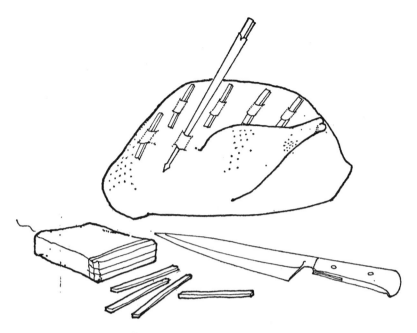

Larding poultry and game

With venison, hare and wild rabbit, roasting is more of a problem. First set the oven to a lower temperature, mark 4, 350°F. It is a good idea both to lard the game, and then to tie a jacket of fat pork round it, which can be removed for the last 15 minutes of cooking time. Allow 30 minutes per pound. With a wild rabbit, it is wiser to braise it or cook it in a casserole—the usual flavourings are onion and thyme. Saddle of hare can be stuffed and roasted successfully—it is a good idea to baste it with butter, bacon fat, red wine or milk, even if it is already larded and covered with a piece of fat. Venison, unless it is really young, should be soaked in a marinade before being cooked.

PHEASANT
roast : 20 mins per lb, plus 10 mins
inside : butter with seasoning and herbs; fillet steak; mushrooms, chopped and cooked first in butter

serve with : bread sauce, etc., see page 185; celery sauce, page 170, or celery salad; chestnuts; game chips, or roast, mashed or boiled potatoes.

PARTRIDGE

roast : 30 minutes

inside : chopped liver, chopped onion and butter; mushrooms chopped and stewed in butter

serve with : bread sauce, etc., as for pheasant

braised : with chestnuts and cabbage and white wine, page 184

GROUSE

roast : 30–45 minutes, covered with vine leaf if possible, then bacon or pork fat in a sheet

inside : bananas; wild raspberries, cranberries; peeled and seeded grapes

serve with : bread sauce, etc., as for pheasant, rowanberry jelly, page 301

PLOVER

roast : 30–45 minutes

inside : *as* grouse

serve with : *as* grouse

PTARMIGAN

roast : 30–35 minutes

inside : *as* grouse

serve with : *as* grouse

WOODCOCK

roast : 18 minutes (rare)

inside : leave the trail

serve with : finish cooking on fried bread; when done, spread trail on the toast—or else draw birds, before roasting, and cook trail with butter and marjoram and spread on fried bread just before serving

SNIPE
>*roast* : 15 minutes (rare)
>*inside* : *as* woodcock
>*serve with* : fried bread soaked in cooking juices, spread with trail as woodcock. Plus redcurrant jelly, orange salad, game chips; or simply with lemon quarters and watercress

WILD DUCK
>*roast* : 30 minutes (rare)
>*inside* : butter with salt, pepper and herbs

serve with : orange sauce, page 302; orange salad; with pan sauce made from stirring a glass of port wine into the cooking juices, skimmed of fat, and a tablespoon of bitter marmalade

WIDGEON AND TEAL
>*roast* : 20–25 minutes (rare)
>*inside* : liver mashed with butter, parsley and lemon
>*serve with* : *as* wild duck. On fried bread put under bird at the end of roasting

QUAIL
>It is now illegal to kill wild quail. Japanese quail are bred for the table : they can be browned in butter and braised with a little stock, port wine and orange peel

WOOD PIGEONS
>Only domestic pigeons or squabs are suitable for roasting. Wild pigeons should be cooked in a casserole—see stewed venison; or stewed with white wine, chestnuts and cabbage, see page 184

VENISON
>*roast* : 30 minutes per lb, after marinading, page 190. Lard, and tie on a jacket of fat
>*serve with* : french beans, well buttered; celery; Cumber-

land sauce, page 294; cherry sauce, page 300; venison sauce, page 298; orange sauce, page 302; mushrooms, particularly wild mushrooms; redcurrant jelly or rowan jelly; orange salad; roast or boiled potatoes

stewed : see page 193

HARE

roast : lard, jacket of pork fat, 30 minutes per lb

inside : herb forcemeat, page 193

serve with : forcemeat balls, redcurrant jelly, port wine sauces, e.g. venison sauce; bacon rolls.

jugged or stewed : page 193

WILD RABBIT

roast : 30 minutes per lb, *as* hare

inside : herb stuffing with thyme predominating

serve with : *see* hare

stewed : page 193

Partridge or Woodpigeons with Chestnuts and Cabbage

For 6

3 partridges, or 6 woodpigeons	¼ pt dry white wine
½ lb fat bacon, cut in strips	Game or beef stock
2 oz butter	Crisp cabbage of Savoy type
24 pickling onions, peeled	½ lb chestnuts

Brown the birds and bacon strips lightly in the butter. Transfer them to a casserole, putting the birds breast down. Brown the onions in the butter and add them to the pot. Finally pour the wine and about half a pint of stock into the frying juices, boil it up and scrape in all the nice brown bits and pour it over the birds. Woodpigeons should be almost covered, as they are a tougher proposition than partridges, so it may be necessary to add more stock—it will depend on the fit of the birds in the casserole. Cover the casserole closely and simmer it gently either on top of the stove or in the oven. Nick and boil the chestnuts for 15 minutes, then peel them. At the same time blanch the cabbage for 15 minutes in boiling salted water. When the birds are almost cooked, remove them from the casserole—put the cabbage in, open it out as best you can and place the birds on top, with the chestnuts. Replace the lid and continue cooking until done. Put the birds, cabbage, bacon and chestnuts on a dish. Skim the fat off the sauce, and if necessary boil it down hard to concentrate the flavour. Pour over the dish and serve.

Roast Pheasant

For 8

Brace of pheasants
4 oz fillet steak or 4 oz butter
2 thin sheets of back pork fat, large enough to cover the pheasant breast and top of the legs
Salt, pepper
Seasoned flour
1 glass port
Watercress

Giblet stock
Pheasant giblets, excluding liver
Light beef stock
1 carrot, sliced

1 onion, sliced
Bouquet garni

Browned crumbs
3 oz white breadcrumbs
1½ oz butter

Bread sauce
see page 290

Potatoes
1½ lb firm potatoes
deep fat for frying

First prepare the pheasants for roasting—cut the fillet steak into strips and put half into each cavity, with salt and pepper; alternatively divide the butter between them. These measures are to add extra moisture, pheasant can be dry. Put the livers into the pheasants, too, having first made sure that any greenish-yellow bits have been cut away. Season the birds and tie the sheets of pork fat in place. It is a good idea to lard the birds too, which means that the fat is introduced right into the lean meat of the breast and legs. Use strips cut from the sheets of fat. Set the pheasants aside until required.

To make the giblet stock, put all the ingredients into a pan and cover them generously with water. Simmer for two hours, strain off the stock and boil it down to half a pint. Season it.

To roast each bird, allow 20 minutes to the pound, plus 10 minutes at mark 7, 425° : this usually means 40–60 minutes. For the last 10 minutes, remove the jackets of pork fat, dredge the breasts lightly with seasoned flour and return to the oven to brown.

When the pheasants are cooked, put them on a serving dish and keep them warm. Skim the fat from the pan juices, pour in the giblet stock and boil hard for a few minutes. Scrape in any of the nice bits and pieces that may have stuck to the bottom of the roasting pan. Add the wine and bring to boiling point again. Season to taste if necessary and strain into a sauceboat.

While the birds are cooking, prepare the other items. The breadcrumbs should be fried in the butter until they are golden brown. This means regularly stirring. Tradition enjoins that they should be served on a doily in a small dish. The doily also absorbs any extra fat, so it is not an idle or pretentious refinement.

The bread sauce can be prepared in advance, and reheated over a pan of boiling water.

The potatoes should be peeled and then sliced very thinly on a mandolin into a bowl of water. If you like, use the ridge blade to produce *gaufrette* slices : for the lattice effect, run the potato one way on to the ridge blade and discard the first slice —then turn the potato and run it at right angles on to the blade to give you the lattice slices. Dry the potato well, and put it in batches into a chip basket. Cook in the deep fat for 2 minutes at 345–360°, then for about 30 seconds at 385–390°, until they're brown and crisp : it is the potato chip technique, but it allows for a briefer cooking time. Drain on crumpled kitchen paper and sprinkle with salt before serving. They too can be prepared in advance and reheated.

Brussels sprouts, mushrooms or celery can all be served with pheasant.

Don't forget to arrange the watercress round the birds before serving them.

A brace of pheasants makes a fine dish for winter celebration. Round about Christmas they are in top condition, falling to the guns in plump splendour.

> *See! from the brake the whirring pheasant springs,*
> *And mounts exulting on triumphant wings:*
> *Short is his joy. . . .*

And it is still this pheasant, Pope's pheasant in Windsor Forest, that you see in the main, hanging outside the game shop, a firebird among the sober ranks of hare and partridge.

Unlike our other game birds, partridge, grouse, woodcock, wild duck, the pheasant is by origin a most un-English creature of wild legend and magic. Its story goes back to the Argonauts who are said to have brought it back to Europe from Medea's Colchis (now part of Georgia), on their return from the quest of the Golden Fleece. The pheasant strutted about in troops on the banks of the River Phasis, at home in a land of glamour and exotic princesses.

It's no legend, though, that the Romans bred pheasant for the table, even at the grey end of the world on Hadrian's Wall (fossilized bones of the bird from Colchis were found in excavations at Corbridge—a long journey to have made, from Phasis to the Tyne). Sadly, it disappeared with the Romans.

The next unassailable pheasant record dates from the eleventh century; presumably the birds had come from France, preceding William the Bastard by a few years. And the French had the pheasant from the Romans. So it's back to Italy, the intermediary for so many things coming from the East to the West.

I had always thought that the pheasant belonged to the eighteenth and nineteenth centuries. And in spite of the Argonauts my impression was not so false after all, because it was then that many new varieties were introduced into this country —Lady Amherst's pheasant, the golden pheasant and so on. They came mainly from the Far East, China in particular, where they had been hunted by falconers since the third century

Unhung pheasant, like many other game birds, and game, isn't fit to eat. There's no need to wait until the back end turns green (though I knew of one parson's wife who thought pheasant wasn't ready for the table until maggots dropped on to the marble slab below), but they must be hung for several days. The exact number depends on temperature and humidity—and personal taste. On the whole it's a matter best left to an expert, in other words a good game butcher. Fix him with a determined eye, and make sure that the bird he presents you with has had a chance to develop the right unmistakable flavour before being plucked. Otherwise your money will be wasted.

Don't be put off by the price—there's a high proportion of meat to carcase. Quite the opposite of duck. A pheasant will go round four people nicely, when the dressed weight is in the region of 2 lb. Older birds can be casseroled in the usual way, but it is best to go for a young roasting bird whatever method you intend to use. The young cock bird has short, rounded spurs; the hen—to be preferred for fatness and fine flavour— has soft feet. Older pheasants have long and pointed spurs, and hard feet.

Pheasant Braised with Celery

1 pheasant	1 large egg yolk
3 oz butter	4 oz single cream
1 onion, chopped	4 oz double cream
3 thin rashers unsmoked bacon, cut in strips	Lemon juice
	Chopped parsley
Salt, pepper	$\frac{1}{4}$ pt port
1 head celery, cleaned, sliced	$\frac{1}{2}$ pt giblet stock (page 185)

Brown the pheasant in the butter with the onion. Put it into a deep ovenproof pot, breast side down. Add the port, stock and bacon to the frying pan, bring everything to the boil, then pour it over the pheasant. Cover the pot with a double lid of foil, and put into the oven for half an hour at mark 4, 350°. Remove the pot from the oven, turn the bird right side up, and pack it round with the sliced celery—slip some underneath as well, and into the cavity. Season well. Replace the lid and return the pot to the oven for another half hour, or until the pheasant is cooked.

Put the pheasant on a serving dish, surrounded by the celery. Beat the egg yolk and creams together, then add the hot liquor from cooking the bird. Pour it into a pan and heat gently, stirring all the time, until the sauce thickens. Taste it for seasoning, and sharpen with a little lemon juice. Scatter the chopped parsley over the celery just before serving. Pour the sauce into a separate sauceboat.

Braised Wild Duck with Apricot Stuffing

2 wild duck, dressed
½ onion, sliced
3 stalks from celery heart
½ teaspoon thyme
1 oz butter
1 tablespoon flour
1 tablespoon bitter orange marmalade (optional salt, pepper)

Stuffing
3 oz dried apricots, preferably the wild apricots with stones from Afghanistan
2 oz breadcrumbs from day-old bread
2 oz butter
2 heaped tablespoons chopped celery
Salt, pepper

First make the stuffing. Soak the apricots overnight. Drain them next day, and if they are the small kind, remove the stones, crack them, and extract the kernels. Chop the apricots roughly and add the kernels. Mix with the bread. In the butter cook the celery very gently for about 10 minutes until it is almost cooked; keep the pan covered. Add to the stuffing, season and put into the cavities of the duck.

Place the duck side by side in a deep pan or roaster. Put in the onion, celery stalks, and thyme and enough boiling water to come half an inch up the duck. Cover and put into a slow oven, mark 3, 325°, for 1 hour. Remove the cover, and top up with more boiling water if necessary to maintain the original level. Put back into the oven for another half hour. Remove the duck to a serving dish and keep them warm. Taste and boil down the cooking liquor to a good flavour. Mash the butter and flour together, and use to thicken the sauce by adding it in small knobs : the sauce should be stirred continuously and kept just below boiling point. Finally correct the seasoning, and add the marmalade gradually to taste, if you decide to use it. If not, serve the duck with redcurrant jelly as well as the sauce.

Roast Venison

Leave the joint in the following marinade for several hours :—

½ bottle red wine	1 onion sliced, or 4 strips orange
¼ pt olive oil	peel
2 tablespoons wine vinegar	12 slightly crushed peppercorns
Bouquet garni	Salt

Alternatively, with smaller joints, lard it with strips of pork or bacon fat.

Remove the venison from the marinade, drain it and brush it with melted butter or oil. Then tie a jacket of fat pork round it—or in the case of a leg or haunch, enclose it in a paste made of flour, water and a little lard (4 lb flour, 8 oz lard, water to mix). The paste is put round the joint, then the whole thing is wrapped in brown paper and tied with string. This keeps the moisture in the meat, and prevents it cooking too fast.

Cook the venison at mark 4, 350°. For smaller joints, allow 30 minutes per pound. As one gets to the larger pieces, the time is considerably reduced as you would expect—it does, after all, depend on the thickness of the meat rather than the acreage. Even a 25 lb haunch will only need from 4½–5 hours.

About half an hour before the meat is likely to be cooked, remove the brown paper, chip off the crust which is not for eating, and brown the meat at a raised temperature—mark 7, 425°. This should also be done with the smaller joints—remove the bacon or pork fat jacket first.

A leg or loin of venison is delicious when allowed to cool before being cut. Serve with Cumberland sauce, page 294, and orange salad, or with the cherry sauce on page 301.

Venison Chops and Steaks

Well-hung venison chops and steaks may be grilled in the same way as beef steaks. Serve them with the usual venison accompaniments, a port-wine sauce or quince jelly, French beans or mushrooms or an orange or celery salad, and roast or fried potatoes or game chips.

It is, however, a good idea to wrap them first in a piece of softened caul fat (page 139), to act as a permanent basting. Season them with a little salt and plenty of black pepper first.

They will take a little longer than beef, on account of the protective caul fat, but should be grilled medium rare. Give them 5 minutes a side under a really fierce heat, then a further 5 minutes a side at a slightly lower temperature.

Venison (or Game) Pie or Pasty

For 6

3 lb shoulder venison, or other game cut in pieces	¼ pt red wine
Flour seasoned with mace, pepper and salt	Game or beef stock
	4 oz chopped onion
4 oz butter	1 tablespoon flour
	Puff pastry and beaten egg to glaze

Turn the venison or other game pieces in the flour, and brown them in half the butter. Add the wine and enough stock to cover the meat. Put in the onion, cover and simmer until the meat is cooked and can be removed, in the case of other game, from the bone. Strain off the sauce. Melt the remaining butter in a small pan, stir in the flour and add the sauce to moisten it. Taste and correct the seasoning and put with the meat into a pie dish.

Roll out the pastry. Put a strip round the rim of the dish, brush it with water and put on the lid. Press the edges firmly together. Make a hole in the centre and decorate with pastry leaves and flowers (venison pasty is always on the ornate side as far as appearance goes). Brush over with beaten egg, and bake at mark 7–8, 425–450°, for about 20–30 minutes, until the crust is well risen and brown, and the contents of the pie heated through and bubbling. Delicious hot or cold.

One of the best of English dishes. It cannot fail to be a success, as the cooking of the contents is done separately beforehand : this means that tenderness and seasoning can be assured.

Jugged Hare (or Rabbit)
For 6

1 hare, jointed
Strips of pork or bacon fat for larding (optional)
Salt, pepper, mace
Bouquet garni
1 onion, stuck with 3 cloves
¼ lb butter
¼ pt red or white wine

1 anchovy, chopped
Pinch Cayenne pepper
1 tablespoon butter
1 tablespoon flour
Blood of hare or rabbit (optional)
Lemon juice (optional)
Triangles of fried bread

Unless your hare or rabbit is young and tender, you will be wise to lard it. Put the pieces into a large jug (the unlipped stoneware jugs still made in France, and widely sold in England, are ideal) after rubbing them with salt, pepper and mace. Add the bouquet, onion and butter. Cover the jug tightly and securely with kitchen foil, and string to make sure it keeps in place. Stand the jug in a pan of boiling water and keep it simmering until the hare is cooked—about 3 hours, but the time depends on the age and toughness of the creature. This can be done on top of the stove (it was an obvious solution to the problems of slow cooking without an oven) or in the oven if this is more convenient.

Remove the cooked pieces to a serving dish. Strain the juices into a pan. Add the wine, anchovy and pepper to taste. Thicken either with the flour and butter mashed together, and added in little knobs, or with the blood of the creature—in the latter case, mix a little of the sauce with the blood, then return it to the pan and stir over a low heat until thick; the sauce must not boil again once the blood has been added. Like eggs, it will curdle. Sharpen with a little lemon juice if you like.

This recipe was the obvious way of cooking game slowly in the days when ovens were not common, and most cooking was done over the hearth fire. Modern 'jugged' hare is really stewed, as in the following recipe.

Stewed Hare, Rabbit, Woodpigeons or Venison, with Forcemeat Balls

For 6

1 hare or rabbit jointed, or six pigeons, or 3 lb stewing venison, cut in pieces
Seasoned flour
½ lb streaky bacon, cut in strips
½ lb chopped onion
3 oz lard
1 heaped teaspoon thyme
1 heaped tablespoon chopped parsley
Half a bay leaf
Game or beef stock
3 oz port

Redcurrant jelly
Salt, pepper

Forcemeat balls
4 oz fresh white breadcrumbs
2 oz chopped suet
1 tablespoon chopped parsley
1 teaspoon thyme
Grated rind ½ lemon
2 oz finely chopped bacon
Salt, pepper
1 large egg

Turn the joints, pigeons, or pieces of venison in seasoned flour (keep the brains, liver and blood for the final thickening, in the case of hare and rabbit). With the bacon and onion, brown them in the lard. Transfer to a casserole. Put in the herbs and just enough stock to cover them. Simmer gently until the meat is tender and parts easily from the bone. Add the port, jelly and seasoning to taste. To thicken the sauce, either mix some of the liquid with a little of the remaining seasoned flour—about a tablespoon—and return it to the pot: alternatively, mash the brains, liver and blood together, pour on a little hot liquid and then return this mixture to the pot, cook without boiling for a few minutes until the sauce is thickened. The second method produces the better flavour—a good game butcher will give you the blood of a hare or wild rabbit.

Meanwhile mix the ingredients for the forcemeat balls, and fry them in lard until brown. Make the balls about an inch in diameter. They are also good with game soups, but should be made smaller. If you do not want to make forcemeat balls, serve the stew with triangles of fried bread.

Boiled Wild Rabbit or Duck with Onion Sauce

Put the trussed rabbit or duck into a pan. Cover it with cold water. Put in a bouquet of herbs, and pepper and salt. Bring to the boil and simmer until done—this will not take long, if the rabbit is a young one.

After half an hour, put 2–3 lb large, whole, skinned onions into the pot. Remove them after 20–30 minutes, drain and chop them and put them into a pan with 4 oz of butter. When they are cooked to a soft golden colour, stir in 4 tablespoons of double cream. Correct the seasoning, adding a little nutmeg if you like.

Put the cooked rabbit or duck on to a serving dish, either whole or cut into serving pieces. Pour the onions over the top so that they are smothered in the rich creamy sauce. Serve with potatoes and spinach.

A favourite eighteenth-century recipe, and a good one. If you cannot get a wild rabbit, use duck instead—domestic rabbit is too insipid for this kind of treatment.

John Farley, who was principal cook at the famous London Tavern, and published a book of his recipes in 1783, went in for startling decoration in the boar's head style. 'Pull out the jaw bones, stick them in their eyes, and serve them up with a sprig of myrtle or barberries in their mouths.' Sucking pig, with an apple in its mouth, and red berries in its eyes, is almost the last survivor of this tradition.

To Dress Rabbits in Casserole

For 4

1 wild rabbit, jointed
Seasoned flour
4 oz butter
¼ pt dry white wine
About 1 pt beef stock
Pepper, salt

Bouquet garni
1 rounded tablespoon flour
Juice of 1 Seville orange
2 whole Seville oranges
Chopped parsley

Dredge the rabbit with seasoned flour, and brown it in half the butter or lard. Transfer the pieces to an earthenware casserole, and add the wine, then enough stock barely to cover the meat. Season and tuck in the herbs. Simmer in a low oven, 250–275°, mark ½–1, until the rabbit is tender. The time will depend on the age of the rabbit, so it is a good idea to cook the dish one day, and reheat it *thoroughly* the next. If you cannot do this, allow three hours at least. Meanwhile mash up a tablespoon of the remaining butter with the flour to make *beurre manié*. Slice the two whole Seville oranges, and nick triangles of peel from the edge of each slice—save all the tiny pieces (this decorative detail can be omitted, but it adds to the final appearance of the dish).

When the rabbit is ready, arrange the pieces on a warm, shallow serving dish and keep them warm. Strain the sauce into a wide pan and reduce it to a good flavour. Lower the heat so that it barely simmers, and add the *beurre manié* in small knobs, stirring them in until the sauce thickens—this takes about 5 minutes. Add the orange juice, correct the seasoning, and, off the heat, beat in the final ounce of butter. Pour this sauce over the rabbit, and sprinkle it with the tiny bits of orange peel and a little chopped parsley. The orange slices go round the edge.

Lard can be used for frying the rabbit in this recipe from Hannah Glasse. A teaspoon of sugar can be added to the sauce as an improver of flavour : stir it in gradually, and stop before it becomes too sweet. Dessert oranges can be used, but Sevilles are the perfect balance for the slightly rank flavour of rabbit.

Puddings

English puddings have had a great reputation since the seventeenth century—perhaps earlier—and they deserve it.

One French visitor, the protestant exile François Maximilien Misson, who came to England at the end of the seventeenth century, was lyrical in his *Mémoires et Observations faites par un voyageur en Angleterre* (published 1698, translated into English by John Ozell, 1719) about the unexpectedness and variety of English puddings. 'They bake them in an oven, they boil them with meat, they make them fifty several ways: BLESSED BE HE THAT INVENTED PUDDING, for it is a manna that hits the palates of all sorts of people.' He had in mind puddings both sweet and plain, mentioning as the most common ingredients flour, milk, eggs, butter, suet, sugar, marrow and raisins. It's rather sad that pudding, among ourselves, inclines to become a word of abuse. It's true that an addiction to puddings hasn't been exactly in favour of English teeth and waistlines, but these wonderful things are some of the most subtle and imaginative combinations, relying on simple and natural ingredients.

Misson has described the heftier puddings including the kind eaten with gravy, or with sugar and butter. Filling, decidedly. But there's much to be said, and more than is usually said nowadays, for a national cooking which has invented Queen of Puddings, summer pudding, syllabubs, gooseberry fool, Bakewell Tart and that sweet concoction we now insist on calling crème brulée as if it were French and not the Burnt Cream of English cooks of the eighteenth century.

A generous hand with the cream—not to mention butter and eggs—has been the making of many of the best English puddings. Equally their downfall has been stinginess with cream and the illusion that nobody notices if you use margarine or vegetable fat instead of butter or lard.

Another blow has been the commercialization of puddings, premixed in packets, with skimmed milk powder, chemical flavour and chemical colour and chemical preservatives. Custard powder made in this way has been one of our minor national tragedies, also the commercial use of cornflour as a thickening substitute for eggs. It's cornflour which has made people loathe the idea of blancmange, turning an ancient and courtly delicacy into those cold shapes derided as 'baby's bottom' ('dead man's leg', 'dead baby', according to shape, are school names I recall for some of the less appetising suet puddings).

Puddings unquestionably were some of the first victims of mass catering and manufacture. But they survive, though in their huge number they are barely explored nowadays. For instance, how many families have sat down to Sussex Pond Pudding (sometimes called Sussex Well Pudding) for which I give the recipe? Yet it is one of the best of our suet puddings. That is a slightly complicated affair, but many of the best puddings are also the simplest. There's nothing simpler than junket flavoured with brandy, sprinkled with nutmeg and spread with clotted cream, and there's nothing simpler than adding a quince, if you can get one, to an apple pie.

People used to talk, still do talk occasionally, of the roast beef of old England, along with the revolting image in their minds of an overfed John Bull. My English family scenario would be candles on the dining-room table, clotted cream in a large triangular Coalport bowl patterned with blue and white flowers about to be added in large helpings to cold apple pie left over from Sunday lunch. The thought of it has buoyed children—and adults too, no doubt—through the tedium of Evensong.

Gooseberry Fool

For 6–8

1 lb young green gooseberries
2 oz butter
Sugar

Either

½ pt double or whipping cream or
¼ pt each single and double cream
Or
½ pt single cream and 3 egg yolks

Top and tail the gooseberries. Melt the butter in a large pan, add the gooseberries, cover and leave to cook gently for about 5 minutes. When the fruit looks yellow and has softened, remove the pan and crush the fruit with a wooden spoon, then a fork. Do not try to produce a smooth purée by sieving or liquidizing the gooseberries; they should be more of a mash. Season with sugar to taste.

Now either whip the cream(s) until they are firm, and fold in the cooled fruit. Taste and add more sugar if necessary, but do not make the fool too sweet. A couple of tablespoons of Frontignan gives a gooseberry fool a delicious, unidentifiable fragrance, but I would not recommend the addition of any other wine. Serve lightly chilled, with almond biscuits.

Or, instead of cream, make a thick custard by boiling the single cream, then stirring it into the egg yolks. Return it to the pan, and keep it over a low to medium heat until it thickens—stir all the time with a wooden spoon, and make sure it doesn't boil. Combine with the fruit purée when cold. Both methods go back to the earliest recipes. What is unforgivable is the use of package custards.

Any crushed soft fruit can make a delicious fool. Gooseberries, though, combine acid tartness and firm but melting texture which makes them the perfect choice. They are also one of the first fruits of the spring. Their early season is the time for food in the garden, within the scent of roses and dame's violet and balsam poplar, before the leaves have coarsened to their hard summer green. Gooseberries, too, are one of our few particular fruits; no other country has appreciated them as we have done, although they will grow happily up to the Arctic Circle. In France, one rarely sees a gooseberry bush in the cherished order of the kitchen garden. In our parish there, we have managed to find two or three, now part of the hedgerow round an old deserted cottage. We go quietly to pick the fruit which everyone else despises, and never seems to notice (although it has a place in French cooking as the *groseille à maquereau*, that is the mackerel gooseberry, see page 66). Then we delight our friends with an English gooseberry fool.

As Bunyard says in his *Anatomy of Dessert*, 'the plebeian origin of the Gooseberry has been, I fear, a handicap to its appreciation at cultured tables.' He remarks that it was first developed, in the early nineteenth century, by Midland workers who raised new seedlings for competitions. The criterion of excellence—as now in village summer fetes—was weight and size . . . 'the Big Gooseberry born in the smoke and moisture of Macclesfield and other great industrial towns.' 'The result of this great interest in the Gooseberry has been to increase its size and possibly its flavour, but best of all to combine these two qualities so that the big fruit of today'—he was writing in the late twenties—'is in many cases of excellent quality and well worthy of the gourmet's attention.'

Nevertheless, the small green gooseberry of old farm-house and cottage gardens is the best for gooseberry fool, and the other gooseberry puddings.

Orange Fool

For 4–6

The juice of 3 oranges	2 oz sugar
3 large eggs	Cinnamon, nutmeg
½ pt double cream	1 oz unsalted butter

Mix all the ingredients except the butter in a basin, stirring them well together. Set the basin over simmering water and stir the mixture until it is very thick. Do not allow it to boil, or the eggs will curdle. Remove the basin from the pan, and when the mixture is tepid, beat in the butter. Taste and add more sugar and spices if necessary. Put into small glasses and serve well chilled. The fool can be decorated with a few pieces of candied orange peel, and a hint of orange-flower water gives a delicious fragrance to the fool.

Worcestershire Pear Soufflé

2 macaroons	4 oz butter
1 large ripe pear	4 oz vanilla sugar, page 299
Juice ¼ lemon	1 oz cornflour
1 tablespoon kirsch or William pear	4 egg yolks
brandy (optional)	4 egg whites

First prepare a 2½ pt soufflé dish, or pyrex dish, or charlotte mould, by greasing it with a buttered paper, and shaking round it one crushed macaroon so that the crumbs form an even coating with the butter. Crush the other macaroon and keep it for the top of the soufflé.

Peel, core and chop the pear to a juicy mash. Mix in lemon, and alcohol if used. Put the butter in a basin, set it over a pan of almost simmering water and stir until it's melted. Sieve the sugar and cornflour together (if you are not using any alcohol, the *concentrated* vanilla is best). Tip it into the butter and stir to a thick buttery mass. Remove basin from heat and whisk in the egg yolks one by one. Then add the chopped pear and its juices. Beat the egg whites until they are stiff; mix a tablespoon of the whites vigorously into the egg and pear, then fold in the rest with a metal spoon—the best way of doing this is to scoop the whites on to the soufflé base, then to scrape up gently from the bottom of the basin, turning it with every scrape of the spoon.

Turn the final mixture into the soufflé dish. Sprinkle the top with the remaining macaroon crumbs. Bake at mark 6, 400°F, for 3 minutes, then reduce the heat to mark 5, 375°. Allow 30 minutes in all, and do not on any account open the oven door before 20 minutes has gone by.

Apricot and Almond Crumble

24 fresh ripe apricots	*Crumble*
2–3 oz sugar	4 oz flour
2 oz blanched, split almonds	3 oz sugar
	4 oz ground almonds
	6 oz butter

Pour boiling water over the apricots, leave them for a few minutes and peel off the skins. Slice them and, if you have the patience, crack the stones and remove the kernels—this is well worth doing. Arrange the apricots in a shallow baking dish, scatter them with sugar and the kernels. To make the crumble, mix flour, sugar and almonds. Rub in the butter to make a crumbly effect, and spread it over the fruit evenly. Arrange the split almonds on top. Bake at mark 6, 400°, for 20 minutes, then lower the heat and leave for another 20 minutes at mark 4, 350°. In fact crumble puddings are very good tempered— they can be cooked for a longer time at a lower temperature if this suits you better. The only thing to make sure of is that the top is nicely browned, and not burned. Serve with cream.

Many other fruits can be used instead. It is a good recipe for pears, but they should first be stewed in a very little water (just enough to prevent them sticking) with the sugar in the first list of ingredients. Tinned peaches are particularly successful, so long as they are drained well and then rinsed under the cold tap before being arranged on the dish—they will not need the sugar.

English Apricot Pie

For 8

36 fine ripe apricots (1½ lb approximately)
2 oz unsalted butter
8 oz caster sugar

8 oz weight puff pastry
1 egg white
Extra sugar

Halve the apricots and remove their stones. Melt the butter in a large frying pan, stir in the sugar. Keep the heat low to moderate, until the mixture begins to melt, then tip in the apricots. Turn them gently so that they are completely coated in the sugary mixture. They will become warm, but should not cook or begin to exude much juice.

Roll out the pastry, and cut from it strips to put round the rim of the pie dish. Allow a little to drop down into the dish itself. Put the apricots carefully into the dish, fitting them together so that there is as little space as possible left between them. Pour over them any juices which might be left in the pan. Brush the pastry rim with egg white. Lay the remaining pastry over the top, to form a lid, and press it down round the edge in a decorative manner. Make a central hole. Brush the lid over with white of egg, sprinkle it evenly with the extra sugar. Put into a hot oven, mark 8, 450°, for about 15 minutes until the pastry has risen and begun to turn golden brown. Lower the heat to mark 3–4, 325–350°, and leave for another 15 minutes. Serve hot or warm with plenty of cream.

This and the following recipe for apple pie are two more of the English dishes so appreciated by the French chef Carême. He gives them in *Le Cuisinier Parisien*, of 1828. He describes a brown-glazed English pie dish most carefully for his French readers, with its wide rim like a soup plate, but twice as deep. He spells out the way of setting strips of pastry on the rim, and covering it over with pastry and pressing the two edges together to make a firm, attractive seal. These two recipes are very simple, but the preliminary coating of the fruit in butter and sugar produces a most delicious flavour.

Carême also recommends this method for other fruit—plums, greengages, damsons, gooseberries and redcurrants, cherries, and pears.

English Apple and Raisin Pie

For 8

20 Reinette or Cox's Orange Pippins (3½ lb)
4 oz unsalted butter
4 oz caster sugar
Grated rind of half a lemon

4 oz seedless raisins, or 2 heaped tablespoons apricot jam
8 oz weight puff pastry
1 beaten egg white
Extra sugar

Peel, core and quarter the apples; then slice each quarter into six and put them into a bowl. Sprinkle over them the sugar and rind and mix together thoroughly. Melt the butter and add that to the apples, turning everything over as you do so. Finally add the raisins or the jam. Finish the pie as given above in the apricot recipe, but cook for at least 45 minutes at the lower temperature, instead of only 15. Apples, being a hard fruit, take longer.

Apple Pie

For 6

Either
1 lb cooking apples, e.g. Bramley's
½ lb Cox's Orange Pippins, or Ellison's Orange
Or
1¼ lb cooking apples
1 large quince

Plus
Sugar
½ pt water approximately
8 oz total weight pastry

Either peel, core and slice the apples, *or* peel, core and slice the apples and peel, core and grate the quince. Fill the fruit into a pie dish, so that it mounds up in the centre, sprinkling each layer of fruit with sugar as you go. Pour the water into the dish, stopping when it comes halfway up or a little less. Roll out the pastry. Cut a strip long enough to go round the edge of the pie dish, brush this edge with water and lay the strip on top, pressing it into place. Brush the strip with water. Use remaining pastry to make a lid over the pie. Cut off surplus pastry, knock up the edges and make a central hole for the steam to escape. Brush over the pastry lid with water, sprinkle it with an even layer of caster sugar and bake in a fairly hot oven, mark 6, 400°F, for 20 minutes. Lower heat to mark 5, 375°, and cook for another 20 minutes. Eat hot or warm, with plenty of cream.

> Many of our dessert apples have sufficient acid to make them good cookers, as in Cox's Orange Pippin, James Grieve and Allington Pippin . . . Two or three apples of Cox's Orange Pippin or Ellison's Orange added to the Bramley's Seedling improve the flavour of an apple pie far better than do cloves . . .
>
> H. V. Taylor, *The Apples of England.*

—and quinces are even better.

Cherry Tarts

Pastry	Filling
5 oz flour	1½ lb cherries, stoned
3 oz butter	¼ pt double cream
2 tablespoons icing sugar	2 eggs
1 large egg yolk	3 oz caster sugar
1 tablespoon lemon juice	

Make the pastry in the usual way and line 18 small tart tins. Stone the cherries with one of those useful fruit and olive stoning machines and put a closely-packed single layer in each pastry case. Beat cream, eggs and sugar together and put about a tablespoon or a little less over the cherries in each tart. Bake for 15–20 minutes at mark 8, 450°. The filling will puff up and brown slightly in the heat, but as the tarts cool, it will shrink. They are best eaten tepid or moderately hot.

In the Middle Ages, the cherry fair was a great festival in England. People wandered about the orchards when the fruit was ripe; they would dance and sing and drink and make love; the cherries were picked and sold. The poignancy of colour and glory in lives which were normally brutish had by the thirteenth century turned the fair into a symbol of the passing moment (like the cherry blossom festival in Japan at an even earlier date):

> *This lyfe, I see, is but a cheyre feyre:*
> *All things passe and so must I algate.*

And so the cherry season is still, though to a lesser degree: it passes too soon, and one never seems—unless one has the fortune to live in Kent—to have made the most of it.

As far as cooking is concerned, the dark acid morellos and the paler amarelles are the varieties to buy. Dessert cherries can be used, so can the tinned morellos sold under the Yugoslavian brand name, Vitaminka, but fresh acid cherries give the deep-flavoured richness that one needs. Incidentally, it is the use of over-sweet canned red cherries that makes so many restaurant dishes of duck with cherries uneatable.

'Cherry' is one of those words which convey a great deal, not just the idea of summer and love and their passing, but the whole history of the fruit. It comes from the Old French *cherise*, which comes in turn from the Latin *cerasus*—and that goes back to *karsu*, the Accadian word used by Assyrians and Babylonians who first cultivated the cherry.

Oldbury Gooseberry Pies

1 lb plain flour	2½ oz water
¼ lb lard	½ lb gooseberries, topped and tailed
¼ lb butter	½ lb demerara sugar

Put flour into a bowl and make a well in the centre. Chop butter and lard into smallish pieces and put into the well. Bring the water to the boil and tip it on to the fats, stirring them about briskly until they dissolve. Now stir in the flour gradually to make a malleable, not too stiff dough, which looks slightly waxy.

Roll out some of the dough and cut out a circle with the aid of a saucer. Bring up the sides about an inch, pressing and moulding the pastry to form a case. Fill with gooseberries and a proportionate amount of sugar. Roll out a smaller piece of dough and cut a lid. Brush the edge of the pastry case, lay the lid on top and pinch the edges decoratively together, to make a firm seal. Cut a small central hole for the steam to escape. Repeat with the rest of the pastry. Bake the pies at mark 6–7, 400–425°, for 25–30 minutes.

This simplified hot-water pastry can be used successfully with other fruit. Try it with peeled, cored and sliced pears—to make a medieval or Shakespearean Warden Pie. Mix powdered ginger and cinnamon with the sugar, and add a squeeze of lemon juice before putting on the lid, to bring out the flavour of the fruit.

A friend gave me this recipe, which she had from a farmer's wife at Shiperdine, near Oldbury on Severn. In *Good Things in England*, Florence White remarks that, in 1931, raised gooseberry pies were still being sold at Mansfield fair in Nottinghamshire.

Raspberry Pie

Pastry
12 oz plain flour
2 tablespoons icing sugar
1 pinch salt
8 oz butter, or butter/lard
1 egg yolk
Ice-cold water to mix

Filling
1 lb raspberries
About 4 oz sugar
4 oz single cream
4 oz double cream
2 large egg yolks

Glaze
1 egg white
Caster sugar

First make the pastry in the usual way. Roll out rather more than half of it, and use to line a 1″ deep pie dish or pyrex plate.

Brush the pastry with egg white and sprinkle evenly with sugar : this helps to prevent the pastry becoming too soggy. Pile in the raspberries, sprinkling them with the sugar according to their natural sweetness. Roll out the remainder of the pastry and cover pie in the usual way, making a hole in the centre wide enough to take the stem of a kitchen funnel. Decorate the pie with the trimmings, brush it over with egg white and sprinkle with caster sugar. Bake at mark 5, 375°, until the pastry is well cooked—about 40 minutes.

Towards the end of cooking time, warm the creams to boiling point, and pour them on to the yolks, beating vigorously. When the pie is done, pour this custard, or 'caudle' as it used to be called, through a funnel into the central hole. Do this gently and stop before the pie overflows. Return to the oven for 5 minutes. Eat warm rather than hot; any cream and egg left over can be used to thicken a soup or sauce.

This was the usual way of making a fruit pie in the eighteenth century, though normally puff pastry would be used. The caudle mixes with the juice in the pie and thickens it slightly, softening the acidity of the fruit. Gooseberries could be substituted, or other soft fruit in season.

Fifteenth-Century Apple Fritters
Fretoure owt of lente

Apples	*Batter*
6 large Cox's Orange Pippins, or other firm eating apple	4 oz flour
Sugar	2 medium eggs
1 liqueur glass brandy	1 tablespoon oil or clarified butter
	Up to $\frac{1}{2}$ pt milk
	Pinch saffron
	Freshly ground black pepper

Peel, core and slice apples $\frac{1}{4}''-\frac{1}{2}''$ thick. Put them into a dish and sprinkle them with sugar, and pour on the brandy. Leave them for several hours—or overnight—turning them occasionally in the liquid. Drain them well before coating them with batter.

For the batter, mix the flour, one whole egg, the second egg yolk and the oil. Beat in about quarter of a pint of milk. Pour 3 tablespoons of almost boiling water over the saffron and leave to steep for a little while; when the water is a good crocus yellow, strain it into the batter. Add more milk if the batter is too thick. Grind the pepper two or three times over the basin and stir it in. Last of all whisk the second egg white until stiff, and fold it into the batter.

Dip the apple slices into the batter and fry them in oil until golden brown. Serve sprinkled with sugar.

Although the saffron and pepper are omitted from modern recipes, this is a shame. The saffron gives the batter a delicate flavour and a beautiful colour: the pepper adds an aromatic piquancy rather in the manner of ginger but with a less assertive taste. Pepper is still used for flavouring pear tarts in the Bourbonnais and Poitou districts of France.

Bananas make good fritters, too. Steep them in sugar and rum instead of brandy.

Pears in Syrup

For 6

6 pears	1 stick cinnamon
Red wine	Pinch of powdered ginger
Sugar	

Peel, core and halve the pears. Place them in a pan in a single layer, and pour in enough red wine to cover them (no need to use the best claret, a wine sold by the litre will do). Add 2 tablespoons of sugar, the cinnamon and ginger. Cover and simmer until the pears are done. Remove them to a dish with a perforated spoon and keep them hot. Boil down their cooking liquor until it is slightly syrupy. Taste it from time to time, and put in more sugar if you like—the flavour should be fairly strong, and sweet, but not over-sweet. Pour, boiling, over the pears and leave to cool. Don't strain out the cinnamon stick: it adds to the appearance, as well as the flavour of the dish.

A medieval recipe which was usually made with Wardens or cooking pears. They were as hard as quinces and were first boiled until just tender, in water. This is not necessary with the pears we buy today, though the hint might be useful if you have a tree of cooking pears.

If wine is out of the question, add three sliced quinces to the pears, and substitute a vanilla pod, split, for the cinnamon stick. Cover with water, and start with 4 tablespoons of sugar. If you cook the dish slowly enough and long enough, the juice will turn a most beautiful deep red.

Summer Pudding

For 8–10

2 lb blackcurrants, or raspberries, or a mixture of raspberries, redcurrants and blackberries	6 oz caster sugar Good quality white bread, one-day old

Put the fruit and sugar into a bowl, and leave overnight. Next day tip the contents of the bowl into a pan, bring to the boil and simmer gently for 2–3 minutes to cook the fruit lightly. It should make a fair amount of juice.

Cut the bread into slices $\frac{1}{4}''$ thick. Remove the crusts. Make a circle from one slice to fit the base of a $2\frac{1}{2}$ pt pudding basin or other bowl. Then cut wedges of bread to fit round the sides. There should be no gaps, so if the wedges do not quite fit together, push in small bits of bread. Pour in half the fruit and juice, put in a slice of bread, then add the rest of the fruit and juice. Cover the top with one or two layers of bread, trimming off the wedges to make a nice neat finish. Put a plate on top, with a couple of tins to weight the whole thing down, and leave overnight—or for several days if you like—in the refrigerator. (If the bread is not thoroughly impregnated with the brilliant fruit juices, boil up a few more blackcurrants or raspberries and strain the liquor over the white bits which will occur at the top of the pudding.) Run a thin knife round between the pudding and the basin, put a serving dish upside down on top, and turn the whole thing over quickly. Remove the basin and serve with a great deal of cream; cream is essential for this very strong-flavoured pudding, which because of its flavour goes a long way and should be served in small slices.

This pudding can be made successfully with frozen black-currants—though it seems a shame. One family I know always has it on Christmas Day, after the turkey, as a reminder that summer will come.

Wild Apricot Fool or Ice Cream

For 4–6

6 oz wild dried apricots from Afghanistan (from Asian food shops and some health food shops)

Or

8 oz apricots dried without sulphur dioxide (from better health food shops)

Plus 1 oz blanched almonds
Icing sugar
Lemon juice
6 oz double cream
3–4 oz single cream

Soak the apricots, then simmer them in their soaking water for 5 minutes until just cooked, without adding any sugar. Remove the stones from the whole wild apricots, crack them and remove the kernels; crush the fruit with a fork and mix in the kernels. Otherwise, mash the ordinary dried apricots, and add the blanched almonds, cut into slivers. Boil down the juice remaining from the fruit until it is syrupy and add that to the fruit. Sweeten further with icing sugar, and add a little lemon juice to bring out the flavour.

Beat the creams together, and when stiff, fold in the fruit. Serve chilled, or frozen as an ice-cream, with almond biscuits.

This is the best winter fool. Make an effort to find the small whole Afghan apricots. They have quite a different flavour from the usual kind, very spicy and delicate, yet the richness pervades the whipped cream. One of the many blessings brought to us by the immigrant Asian communities since the war. In fact they are grown in a wide stretch of land from Persia across to the Hunza valley of Kashmir. They have a flavour of long civilization.

Brown Bread Ice Cream

For 6–8

6 oz wholemeal breadcrumbs	2 egg yolks
½ pt double cream	1 tablespoon rum (optional)
8 oz single cream	2 egg whites
4 oz icing sugar, or pale brown sugar	

Spread the breadcrumbs out on a baking tray and toast in a moderately hot oven. They should become crisp and slightly browned. Meanwhile beat the creams with the sugar. Mix the yolks and rum, if used, and add to the cream mixture beating it in well. When the breadcrumbs are cool, fold them in gently and thoroughly, so that they are evenly distributed. Lastly, whip the whites of the eggs stiff and fold into the mixture. Freeze in the usual way, at the lowest temperature. There is no need to stir up this ice-cream.

After too much experience of creamless ice-creams, we were startled one day in our small village in France by the hotel-keeper's wife. She had spent a holiday in England during the thirties, as a child. 'It was marvellous,' she said. 'Your ice-creams are so wonderful. We have nothing like them here. I remember at Gunter's. . . .' We bowed our heads over an especially good coffee ice-cream that she had made herself, and kept quiet as her memories wafted round the room. A year or two later, I managed to buy a copy of *Gunter's Modern Confectioner* of 1861. I see what she meant, and think of her every time I use it. This recipe in particular was popular in the nineteenth century, and has recently had a revival—which I imagine we owe to the excellent wholemeal bread now on sale in so many bakers' shops. The original recipe made no use of eggs or rum, it was just brown breadcrumbs, syrup and cream, but I think this version gives a lighter result and it needs no attention while freezing.

Ginger Ice Cream

For 6–8

8 oz milk	3–4 oz preserved ginger, chopped
2 egg yolks	8 oz double cream, whipped
1 egg	2 tablespoons icing or soft brown
2 oz ginger syrup	sugar

Bring the milk to the boil and pour it on to the yolks and egg very gradually, beating the whole thing together (small wire whisks are the best for this kind of operation). Return to the pan and cook slowly over a low heat until the custard thickens: it must not boil or the egg will curdle. Immediately the thickness seems right, dip the base of the pan into a bowl of very cold water. This prevents the mixture continuing to cook in its own heat. Add the ginger syrup immediately after this, to hurry further the cooling process. If I sound fussy, I apologise, but even after 20 years' experience with custards things can go wrong, and one may as well minimize the risks.

Place this mixture in the freezing compartment of the refrigerator, which should be set at the coldest possible temperature. When it has set solid round the edges, remove it to a bowl, stir it up well and quickly incorporate the ginger pieces and whipped cream. Taste and add sugar gradually—ices should not be too sickly-sweet, mainly on account of the flavour, but also because an oversweetened mixture freezes less well.

Return to the freezer and leave until hard. If the custard was frozen to the right amount before the ginger and cream was added, it should not be necessary to stir it at all during the second freezing process. If there was any doubt about this, stir it up gently after an hour, so that the ginger pieces do not sink to the bottom.

I think that ginger ice-cream is very much a Christmas-time

pudding, even a substitute for plum pudding. Those tubby porcelain and decorated jars of preserved ginger, often suspended by their rush lattice nets from the beams of old-fashioned grocery stores, are as much a sign of the season as tangerines and nuts. For those who are likely to suffer from too-much-ness, I offer a comforting thought from Dioscorides, the great Greek herbalist of the first century A.D., who still influences some odd corners of our minds: he recommends ginger, for it has 'a warming, concocting power, mollifying of the belly gently, and good for the stomach.'

Preserved ginger, which comes mainly from China, is the young rhizome, succulent, green, not yet fibrous, of *Zingiber officinale*, which is native to South-East Asia, but is now grown throughout the tropics (much of our powdered ginger comes from the West Indies; so do the 'hands' of fresh root ginger which can be bought at the best greengrocers these days, and those dry, whitish bits of 'root' ginger used in pickling and chutney-making).

There is one extraordinary fact about ginger—not its ancient use, nor even its universal importance (second only to pepper), but the persistence of its name. The words *singi vera*, meaning horn stem, were borrowed into Sanskrit from the Dravidian languages which were spoken in India before the Indo-Aryan invasions of about 1200 B.C. (and it seems that the Dravidian languages had it from south-east Asia where ginger is native). From India the name travelled west by two routes: via Greek and Latin (*Zingiber*) into Europe, and via Persian and Arabic into Africa, so that even the Swahili word is similar to ours.

Melon Water Ice

4 oz sugar

8 oz water

½ pt liquidized melon pulp

Lemon juice

1 large egg white

Simmer sugar and water for four minutes to make a syrup. Cool, then add gradually to the melon until the mixture tastes sweet enough—this will depend on the variety of melon used, and on its ripeness. If the mixture tastes too sweet, it can be diluted with a little water.

Add lemon juice to bring out the flavour. Freeze at the lowest possible temperature, in the usual way. When the mixture is just firm, whip the egg white until stiff with an electric beater and add the ice to it spoonful by spoonful. It should blow up into a foamy mass. Re-freeze. The mixture can be spooned into the emptied melon skins for serving.

The English became adventurous gardeners in the sixteenth century, and many tried, without great success, to grow melons. Few of them attained perfection, as John Parkinson observed (he was apothecary to King James I, and dedicated his famous gardening book, *Paradisi in sole* to Queen Henrietta Maria—the wife of Charles I—the title is a pun on his name). Melons were eaten then with pepper and salt, and with plenty of wine because everyone was nervous of their effect on the stomach. Catherine de'Medici, Queen-mother of France from 1559 to 1588, once complained of feeling unwell to the Queen of Navarre, and received the sharp retort that it was no wonder, seeing how many melons she ate.

In spite of the climate and nervous digestions, the English persisted and now there are a number of hardy varieties which can be raised under glass in this country. We still eat them with pepper sometimes, or ginger, or with port, though we have forgotten why, and do so because such seasonings bring out the flavour and emphasize the melon's coolness.

Elizabeth Raffald's Orange Custards

For 8–10

Rind of ½ Seville orange	4 large egg yolks, or extra large for
1 tablespoon brandy (or orange liqueur)	preference
	½ pt double cream
Juice of 1 Seville orange	½ pt single cream
4 oz granulated sugar	Candied orange peel

The rind can be removed from half the orange with a potato

peeler: simmer it in water for 2 minutes, then drain it and place in the liquidizer with the brandy (or liqueur) and the orange juice, sugar and egg yolks. Blend at top speed until the peel is reduced to a very slight grittiness in the liquid. Bring creams to the boil, and add gradually to the mixture in the blender. Check the seasoning, and add more sugar and orange juice if necessary.

Pour into 8 or 10 custard cups or small soufflé dishes. Stand them in a pan of hot water and put into a warm oven, mark 3, 325°, until just set. About 30 minutes, or a little longer depending on the depth of the mixture in the pots.

Serve warm or chilled, with a decorative piece of candied orange peel in the centre of each one.

Most of the best cookery books in this country have been written by women (or by foreigners). And of this energetic tribe, the most energetic of all was Elizabeth Raffald. Consider her career. She started work at fifteen, in 1748, ending up as housekeeper at Arley Hall in Cheshire. At thirty she married. Eighteen years later she was dead. During those eighteen years she organized:

(a) a cooked food shop selling pies, brawn, pickles, etc.;

(b) an enlarged cooked-food shop, with a confectionery department;

(c) the first domestic servants' employment agency;

(d) two important Manchester inns, or rather posting-houses;

(e) the first street and trade directory in Manchester (then a town of something over twenty thousand inhabitants);

(f) a couple of newspapers, as an *eminence rose*;

(g) an unreliable husband;

(h) fifteen (or sixteen—some conflict of evidence) daughters;

(i) her cookery book, *The Experienced English Housekeeper*, published in 1769 (a facsimile of the 8th edition is available from E & W Books, at £3.50). Many of her recipes can be adapted to modern kitchen machinery, which she would thoroughly have approved of. She could always see the advantages of the latest thing, and added her own contribution to progress.

Gooseberry, Pear, Apple or Quince Cream

For 4–6

1 lb fruit	3 egg yolks
Sugar	2 oz butter, melted
½ pt cream	An appropriate spice or wine

Prepare and cook the fruit, starting it off with three tablespoons of water. No need to remove peel or cores, just cut it up if necessary. Sieve the fruit into a bowl. Add sugar to taste, making it on the sweet side. Beat in the cream, then the egg yolks and butter. Flavour with a spice appropriate to the fruit you choose, or, in the case of gooseberries, a little muscat wine such as Frontignan, or some orange-flower water for an especially eighteenth-century flavour.

This mixture can either be cooked over a low heat until very thick, without boiling or the eggs will curdle; or it can be turned into a pastry case, or a pyrex dish, and baked in the oven until just set—mark 5, 375°. Eat hot, warm or cold.

A head of elderflowers, tied in a piece of muslin, is always a good aromatic addition to gooseberries as they cook. Keep tasting the mixture, and remove the elderflowers before the flavour is too strong. A substitute for Frontignan. This should also be done when making gooseberry jelly, or cooking the fruit for gooseberry fool. Home-made elderflower wine used to be known in the past as 'English Frontignan'. There is a remarkable affinity between these muscat flavours and gooseberries.

Elizabeth David's Everlasting Syllabub

For 4–6

4 oz white wine or sherry	2 oz sugar
2 tablespoons brandy	½ pt double cream
Pared rind and juice of 1 lemon	Nutmeg

Put the first three ingredients into a bowl and leave overnight. Next day strain the liquid into a bowl and stir in the sugar until it has dissolved. Still stirring, pour in the cream slowly. Add finally a grating of nutmeg. Beat the syllabub with a wire whisk until it holds its shape—do not go on too long, or too vigorously, or the cream will curdle and separate into a buttery mass.

Spoon the syllabub into small glasses or custard cups—there is enough for four to six people—and keep in a cool place (not the refrigerator) for two days or more. Of course they can also be served straightaway, but it is usually more convenient to make puddings in advance and this one keeps well. 'A tiny sprig of rosemary or a little twist of lemon peel, can, as suggested by Sir Kenelm Digby, be stuck into each little filled glass.' Serve with almond or sponge biscuits.

The recipe comes from Elizabeth David's pamphlet *Syllabubs and Fruit Fools* (which also includes some delicious Scottish specialities). She traces the history of syllabubs back to the seventeenth century. The simplest of all was a pastoral affair, a picturesque treat for town visitors to the country; a milkmaid would direct a stream of new, warm milk into a bowl of spiced cider or ale. After a while a light curd formed on top, with a delicious whey underneath.

The more solid syllabub, the kind we eat today, the Everlasting Syllabub as opposed to the milkmaid's simple affair of milk and cider, also goes back to the seventeenth century. In grander kitchens, cream and wine were used, though Sir Kenelm Digby, in *The Closet . . . Opened*, his notebook of recipes which was published, after his death, in 1669, does remark that concentrated fruit syrups could be substituted for the wine. They should be on the tart side, 'very weak of sugar'.

Trifle

For 8

6 large macaroons
Frontignan, Malaga or Madeira Wine
Glass brandy
1 pt single cream
2 large egg yolks
2 large eggs
1 tablespoon ground rice or flour
Caster sugar

Raspberry jam
Everlasting syllabub, page 217, made with the wines above
Ratafia biscuits (Atkinsons of Windermere still make them—to be found at good confectioners and cake shops)
Candied peel and other decorations

Put the macaroons into the base of a deep glass dish, cutting them to fit if necessary. Pour 4 oz of wine over them—the muscat-flavoured Frontignan is best—and the brandy. Allow it to soak in, then add more if the macaroons are still on the dry side. Next make the custard—bring the single cream to the boil, and pour it on to the egg yolks and eggs which have been beaten together with the ground rice or flour. Return this mixture to the pan and cook gently without boiling until very thick; keep stirring with a wooden spoon. Season with sugar to taste. Pour over the macaroons and leave in a cool place to set. When firm, spread with a layer of raspberry jam. Make the Everlasting Syllabub on page 217 and put it on top. Decorate with nicely cut shapes of peel and other decorations. Try and avoid the brassy effect of angelica and glacé cherries: many confectioners still sell the more delicate kind of cake and pudding decorations which are closer in style to the old-fashioned sweetmeats and comfits. Leave in a *cool larder* overnight.

A pudding worth eating, not the mean travesty made with yellow, packaged sponge cakes, poor sherry and powdered custards.

Mrs Beeton's Chocolate Soufflé

For 4

4 egg yolks	3 oz plain chocolate, grated
3 heaped teaspoons caster sugar	4 egg whites, stiffly whipped
1 heaped teaspoon of flour	Extra caster sugar

Beat the first four ingredients together well. Fold in the egg whites. Pour into a greased cake tin and bake at mark 5, 375°, for 20 minutes. Pin a white napkin round the tin quickly, sprinkle the top of the soufflé with caster sugar and serve immediately. Cream goes well with this soufflé, which should be taken straight from oven to table before it has a chance to fall.

A splendid pudding, rich in flavour and easy to make.

Payn pur-dew (1420)

Take fair yolks of eggs, and separate them from the white, and drawn them through a strainer, and take salt [a pinch] and cast thereto; then take fair bread, and cut it in round slices; then take fair butter that is clarified, or else fresh grease, and put it in a pot, and make it hot; then take and wet well the slices in the yolks, and put them in the pan, and so fry them up; but be ware of them cleaving to the pan; and when it is fried, lay them on a dish, and lay plenty of sugar thereon, and then serve it forth.

Poor Knights of Windsor (1937)

Cut a French roll in slices and soak them in sherry. Then dip them in beaten yolks of eggs and fry them. Make a sauce of butter, sherry and sugar to serve with them.

Ambrose Heath, *Good Sweets*

You may be surprised to observe that the medieval instructions are more precise than the modern ones. It is important, for instance, to use clarified butter as this reduces the likelihood of the bread burning. I like, too, the stress on the quality of the ingredients—they are to be fair, or fresh. Certainly the finer the bread you use the better the dish will be. If you can find brioche, for instance, you will understand how this simple pudding delighted the court of Henry V. No wonder it has lasted down the centuries, even with its mangled French title (which means *pain perdu*, lost, i.e. smothered bread), and become a family pudding in this country. I do not know when the second title was given to the dish—it certainly contains a memory of its original grandeur as well as the feeling of having come down in the world.

Hannah Glasse flavoured her *Pain perdu* with cinnamon. It can also be served with fresh fruit :—

Poor Knight's Pudding with Raspberries

For 6–8

1 lb raspberries	6 oz butter
¼ lb icing sugar	6 oz whipping cream, or 3 oz each
Cinnamon	double and single cream
8 slices white bread	1 heaped tablespoon caster sugar

Sprinkle raspberries with the icing sugar and about half a teaspoon of cinnamon. Leave until they produce some liquid and look like a slightly runny whole-fruit jam. Taste and add more cinnamon and sugar if necessary.

Cut the crusts off the bread. Bring the butter to the boil in a small pan, then pour it, through a muslin-lined sieve, into a frying pan; fry the bread in it. This sounds laborious, but it is quickly done, and avoids the risk of the bread browning too much—it should look golden, and be crisp.

Keep the bread warm in the oven, while you whip the creams together and sweeten them to taste with the sugar. Sandwich the bread with raspberries, and top with a generous swirl of whipped cream. You have a delicious contrast between the keen, buttery heat of the bread, and the keen cold of the raspberries, softened by the whipped cream.

Before the last war, when tea was an occasion for enjoyment and not for guilt, we often used to have home-made raspberry jam sandwiches at my grandmother's house. There were always too many—raspberry jam being her favourite—and next day they would appear as a pudding, having been fried in butter. I always thought, and still do think, that their latter end was more glorious than their debut. This recipe is my adaptation of her economy. It works well, too, with really ripe apricots and peaches. In winter one can use a really good jam, but I find this too sweet.

Whim-Wham

For each person

1 boudoir biscuit (sponge finger biscuit)	2 tablespoons double cream
	½ teaspoon chopped roasted hazel-
1 tablespoon muscatel dessert wine or sweet sherry	nuts
	2 small leaves cut from angelica

Break the biscuit in four and place the pieces in a small custard cup. Pour over the wine and leave it to soak in. Whip the cream and pile it on top. Decorate discreetly with the nuts and angelica—candied citron or orange peel can be used instead of angelica, but avoid glacé cherries which would be out of style.

A popular eighteenth-century emergency recipe, which is delicious and not too heavy. Whim-wham means something trifling, i.e. a trifle. Double the quantities if you like, but this kind of thing is more a delicious mouthful at the end of a meal, than a pudding.

Burnt Cream or Crème Brulée

I: 1909, from The Ocklye Cookery Book, *by Eleanor L. Jenkinson*

1 pt double cream, or ½ pt each double and single	4 large egg yolks Caster sugar

Bring cream(s) to the boil, and boil for about 30 seconds. Pour immediately on to the 4 yolks, which have been well beaten, and whisk them together. (At this point, although the recipe doesn't say so, I return the mixture to the pan, and cook it *without allowing it to boil*, until it thickens and coats the spoon.) Pour it into a shallow heat-proof gratin dish. Leave to chill overnight. Two hours before the meal, sprinkle the cream with an even layer of caster sugar, and place it under a pre-heated grill at maximum temperature. The sugar will caramelize to a sheet of brown smoothness: it may be necessary to turn the dish about to achieve an even effect.

II: 1848, from Domestic Cookery, *by a lady* (*Maria Rundell*)

'Boil a pint of cream with a stick of cinnamon, and some lemon peel; take it off the fire, and pour it very slowly into the yolks of four eggs, stirring until half cold; sweeten, and take out the spice, etc.; pour it into the dish; when cold, strew white pounded sugar over, and brown it with a salamander.'

In professional kitchens in France and England, the overhead grill of the kind that most of us have, is always referred to as 'the salamander'.

III: 1769, from The Experienced English Housekeeper, *by Elizabeth Raffald*

'Boil a pint of cream with sugar, and a little lemon peel shred fine, then beat the yolks of six and the whites of four eggs separately; when your cream is cooled, put in your eggs, with a spoonful of orange flower-water, and one of fine flour, set it over the fire, keep stirring it till it is thick, put it into a dish; when it is cold sift a quarter of a pound of sugar all over, hold a hot salamander over it till it is very brown, and looks like a glass plate put over your cream.'

The custard here is very thick with the extra eggs and the flour. The first recipe can also be enriched with more yolks, but I think that the whites make the consistency rather too firm. Mrs Raffald's orange flower-water gives the authentic eighteenth-century flavour to custards—good chemists often stock it; it is also used with fruit creams, and gives a deep-flavoured muskiness almost like Frontignan. Always add it gradually, because it easily becomes too dominant.

This best of all English puddings, the apotheosis of the custard, is usually accredited to Trinity College, Cambridge, on the strength of the first recipe which comes from the sister of a former librarian. Florence White quoted it in her *Good Things in England* of 1932, and repeats the story that an undergraduate offered the recipe—which came from a country house in Aberdeenshire—to the college kitchens in the 1860s. It was refused without trial, coming from such a lowly source. When the undergraduate became a fellow, it was a different matter, and the pudding rapidly became a favourite dish of the May Week celebrations. It goes particularly well with strawberries, which are in their first glory at that time of the year; indeed, it is always a good idea to serve fresh or lightly cooked fruit with it.

The story worried me, though, not on account of its exact truthfulness, but because *crème brulée* seemed such an eighteenth-century kind of pudding. And I soon found the second and third recipes, plus one in a cookery book of 1812, which was obviously taken from Mrs Raffald although the French title of *crème brulée* was used (she called it Burnt Cream). But where did Mrs Raffald get it from? One can see from the last sentence of her recipe that she enjoyed making it. Is it a French dish after all? Did she get it from the Warburton family, at Arley Hall in Cheshire, where she worked as housekeeper with such success that she remained on friendly terms with them for years afterwards (she dedicated her book to Lady Elizabeth Warburton)?

This doubt is typical of much of our cooking. The French and English strands are interwoven from at least the time of the Conquest. The French influence became strong in the seventeenth century, in particular when Charles II and his court returned from exile in Versailles, and again at the end of the eighteenth and during the nineteenth centuries when French chefs like Ude, Carême, Soyer, Francatelli and Escoffier came to England to work.

Tea Cream

For 4–6

Scant 1 oz green (gunpowder) tea
3 tablespoons sugar
½ pt each single and double cream

Packet gelatine (½ oz) or 5 leaves
4 tablespoons very hot water

Put tea and sugar into a pan. Mix the creams together and pour about ¾ pt into the pan (the remaining ¼ pt is a safety measure, in case you inadvertently make the tea flavour too strong and sickly). Bring slowly to the boil—keep tasting, so that the pan can be removed when the infusion seems right, but remember that flavours diminish in strength as they cool. Pour through a sieve into a basin. Add remaining cream and taste, adding more sugar if required. The flavour can be strengthened by pressing gently on the tea debris to extract the last sludge-green drops. Don't overdo the sugar: this is a dish for adults.

Melt the gelatine in water and beat into the warm cream. Brush the inside of a mould with corn oil (preferably one of those elaborate Victorian china moulds). If oil collects in the intricacies of the design, turn it upside down to drain. Pour in the cream when cold. Serve chilled, in small quantities, with not-too-sweet plain or almond biscuits, very crisp. The flavour will be subtle, with an aftertaste of tea (gunpowder tea contains the pure tea-flavour), the texture very smooth, and the colour that fawnish dove-grey that the Victorians loved.

When you buy green or gunpowder tea, the dried but unfermented tea required for this recipe, you will understand the names. And also the earlier Hyson, which is a corruption of the Chinese name, *hsi-ch'un*, meaning 'bright spring'. 'Andrews the Smuggler'—this is a parson, Parson Woodforde of Weston Longeville in Norfolk, writing up his diary in Norfolk for March 29th, 1777—'brought me this night about 11 o'clock a bagg of Hyson Tea 6 Pd weight. He frightened us a little by whistling under the Parlour Window just as we were going to bed. I gave him some Geneva [gin] and paid him for the tea at 10/6 per Pd.' Nowadays green tea disappears into many blends, but it can be bought from tea merchants or Far Eastern stores. The curly mass of green withered leaves has the true essence of tea in its flavour.

Incidentally, the widely tolerated custom of buying smuggled tea came to an end not long afterwards in 1784, when the high customs duties on tea were repealed. It also put an end to the habit of adulterating tea—elder buds were dried and added to green tea—which had given a profitable employment to a number of small villages. According to Gervas Huxley in *Talking of Tea* (Thames & Hudson, 1956), one village produced twenty tons a year of 'tea'—or 'smouch' which was made 'from the leaf of ash trees, steeped or boiled in copperas and sheep's dung'.

The mixture, minus gelatine, can also be frozen. Or you can use green tea to flavour the conventional egg custard and cream mixture. In the former case, the texture is best lightened by beating the almost-set ice with a couple of stiffly whisked egg whites.

Devonshire Junket

For 4–6

1 pint Channel Island milk	1 teaspoon rennet
1 dessertspoon sugar	4 oz clotted cream
2 tablespoons brandy	cinnamon or nutmeg

Bring milk slowly to blood heat—if you are not used to judging this, use a thermometer; it is surprising how hot a liquid at

98.4° feels. Meanwhile mix the sugar and brandy in the china bowl in which you intend to serve the junket. And put it in a convenient place in the kitchen, where it can stay until required (junket sets best at room temperature). Pour the warmed milk into the bowl, then stir in the rennet gently. Do not disturb until the junket is firmly set.

If the clotted cream is stiff, mix it with a little fresh cream, so that it can be spread over the surface of the junket without disturbing it. Sprinkle the cream with ground cinnamon or nutmeg.

If the junket tastes salty, your teaspoonful of rennet was too generous.

Not a nursery pudding. Junket is an English version of those curd and cream dishes that the French still make in such delicious variety (*cremets d'Angers, maingaux, coeurs à la crème*). Like their *fromage frais*, junket is produced by curdling warm milk with rennet. Then it is left to set to a smooth jelly. The curd is not broken up and drained of whey as it would be in France, and as it once was in England (junket derives from old Norman French, *jonquet*, a little basket made from *jonques* or rushes and used for draining cheeses until recent times).

When we had the idea of leaving the curd alone in its smoothness, I do not know. In *Food and Drink in Britain*, C. Anne Wilson quotes the earliest recipe she can find, from 1653, in which the junket was not drained, but eaten with cream and cinnamon just as in the recipe above. She suggests that it was the popularity of unrenneted creams in the eighteenth century, the syllabubs, fools, fruit creams, which sent the junket into eclipse. Like many old dishes which have survived at the fringes of the country, it has acquired the reputation of being a local speciality, in this case of Devonshire, which is really unjustified —or perhaps one should rather say misleading. The production of rennet in convenient bottled form—rennet extract was first prepared by a chemist in Denmark in the 1870s and was in production from 1878 onwards—unfortunately meant that junket could become the bane of every nursery, with an ultimate degradation of artificial colouring and flavour. From my own experience, I recall hating the texture of junket as a child. Like apricots and rice pudding, it used to end up in the aspidistra pot which stood so helpfully in the middle of the junior dining-table at school.

Baked Almond Pudding I

For 4–6

4 oz butter	2 tablespoons double cream
8 oz ground almonds	1 tablespoon brandy
5 bitter almonds, or a few drops of bitter almond essence (from German delicatessen shops)	4–5 heaped tablespoons sugar
	2 egg yolks
	2 eggs

Melt the butter, pour it into a bowl, and add the remaining ingredients in the order given. Grease a shallow pie-dish or pyrex with a butter paper, ladle in the mixture and bake at mark 5, 375°, for about 45 minutes. The time will depend on the depth of the mixture; allow room for it to rise a little. The surface will brown lightly and acquire that appetising baked almond crust which makes this and the following pudding so delicious. Serve with sugar, butter and a sweet wine like Marsala, Madeira, muscat wine or sherry.

A firm, cake-like pudding with a 'sad' centre and crisp outside. If you want to make it go further, bake it in a sweet shortcrust.

Baked Almond Pudding II

For 4–6

4 oz butter	1 glass sweet sherry, or other similar wine
¼ lb ground almonds	
4 bitter almonds or almond essence (see above)	4 oz sugar
4 large eggs	1 pt single cream or half cream/half milk, plus 1 oz breadcrumbs
Rind and juice of ½ a lemon	

Melt the butter, and add other ingredients. Bake as above. This pudding, being of the custard type, is best when the centre part stays rather liquid to provide its own sauce. Aim to have the mixture 1½″ deep or a little more. A marvellous pudding.

Kickshaws

Roll out half a pound of puff pastry thinly on a floured board. Cut out circles or squares about 3″ across and put a teaspoonful of firm home-made jam in the middle—quince butter is ideal, or some large pieces of fruit from home-made apricot jam. Fold the pastry over, sealing the edges with a little beaten egg. Pinch the edges as decoratively as you like. Deep fry the kickshaws a few at a time until puffed up and golden brown. Serve them sprinkled with sugar.

A most delicious ending to a meal. Little fried pies and dumplings were a favourite part of medieval food, but this seems to be a last survivor all on its own in the eighteenth century. Kickshaws are a sweet version of Turkish *börek* and Chinese *hun t'un*. The word is a slightly scornful anglicization of 'quelque chose', some odd thing or other. Indeed kickshaws are small delights which need skilful hands, the refined frivolities of a well-established cooking tradition.

Sweetmeat Cake

6 oz puff or shortcrust pastry	2 large eggs
4 oz chopped peel	2 large egg yolks
2 oz chopped roasted hazelnuts (optional)	6 oz caster sugar
	6 oz lightly salted butter, melted

Line a 9″ flan tin with the pastry. Scatter the chopped peel over it, then the hazelnuts if used. Beat the remaining ingredients thoroughly together and pour the mixture over the peel. Bake at mark 4, 350°, for 35–40 minutes. The top should be crusted with a rich golden brown all over—so keep an eye on it after 30 minutes in the oven. At first the filling will rise with the baking, but once the cake is removed from the oven and transferred to a plate, it will sink again as these egg mixtures usually do. Do not worry if the centre part of the filling is a little liquid beneath the crust, as it makes a delicious sauce. The consistency is a matter for individual taste.

Like most sweet tarts, this one is best eaten warm. Serve cream with it.

This delicious cake with its butterscotch flavour and semi-transparent filling is my own favourite of the eighteenth century open tarts. Candied peel provides the 'sweetmeat': it can be augmented with angelica, and with the hazelnuts mentioned in the ingredients, but don't be tempted to add glacé cherries as they spoil the subtle flavour.

This recipe is a forerunner of the nursery favourite, treacle tart, but it has a much superior flavour. Treacle tart is filled with a mixture of 3 tablespoons golden syrup, 3 tablespoons white breadcrumbs and the grated rind of a lemon: bake it at mark 7, 425°, for 20–30 minutes.

John Farley's Fine Cheesecake

6 oz puff or shortcrust pastry
8 oz full fat cream cheese
2 generous tablespoons double cream
1 tablespoon orange-flower water, or rose water

4 large egg yolks
2 oz lightly salted butter, melted
3 oz crushed macaroon crumbs
3 oz almonds, blanched, ground
3 oz caster sugar
Up to half a grated nutmeg

Line a 9″ flan tin with the pastry—John Farley and every other cook of the eighteenth century used puff pastry, but we prefer a rich shortcrust these days, I think, on account of its crispness.

Mix the remaining ingredients in the order given, adding the nutmeg to taste. Turn the mixture into the pastry case. Bake at mark 4, 350°, for 30–40 minutes. The top will be nicely browned all over. Eat hot or warm, with cream.

In England, we are too busy with a United Nations of cheese-cakes—American, Polish, Israeli, Dutch—to remember that John Farley, of the London Tavern, and one of the best-known cooks of his time in the eighteenth century, gave eight quite different cheesecake recipes in his *London Art of Cookery.* Among them was the following simple mixture of cheese, eggs and raisins, which is now often called :—

Yorkshire Curd Tart

8 oz weight shortcrust pastry, made with lard and sour milk

Filling
4 oz butter
2 oz sugar
8 oz curd cheese (not cottage or cream cheese)

4 oz seedless raisins, or currants
1 rounded tablespoon wholemeal breadcrumbs
Pinch salt
Grated nutmeg to taste
2 well-beaten eggs

Line an 8″–10″ tart tin with the pastry—use the kind with a removable base. Cream butter and sugar together, mix in the curds, raisins or currants and breadcrumbs. Add the salt and nutmeg and lastly the eggs. Taste and adjust nutmeg, add a little more sugar if you like (I find most recipes too sweet). Pour into the pastry case and bake for 20–30 minutes at mark 7, 425°. The pastry should be a nice brown.

Yorkshire Almond Tart

6 oz weight puff pastry

Filling
2 egg yolks
2 oz sugar

Rind and juice of half a lemon
1 oz ground almonds
1 oz melted butter
2 egg whites
Pinch salt
Extra sugar

Roll out the pastry and line a pie plate with it. Beat the yolks, sugar, lemon juice and rind together in a basin. When they are thick and creamy add the almonds and butter. Put the basin over a pan of simmering water and stir until the mixture thickens

—about 10 minutes. Pour this mixture into the centre of the pie plate, and bake at mark 5, 375°, for half an hour. Whisk the egg whites with the salt until stiff. Spread over the pie, sprinkle about a tablespoon of sugar on top and return to the oven to set and brown on top—about 5–10 minutes.

Queen of Puddings

For 4–6

5 oz fresh brown or white bread-crumbs
1 heaped tablespoon vanilla sugar
Grated rind of 1 large lemon
1 pt milk
2 oz lightly salted butter

4 large egg yolks
2 tablespoons blackcurrant jelly, or raspberry jelly
4 large egg whites
4 oz caster sugar, plus 1 extra tea-spoonful

Put breadcrumbs, vanilla, sugar and lemon rind into a pudding basin. Bring the milk and butter to just below boiling point and stir it into the crumbs. Leave for 10 minutes, then beat in the egg yolks thoroughly. Grease a shallow dish which holds about 2½ pints with a buttery paper, and pour in the breadcrumb custard. Bake at mark 4, 350°, for 30 minutes, or a little less, until just firm—the time will depend on the depth of the dish, and remember that the custard will continue to cook a little in its own heat so that if the centre looks runny underneath the skin do not feel anxious. Warm the jelly (if you use jam, warm it and sieve it) and spread it over the custard without breaking the surface. Whisk the whites until stiff, mix in half the caster sugar, then whisk again until slightly satiny. With a metal spoon, fold in the rest of the 4 oz of sugar. Pile on to the pudding, sprinkle with the extra teaspoonful of sugar and return to the oven for 15 minutes until the meringue is slightly browned and crisp. Serve hot with plenty of cream.

A pudding which deserves its name for the perfect combination of flavours and textures, a most subtle and lovely way to end a meal.

Sussex Pond Pudding

For 4–6

8 oz self-raising flour	Milk and water
4 oz chopped fresh beef suet	4 oz Demerara sugar
4 oz slightly salted butter	1 large lemon, or 2 limes

Mix the flour and suet together in a bowl. Make into a dough with milk and water, half and half; ¼ pt should be plenty. The dough should be soft, but not too soft to roll out into a large circle. Cut a quarter out of this circle, to be used later as the lid of the pudding. Butter a pudding basin lavishly. It should contain about 2½ pints. Drop the three-quarter circle of pastry into it and press the cut sides together to make a perfect join. Put half the butter, cut up, into the pastry, with half the sugar. Prick the lemon (or limes) all over with a larding needle, so that the juices will be able to escape, then put it on to the butter and sugar. Add the remaining butter, again cut in pieces, and sugar. Roll out the pastry which was set aside to make a lid. Lay it on top of the filling, and press the edges together so that the pudding is sealed in completely. Put a piece of foil right over the basin, with a pleat in the middle. Tie it in place with string, and make a string handle over the top so that the pudding can be lifted about easily. Put a large pan of water on to boil, and lower the pudding into it; the water must be boiling, and it should come halfway, or a little further, up the basin. Cover and leave to boil for 3–4 hours. If the water gets low, replenish it with *boiling* water. To serve, put a deep dish over the basin after removing the foil lid, and quickly turn the whole thing upside down : it is a good idea to ease the pudding from the sides of the basin with a knife first. Put on the table immediately.

The best of all English boiled suet puddings. In the middle the butter and sugar melt to a rich sauce, which is sharpened with the juice from the lemon. The genius of the pudding is the lemon. Its citrus bitter flavour is a subtlety which raises the pudding to the highest class. When you serve it, make sure that

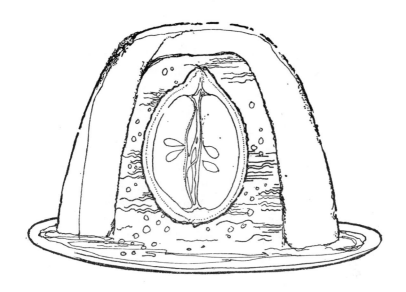

everyone has a piece of the lemon, which will be much softened by the cooking, but still vigorous.

Once when I had no lemons, I used a couple of small limes, which were equally successful.

The name of the pudding refers to the sauce, which runs out of it, when it is turned on to a serving dish, and provides it with a moat of buttery brown liquid.

Steamed Ginger Pudding

For 4

3 oz butter
3 oz castor sugar
1 large or 2 small eggs
4 oz self-raising flour

4 oz preserved ginger, chopped
1 tablespoon ginger syrup
¼ teaspoonful ground ginger
Scant ¼ pt milk

Cream butter and sugar until light, add the egg(s), then the flour, ginger, syrup and ground ginger. Mix to a soft cake dough with the milk. Put into a pudding basin leaving plenty of room for the pudding to rise. Cover and steam for 2 hours. Turn out and serve with a thin egg custard sauce, or with this wine sauce :—

2 yolks of eggs	$\frac{1}{4}$ pt sherry
Half a tablespoon sugar	3 oz cream

Put the yolks, sugar and sherry into a basin. Whisk them together, then stand the basin over a pan of just simmering water. Continue to whisk until it thickens, adding the cream gradually. It should be light and frothy. The snag with this kind of sauce is that it should be served immediately it is made—which leaves rather a gap in the meal. On the other hand, it is a sauce worth waiting for.

Homelier versions of this pudding use 1 teaspoonful of ground ginger and 1 tablespoonful of golden syrup as a substitute for the preserved ginger and ginger syrup.

Baked Semolina Pudding

2 oz semolina	Vanilla pod
1½ pts milk	2 eggs
Pinch salt	Extra sugar
2 tablespoons sugar	

Mix semolina with a little of the milk to make a smooth paste. Bring the rest to the boil with the salt, sugar and vanilla pod; do this slowly. When the milk is boiling, tip it into the semolina paste, working it in well to avoid lumps. Turn this mixture back into the pan and simmer gently for about 5 or 10 minutes until the mixture is thick. Remove it from the heat, and whisk in the egg yolks, then fold in the stiffly beaten whites. Pour it into a buttered dish and bake for 20 minutes in the oven at mark 5, 375°, until the top is brown and the pudding set. Do not remove the vanilla pod—it can be rescued later for washing and drying.

Baked Rice Pudding

2½ oz round pudding rice
1½–2 pints Channel Island milk
1 oz butter

2 tablespoons sugar
1 vanilla pod, split, or 1 cinnamon
stick

Put the rice with 1 pt of the milk and the remaining ingredients into a heatproof stoneware or glass dish. Leave in a gentle oven, mark 1, 275°, for 3 hours. After one hour, stir up the pudding and add more milk to slacken the mixture. After two hours, do the same thing again and, if you like, add some single cream. The butter and the cream are what form the delicious skin. Serve with a jug of double cream.

If you reduce the heat, say, to mark ½, 250°, or even lower, you can leave the rice pudding in the oven for twice as long. Add more milk occasionally; you may need 2½–3 pints. Beneath the crust, the rice will caramelize slightly to an appetising brown.

Some people add currants or sultanas to rice pudding, but I find this distasteful. Another way of enriching the pudding is to make it fairly liquid, and then finally to beat it up with 2 whole eggs and 2 egg yolks. Another 10 minutes in the oven, and you have quite a different pudding, a knobbly yellow custard.

I am a recent convert to rice pudding. All our childhood, my sister and I were carefully shielded from the horrors which my mother had had to eat at the same age. This meant that rice, sago and tapioca pudding hit us with full institutional force when we were sent to boarding school in wartime (shielding children from the realities of life often ends disastrously). For twenty-five years the thought of milk puddings made me queasy. Then a while ago, an American friend made us eat 'quick' tapioca—it was delicious. And not long afterwards, passing through Normandy, we saw some puddings with a rich dark skin on top, in a pastry-cook's shop in Isigny. It turned out that they were nothing more nor less than rice puddings—known locally as *terregoule*, which seems to mean 'mud in the throat'. The look and smell belied the name, and as soon as we got home, I set to work. Three conclusions—a rice pudding must be flavoured with a vanilla pod or cinnamon stick, it must be cooked long and slowly, it must be eaten with plenty of double cream. Like so many other English dishes, it has been wrecked by meanness and lack of thought.

Baked Custard Tart

8 oz weight shortcrust pastry

Filling
¾ pt single cream (or Channel Island milk, or a mixture of both)
2 small pieces of mace
1 inch stick cinnamon

2 large eggs
1 large egg yolk
Generous oz sugar
2 teaspoons orange-flower or rose water (optional)
Grated nutmeg

Roll out the pastry and line an 8"–9" tart tin with a removable base. Prick it all over with a fork, and bake it blind at mark 6, 400°, for 10–15 minutes. It should colour very slightly, but no more.

Meanwhile bring the cream or milk, or both, to the boil together with the mace and cinnamon. Beat the eggs and yolk together with the sugar and pour on the contents of the pan, whisking everything thoroughly together. Taste and adjust the spices with powdered mace or cinnamon, and add the orange-flower or rose water if you want to give the tart an eighteenth-century flavour. Pour the mixture into the pastry case, sprinkle it with a little nutmeg and bake at mark 3, 325°, for 30–40 minutes until the custard is just set—remember that it will become firmer as it cools down. I think that all custards taste best when eaten warm, rather than hot or cold. This means that you can time the cooking to end when you are ready to serve the first part of the meal, and leave the tart in its tin to keep warm in the plate-warming oven, or on the rack above the stove. Serve on its own or with cream.

The filling can be baked without pastry—pour it into small pots or ramekins, stand them in a pan of hot water and put into the oven for 30 minutes, mark 3, 325°.

A Coronation Doucet or Custard Tart

8 oz shortcrust pastry

Filling
12 oz double cream
3 oz Channel Island milk

A good pinch of saffron
Honey or sugar
6 egg yolks, or 2 eggs, plus 2 yolks
   well beaten

Line an 8″–10″ tart tin with a removable base with the pastry. Bake blind as in the recipe above.

Bring the cream, milk, saffron and about a tablespoon of honey or 1 oz of sugar slowly to the boil. Stir it to get the best colour possible from the saffron. Pour it on to the eggs, whisking the mixture together. Taste it and add more honey or sugar if you like. Strain the mixture into the pastry case and bake at mark 4, 350°, or until the mixture has set—it will also rise, then collapse when you take it out of the oven. Best eaten warm.

A doucet was served as part of the third course at Henry IV's coronation banquet. There was candied quince as well (page 305) and fritters, all set on the table with curlews and partridges and quails and rabbits and small birds of many kinds. Chaucer was present.

Doucet, which means something sweet, was always a kind of custard, though it might be made in many different ways. Sometimes the mixture was thick with minced pork or beef marrow, but the flavourings would include sugar just the same. Sometimes almond milk was used instead of cow's milk and cream : this was an infusion of blanched, ground almonds and syrup, or plain water, or water and wine. The mixture was brought slowly to the boil and simmered for a little while to extract as much almond juice as possible. It was then sieved to make a 'milk'. Medieval cooks used it a great deal, especially for dishes on fast days when rich dairy products were avoided. The mixture could be made thicker by increasing the cooking time. I find that whirling the mixture in the blender, before sieving it, gives a richly-flavoured 'milk'—see almond soup, on page 6.

Bakewell Tart

8 oz weight rich shortcrust pastry	4 oz butter
	4 oz sugar
Filling	4 egg yolks
Strawberry jam	3 egg whites

Roll out the pastry and line one large tart tin or several small patty pans. Spread the pastry with jam. Melt the butter (the flavour will be even more delicious if you allow it to cook to a golden brown), then mix it boiling hot with the sugar and egg yolks and whites which have been beaten together in a bowl. Put this mixture over the pastry. Bake at mark 6–7, 400–425°, for 20–30 minutes until lightly browned. Eat immediately.

Commercially-produced Bakewell tarts often contain ground almonds which is quite wrong. The real filling is a rich custard of butter and eggs, which is closer to the *mirliton* tarts made at Rouen than to English almond tarts. This recipe was a speciality of the inn at Bakewell when Jane Austen stayed (do you remember Mr Darcy's estate at Pemberley in Derbyshire, where Elizabeth Bennet began to realize her love for him? She and her uncle and aunt had driven to the top of a hill, where the wood ceased :

'. . . and the eye was instantly caught by Pemberley House, situated on the opposite side of the valley, into which the road with some abruptness wound. It was a large, handsome stone building, standing well on rising ground, and backed by a ridge of high woody hills; and in front a stream of some natural importance was swelled into greater, but without any artificial appearance. Its banks were neither formal nor falsely adorned. Elizabeth was delighted. She had never seen a place for which nature had done more, or where natural beauty had been so little counteracted by an awkward taste').

Chocolate Pie

For 6–8

Crust
6 oz almonds, blanched ground
2 oz caster sugar
1 egg white

Filling
½ pt single cream

½ lb plain chocolate, preferably Menier, Velma Suchard or Côte d'or
½ pt double cream
1 tablespoon rum
1 tablespoon icing sugar
Chocolate flakes, toasted almonds

This is one recipe for a tart which must be eaten the day it is made : if you keep it, the crackling crust becomes tough. It is also a good idea to delay putting in the chocolate filling until a couple of hours before the meal.

Mix the crust ingredients to a stiff paste. Chill it for half an hour, and then roll it out on a lightly floured board. Fit it into an 8″–9″ flan tin. The crust is likely to break, unlike pastry, but don't worry—just press the pieces gently together in the tin to close the joins. Bake blind for 25–30 minutes at mark 4, 350°. The crust should be as golden brown as possible without scorch marks.

To make the filling, stir the single cream and chocolate, broken into pieces, in a double boiler until they are melted into a smooth sauce. Cool it quickly, then whisk until the sauce froths into a foamy bulk. Pour it into the cooled crust. Decorate with the double cream, whipped with the rum and icing sugar, and with the chocolate flakes and toasted almonds.

The pie does not cut easily into tidy pieces, but it tastes so good that you need not be apologetic.

Of the many books on our own food which have appeared in the last few years, my favourite, the one I use most, is Michael Smith's *Fine English Cookery* (Faber). He starts from the reasonable assumption that people who sat on Chippendale chairs in elegant houses, were unlikely to be eating filthy food from their Wedgwood dinner services. Therefore what they ate is worth exploring.

He adapts the recipes slightly, but keeps their originality : in this exceptionally good chocolate pie, he puts together two recipes—the crackling crust from Hannah Glasse, and the chocolate cream filling from John Farley—to make a rich and unusual **pudding.**

Cakes, Biscuits and Pancakes

Cakes have come with tea, or tea with cakes—on balance probably the first. At any rate the afternoon tea habit became universal in the upper and middle classes after the discovery of the Indian tea plant in Assam in the 1820s (Chinese varieties not having succeeded in India). Tea needs its light accompaniment—cucumber sandwiches for Lady. Bracknell—but also something sweet in spite of what Oscar Wilde's Gwendolen might have to say. And then, conveniently, raising powders made their appearance.

A really effective raising powder was developed in America in the mid-1850s. So the light cake and the light scone and the light griddle cake were born, and the old yeast confections—delightful as they were, and are, if one troubles to make them—were reduced to muffins, teacakes and such regional survivals as the lardy cakes of Wiltshire and Gloucestershire and the saffron cake of West Devon and Cornwall.

Cake-making had originally come into existence as a fanciful sideline of breadmaking. The dough of flour raised with yeast

241

was made more agreeable, a pleasure for the end of a meal perhaps, by the addition of sugar, fruit, spice and caraway seeds. Then it was made even lighter and more spongy with eggs, which have their own raising power. Paradoxically it is now much easier to bake with yeast than when yeast cakes were going out. Through most of the nineteenth century the yeast available was ale barm, not our modern compressed yeast which is so easy to use. The difficulty was to keep the ale barm going from week to week in sufficient quantity for the next baking. Eighteenth-century books of household management are full of lengthy advice on this matter. By the time that compressed yeast could be bought, self-raising powder had triumphed in most English kitchens, and then the self-raising flours (in France where cakes are not often made at home, they still add baking powder to ordinary flour).

In the past I think that cake very often meant seed cake, that is cake flavoured with caraway seeds. Manuscript recipe books of the early eighteenth century nearly always have their seed cake recipes. Of course they were made with yeast, but at their best I suppose they could have been as light as French brioche.

Biscuits, too, were an adjunct to the baking process, the baker making use of the last heat of the oven—the kind of brick or clay oven that was heated by lighting faggot wood inside. Early biscuits were rusks, in other words bread, yesterday's bread, baked a second time—hence the name *bis cuit*, twice cooked—until they were crisp, similar in style to the modern French *biscotte*. Later, biscuits became, and have remained, some of the best of manufactured food. This has meant less temptation to make biscuits at home; a pity, in some ways. It's true that you have to stand over the baking, but biscuits are entertaining to make, they can be endlessly varied in texture and flavouring, and they store well. Water biscuits, Bath Olivers, crackers and the like are particularly English. They seem to be a refinement of ship's biscuits which were made thick and baked as many as four times to discourage weevils with their hardness. The light flaky plain biscuits made in the last century in the Palladian kitchens of Mereworth Castle in Kent (page 280) have come a long way from hard tack. They are the lightest and sharpest of all our biscuits, too fragile to butter smoothly.

The American practice of making up rolls of biscuit dough and storing them in the refrigerator or deep freeze is very sensible. In any case, most biscuit doughs should be chilled when possible, and with a ready-prepared roll you can always slice off a few rounds and bake them as the need arises. But there's not much about biscuit-making which the Americans don't know.

Sponge Cake I

3 eggs	3 oz plain flour, well sieved
3 oz sugar	Pinch salt

Whisk eggs and sugar in a large bowl, set over a pan of warm water—not boiling—until they are creamy and frothed up into a pale-coloured bulky mass. If you use an electric beater, it is not necessary to place the bowl over the water. Mix the flour and salt and gradually fold it into the eggs and sugar with a metal spoon : do this lightly so that as little air as possible is lost from the mixture.

Grease either a 7″ cake tin, or two 7″ sandwich tins, and sprinkle them with flour. Pour in the mixture. If you are making one large cake, sprinkle it evenly with caster sugar and cook it for 45 minutes at mark 4, 350° : the smaller cakes will need about 15 minutes at mark 5, 375°, and they are usually sprinkled with sugar after baking. To cool the cake or cakes, remove from the tin and place on a wire rack.

Although sponge cakes of this kind are often used as the basis for much elaboration, they are best when served plain and unadorned with a filling of some good home-made jam, or with strawberries and cream in the summer. Then they are really a **treat**.

Sponge Cake II (with melted butter)

3 fresh eggs	2 tablespoons water
6 oz caster sugar	4 oz self-raising flour
2 oz slightly salted butter	

Whisk eggs and sugar together until they foam up to a creamy bulk. Use an electric beater if possible. Melt butter with water over the lowest heat, so that it never becomes really hot. Stir it when tepid or cool into the eggs and sugar. Fold in the flour lightly with a metal spoon—the best way to do this is to sieve a little of it on to the eggs, etc., and fold it in gently, then to repeat the process until all the flour is used up.

Pour it into two greased and floured sandwich tins—8″ ones are the best size, but 7″ ones will do. Bake at mark 5, 375°, for 20 minutes. Fill with home-made jam and whipped cream.

This delicate, foolproof cake of the genoese type is worth knowing about (the recipe came originally from *Come Cooking!* compiled by the West Sussex Women's Institutes). It makes the ideal basis for all kinds of cakes in the elegant French style, when baked in a large oblong tin and cut into squares or circles as required. In the summer time, cover the underside of each cake with whipped cream and strawberries, or raspberries, which have been sprinkled with sugar and kirsch or an orange liqueur. Try it with peaches, too.

Whatever else you do, don't fill it with that coarse mixture we have the effrontery to call 'butter cream'—a mash of salted butter, or even margarine, and far too much icing sugar. Nothing demonstrates better the English love of positively unpleasant food, except the habit of extinguishing fish with malt vinegar.

Here are two recipes for a proper butter cream—be careful to buy an unsalted or very slightly salted butter of the unblended European type, as their flavour and consistency are better for this kind of recipe :—

Butter Cream I

4 oz caster sugar	2 egg yolks
1 tablespoon water	4 oz unsalted butter

Melt the sugar and water together over a low heat, in a small heavy pan. Then raise the heat and boil until the sugar reaches 280°F, the 'soft crack' stage. If you do not possess a thermometer, I do recommend you to save up and buy one. Until you do, the 'soft crack' stage means that some of the sugar dropped into a mug of cold water will form hard but not brittle threads. Pour this boiling mixture quickly on to the egg yolks, beating vigorously so that the whole thing is well amalgamated : the heat of the sugar cooks the egg yolks slightly and thickens them. When the mixture is tepid, add the butter in small bits, whisking it in so that it melts into the cream without oiling.

The mixture can now be flavoured in various ways—add 3–4 oz of melted, cooled plain chocolate; or a tablespoon of Nescafé mixed with the least possible amount of water to form a paste; or with a liqueur to taste.

Butter Cream II (made with custard)

4 oz milk	4 oz sugar
3 large egg yolks	8 oz unsalted butter

Pour milk into a heavy pan and bring to the boil. Beat egg yolks and sugar to a thick foam, preferably with an electric beater. Keep the beater going, while you pour in the boiling milk. Return the mixture to the pan and cook over a low heat until it is very thick and thickly coats a wooden spoon—it is important to keep stirring, and to keep the custard well below boiling point so that the eggs do not scramble to graininess and spoil the smooth texture. Strain into a clean bowl.

As the custard cools down, soften the butter in a bowl. Do this by beating it, or by standing the bowl over a pan of hot water if the butter is straight from the refrigerator. The thing is not to let it melt to oiliness, merely to soften it to a creamy state.

Combine the cool, or barely warm custard with the butter, and flavour according to taste (see previous recipe).

Saffron Cake from Cornwall

½ drachm saffron
Warm water
1 oz fresh yeast (*not dried*)
2 lb plain flour
8 oz sugar
½ teaspoon nutmeg
½ teaspoon cinnamon

Pinch salt
6 oz lard
6 oz butter
½ pt milk
8 oz mixed dried fruit
2 oz chopped lemon peel

Put the saffron into ¼ teacupful of warm water and leave it to infuse overnight. Next day, crumble the yeast into a bowl with 2 heaped tablespoons from the 2 lb of flour. Add 4 oz of warm water mixed with 1 heaped teaspoonful from the 8 oz sugar. Mix it all together thoroughly and put in a warm, draught-free corner for half an hour to rise : this is the leaven.

Put the rest of the flour into a warmed mixing bowl, add the sugar, spice and salt. Rub in the lard and butter. Make a well in the centre and pour in the risen leaven. Add, too, the milk which has been warmed to blood heat and the saffron liquid (some people strain out the saffron : others leave it in). Mix thoroughly to make a soft dough. Put it into a clean bowl, cover it with a cloth and leave in a warm draught-free place until it doubles its bulk.

Break down the dough, add the dried fruit and peel, and put into 2 well-greased loaf tins. Leave in a warm place for about half an hour for the dough to prove and rise in the tins. Bake at mark 7, 425°, for 40 minutes.

Saffron has always been expensive, even during the Middle Ages when it was at its height of European popularity for flavouring dishes, and even more for the colour it gave them. People liked their food to look gay, so that saffron (as well as sanders from sandalwood and alkanet, which both gave reddish colours) was found in every prosperous household. Saffron can never be cheap: it consists of the bright orange-red stigmas of the saffron crocus (*Crocus sativus*) which have to be gathered by hand and then dried. It has been estimated that it takes a quarter of a million flowers to produce one pound. Such an expensive product has always been a temptation to cheating merchants— never buy powdered saffron on this account, always go for the orange-red hairy kind sold in tiny thimbles or small packages.

The plant was introduced into England in the sixteenth century from Asia Minor (saffron goes back ultimately to the Arabic *za-farān*) and grown here at Saffron Walden in Essex and Stratton in north Cornwall—and in other places too—until the beginning of this century. Saffron cake has hung on in Cornwall and Devonshire from the days when all cakes were raised with yeast rather than eggs or baking powder. Like *bouillabaisse* or *mourtayrol* in France, and *paella* in Spain, it is a last survivor of an earlier grand passion for the flavour and colour of this elegant exotic.

Wiltshire Lardy Cake

1 lb bread dough, which has risen for 1 hour until doubled in bulk	6 oz mixed dried fruit
	2 oz mixed peel
6 oz lard	6 oz granulated sugar

Roll out the dough into an oblong, spread two-thirds of it with one-third each of the lard, fruit and peel, and sugar. Fold it into three. Press the ends down together with a rolling pin, and give the dough a half turn. Repeat twice more.

Place the folded dough into a large square or oblong tin which allows enough room for it to rise. Leave in a warm, draught-free place for 20–30 minutes, then bake at mark 7, 425°, for about 45 minutes. Take out of the oven, leave it to stand for 10 minutes, then put it on to a plate. Lardy cake is best eaten warm from the oven, cut into generous sticky squares.

Like saffron cake, lardies are a survival of older baking habits. They are a kind of rural Chelsea bun, very good, very fattening.

Welsh Cinnamon Cake

4 oz butter
4 oz granulated sugar
2 egg yolks
½ lb flour
½ teaspoon baking powder

1 rounded teaspoon cinnamon
Apricot jam
3 egg whites
3 tablespoons caster sugar

Cream butter and granulated sugar, beat in the yolks. Sift flour, baking powder and cinnamon together, then mix into the butter, etc. Knead to a dough and roll out to fit into an 8½″ tart tin with a removable base. Bake at mark 6, 400°, for 20 minutes. Cool the cake on a wire rack after removing it from the tin. Heat a good tablespoon of apricot jam with a little water, sieve it and brush thinly over the cake. Beat the egg whites until they are stiff, fold in the caster sugar and beat again until the mixture is thick and creamy. Pile on to the cake, swirling the top into decorative points. Bake at mark 4, 350°, until the meringue is golden and set—about 15 minutes.

The traditional recipe has been altered slightly and improved by Mrs Bobby Freeman who used to run the Compton House Hotel at Fishguard. The sad thing is, that apart from a few enthusiasts who are not always Welsh, it is difficult to find restaurateurs in Wales who are prepared to make a speciality of the dishes of their own region.

Cider Cake

½ lb plain flour
1 rounded teaspoon grated nutmeg
1 teaspoon baking powder
Pinch of salt
5 oz butter
5 oz caster sugar

2 medium eggs
2–3 tablespoons Calvados or brandy (optional)
¼ pt dry or medium sweet cider (the better the flavour, the better the cake)

Sift the flour, nutmeg, baking powder and salt together. Cream the butter and sugar until light and fluffy, add the eggs and beat until the mixture is coherent. Put the Calvados or brandy, if used, into a measuring jug and add enough cider to make $\frac{1}{4}$ pt liquid. Otherwise just measure out the $\frac{1}{4}$ pt cider. Beat half the flour into the butter and egg mixture, then half the cider. When everything is well mixed, repeat with the remaining flour and cider.

Line a shallow cake tin with vegetable parchment (Bakewell paper)—I use a tin 11″ × 7″ × 1¼″—and pour in the cake mixture, spreading it out evenly with a spoon. Bake for 45 minutes at mark 4, 350°. Cool for a few moments in the tin, then remove to a rack to become quite cold. This is a delicious plain cake, which tastes particularly good when buttered. The blend of cider, Calvados and nutmeg gives an unusual and delicate flavour.

Carrot Cake

4 egg yolks	$\frac{1}{2}$ lb finely grated raw carrots
$\frac{1}{2}$ lb caster sugar	Rounded tablespoon self-raising
Grated rind one lemon	flour
$\frac{1}{2}$ lb coarsely grated, unblanched almonds	4 stiffly beaten egg whites

Beat the yolks, sugar and rind for 10 minutes (5 minutes with an electric beater). Add almonds and carrots. Fold in the flour lightly, then the egg whites. Turn into an oblong or roasting tin, lined with non-stick Bakewell parchment: it should be about $9\frac{1}{2}″$ × 12″. Bake 45 minutes at mark 4, 350°. Leave to cool in the pan. Serve cut in slices.

Now that cooking is a national hobby, monasteries, women's organizations, universities, museums and schools are producing cookery books as a certain way of making money. They give a genuine picture of what we really like to eat. This unusual and delicious carrot cake comes from the *Oxford High School Cook Book*.

Madeira Cake

6 oz butter
6 oz caster sugar
9 oz flour
¼ teaspoon baking powder

4 large eggs
Grated rind of half a large lemon
2 strips of lemon or citron peel

Cream the butter and sugar together until the mixture is light and fluffy. Sift the flour and baking powder together. Beat the eggs into the butter and sugar, one at a time, adding a little flour if the mixture seems to be separating. Stir in the rest of the flour and the grated lemon rind. Turn the mixture into an 8″ cake tin which has been lined with Bakewell paper or greased and floured. Bake for 1½–2 hours at mark 4, 350°. After 1 hour place the two pieces of peel on top, and complete the baking.

This cake was served with Madeira and other sweet wines in the nineteenth century, hence the name. Although it is now a popular cake at tea time, to enjoy it at its best serve it with Madeira in the old style.

Mrs Sleightholme's Seed Cake

6 oz butter
6 oz caster sugar
3 eggs
1 rounded dessertspoon of caraway
   seeds

1 level tablespoon ground almonds
8 oz self-raising flour
A little milk

Cream the butter and sugar, and stir into it the caraway seeds —if you are not sure about the tastes of the people likely to eat the cake, use a level dessertspoonful the first time. Separate the eggs. Whisk the whites until they are stiff, but creamy rather than dry. Beat the yolks together and fold them into the whites carefully, until they are mixed together. Add to the butter and sugar. Lastly stir in the ground almonds and flour, adding a little milk if the mixture doesn't fall off the spoon when you shake it with a firm flick of the wrist.

Line a 2 lb loaf tin with Bakewell paper. Pour in the cake mixture and smooth it down with the back of a spoon. Bake it at mark 4, 350°, for 1 hour 5 minutes. It should spring back when pressed lightly with a finger, and if you stick a larding needle into it, it should come out clean. Allow the cake to cool in the tin for 20 minutes, before removing it to a wire rack.

A few blanched, slivered almonds can be put on top of the cake before baking.

I had been reading a family manuscript recipe book compiled between 1705 and 1730, in which there were five recipes for seed cake, when I saw this recipe in a copy of *Woman* magazine. The ingredient that set this recipe apart from the many other seed cakes of English cookery, was the ground almonds. And when I made the cake it was indeed the almonds which made it moist and delicious and quite exceptional.

The recipe was given in a series of farmhouse cakes by Mrs Dorothy Sleightholme, who frequently appears on Yorkshire Television. She had had the cake from a Somerset family, but thought that it needed something extra and added the ground almonds—which make all the difference.

Ginger Cake

4 oz butter	1 teaspoon ground ginger
4 oz Barbados or Demerara sugar	2 oz sultanas
2 eggs	2 oz preserved ginger, sliced
10 oz black treacle	2 tablespoons milk
8 oz flour	$\frac{1}{2}$ teaspoon bicarbonate of soda

Cream the butter, add the sugar and continue beating for a few moments. Mix in the eggs and treacle. Sift the flour and ginger together, stir in the sultanas and ginger pieces, then tip into the cake mixture. Warm the milk very slightly with the bicarbonate of soda and mix that in last of all.

Pour into a 7" cake tin, lined with Bakewell paper, or else buttered and floured. Bake at Mark 3, 325°F, for $1\frac{1}{2}$ hours if you like a sticky gingerbread, for $1\frac{3}{4}$ hours if you like it a little drier. The cake will come away from the side of the tin in a rounded shape, and may sink in the middle if you take it out after $1\frac{1}{2}$ hours. Don't worry—it will taste delicious, all the same. Let it cool for a few moments in the tin, then turn it on to a rack.

The darkest, richest gingerbread of them all. It keeps beautifully, in fact I think it tastes better after three or four days. Serve it in slices with coffee, or with whipped cream as a pudding. The recipe comes from *Au Petit Cordon Bleu*, by Dione Lucas and Rosemary Hume.

If you do not like the idea of a strong-tasting, gooey cake, which will almost certainly sink in the middle, cut the quantity of treacle to 7 oz. One ounce of coarsely-chopped walnuts, added with the ginger and sultanas, gives a most agreeable bite to the cake.

Country Christmas Cake

1st list
$2\frac{1}{2}$ lb mixed dried fruit
2 oz chopped candied peel
2 oz glacé cherries, rinsed and halved
3 oz preserved ginger, drained and chopped
Grated rind and juice of 1 large orange
Grated rind and juice of 1 large lemon
1 tablespoon bitter orange marmalade
1 tablespoon apricot jam
1 cup (8 oz) stewed apple
2 tablespoons sweet brown sherry

2nd list
$\frac{1}{2}$ lb lightly salted butter
$\frac{1}{2}$ lb brown sugar, soft, dark
4 eggs
1 teaspoon pure vanilla essence
Few drops almond essence

3rd list
12 oz plain flour, sifted
1 teaspoon ground cinnamon
1 teaspoon ground ginger
1 teaspoon baking powder
1 teaspoon nutmeg
1 teaspoon ground cloves
1 teaspoon mixed spice
Plus
1 tablespoon whisky or brandy

Mix all the ingredients in the first list in a large basin. Turn them over thoroughly. Cover and leave overnight.

Next day, start with the second list: cream the butter and sugar until light and fluffy. Beat in the eggs one by one, and add the essence.

Put all the ingredients in the third list into a bowl and stir them together.

Mix the fruit and flour alternately into the creamed butter and sugar, a little at a time.

Line an 8″–9″ cake tin with three layers of greaseproof paper, and then a final layer of Bakewell paper. Pour in the mixture, and decorate with blanched almonds unless you intend to cover the cake eventually with marzipan and icing.

Bake 2 hours at mark 3, 325°, then lower the heat to mark 2, 300°, for a further 2 hours. Remove the cake from the oven, puncture it with a few holes and pour in the whisky or brandy (2 or 3 tablespoons won't do any harm). Leave the cake to cool in its tin.

Next day, remove the cake and peel off the greaseproof and Bakewell paper. Wrap it in fresh greaseproof paper and keep it in an airtight tin (or in firmly sealed foil) for at least a month before using it.

To finish off the cake for Christmas, you will need marzipan and icing. Do not buy the marzipan ready made—your own may not look so yellow as it does in the shop, but it will taste much better. Moreover you can reduce the sweetness by putting in less sugar :—

Almond Paste or Marzipan

½ lb icing sugar
1 lb ground almonds
1 large egg (weighing about 2½ oz)
3–4 teaspoons lemon juice

Glaze
1 tablespoon apricot jam
1 tablespoon water

Sift the icing sugar and mix it with the almonds. Beat the egg thoroughly, then add the lemon juice and the dry ingredients. Use a wooden spoon to beat everything to a firm paste, then knead it on a board or formica surface, which has been sprinkled with icing sugar. (Incidentally, if you do not agree with me that most almond paste is too sweet, add another half pound of sugar and use two medium eggs instead of one large one.)

Slice the top from the cake to make it even, then turn it upside down and put on a wire rack. Boil the jam and water in a small pan, sieve it into a bowl and while still hot brush it over the top of the cake (that is, over what *was* the bottom).

Set aside a third of the almond paste, and roll out the rest to a circle just a little larger than the cake—do this on a sheet of clean greaseproof paper and use the cake tin as a guide. Press the glazed side of the cake down on to the circle of almond marzipan; reverse it so that you now have the greaseproof paper on top, then the marzipan and then the cake—remove the paper and smooth the marzipan down over the sides. Measure the depth of the cake and its circumference. Roll out the remaining marzipan to these measurements, again on a sheet of greaseproof paper. Brush the cake sides with apricot glaze and roll it slowly along the strip of marzipan. Pat everything into place, closing the cracks and so on, and replace the cake on its rack. Leave for two days before icing it.

Royal Icing

2 small egg whites   1 lb icing sugar
2 teaspoons lemon juice

Whisk the eggs until they are white and foamy, but not stiff. Stir in the lemon juice, then the sugar which should first be sieved. Do this bit by bit, using a wooden spoon. When everything is mixed together, continue to beat the mixture until it is a dazzling white. Cover the basin and leave it for an hour or two before using it.

To ice the cake, put a bowl of hot water beside it. Put about half the icing on the cake and spread it about with a palette knife which you have dipped in the water. It should be hot and wet, but not wet enough to soak the cake and ruin the icing.

Cover the cake all over, then put on the remaining icing, either roughly to make a snowy effect, or in an elegant design with the aid of a forcing bag and nozzles.

To Make Mince Pies

Line small tart tins with shortcrust pastry. Put a spoonful of mincemeat in each one, but be careful not to put in too much, as the suet will melt and bubble out if it has no room to spare. Brush the edges of the pastry with beaten white of an egg, and add pastry lids, pinching the two edges together. Make a small cross with a knife in the centre of each pie. Brush over with white of egg, sprinkle with sugar and bake at mark 7, 425°, for 15 to 20 minutes.

Mince pies are sometimes served with brandy or rum butter (page 298). Very good.

Puff pastry can be used instead of shortcrust, but I find this is too fatty unless the pies are eaten straight from the oven and not allowed to cool down.

Mrs Beeton's Traditional Mincemeat

1 lb seedless raisins
1½ lb currants
¾ lb lean rump steak, minced
1½ lb beef suet, chopped
1 lb dark brown sugar
1 oz candied citron peel, chopped
1 oz candied lemon peel, chopped

1 oz candied orange peel, chopped
½ small nutmeg, grated
1½ lb apples, weighed after peeling and coring
The rind of 1 lemon
The juice of ½ a lemon
¼ pt brandy

Mix all the ingredients together in the order given. Chop or mince the apples before adding them to the fruit and peel. Pour in the brandy when everything else is well mixed together. Press closely into jars, to exclude the air. Cover and leave for at least a fortnight.

I can recommend this recipe for a real mince *meat*. It is particularly good. The steak is perfectly preserved by the sugar and brandy, and seems to give the mixture a moist texture and extra delicious flavour. I have noticed that the years when I make this mincemeat for Christmas, the mince pies disappear more quickly than usual.

Orange Mincemeat

½ lb candied orange and lemon peel, chopped
2 lb apples, peeled, cored, chopped
1 lb suet, chopped
1 lb raisins
1 lb sultanas
1 lb currants
1 lb dark brown sugar
1 whole nutmeg, grated
4 oz blanched, slivered almonds
The rind and juice of 2 oranges
4 tablespoons brandy
6–8 tablespoons orange liqueur

Mix the ingredients together in the order given. Pot and cover the mixture, as above.

Eccles Cakes

1 lb shortcrust pastry made with lard

Filling
4 oz currants
1 oz chopped candied peel
½ teaspoonful each allspice and nutmeg
2 oz sugar
1 oz butter
Plus
Egg white and extra sugar

Roll out the pastry and cut into circles about 4″ round. Mix currants, peel and spices. Put the sugar and butter into a small pan. When they are melted, mix in the currants, etc., and heat through. Leave until cold, then put a spoonful into the centre of each pastry round. Draw the circles together, pinching the edges over the filling. Turn them over, then press gently with a rolling pin to flatten the cakes. Make a hole in the centre. Brush over with egg white, sprinkle with sugar, and bake at mark 7, 425°, for 15 minutes.

Banbury Cakes

1 lb puff pastry

Filling
As above, plus an extra ounce of
   butter, ¼ teaspoon cinnamon and
   a tablespoon of rum
Plus
White of egg and extra sugar

Roll out the pastry thinly and cut into 7″ circles. Melt the butter, and mix in remaining ingredients without heating them. Put a spoonful of the mixture in the centre of each circle in a band of filling about 5″ long. Bring the pastry round it, as for Eccles cakes, but form an oval shape, cut away surplus pastry. Turn over, flatten slightly with the rolling pin and make three slashes across the top. Brush with egg white, sprinkle with sugar, and bake at mark 7–8, 425–450°.

In the *English Hus-wife* of 1615, Gervase Markham gives a recipe for Banbury cakes which is quite different. The modern ones, sold at Banbury, are more like the northern Eccles and Chorley cakes in type, though the puff pastry and rum makes them seem lighter.

Cumberland Currant Cake

Pastry	*Filling*
16 oz flour	10 oz currants or raisins
5 oz butter	4 oz mixed peel
5 oz lard	6 oz cooking apples
Pinch salt	5 oz butter
Cold water to mix	4 oz pale or dark brown sugar
	$\frac{1}{2}$ gill rum (2$\frac{1}{2}$ oz)
	1 teaspoon allspice
	$\frac{1}{2}$ teaspoon each cinnamon and mace

Make the pastry in the usual way. Roll out half and line an oblong tin about 7″ × 11″ × 1″. Spread currants or raisins and peel on top. Peel, core and grate the apples before weighing them, and put them over the currants, etc. Melt the butter, and, off the heat, stir in the remaining ingredients—if your hand slips with the rum, it doesn't matter. Taste this mixture and add more spices if you like. Pour over the fruit. Roll out the remaining pastry and cover the filling. If you like, brush the pastry over with top of the milk, or beaten egg glaze, and sprinkle with caster sugar. Put into a mark 6, 400°, oven for 30–35 minutes. Eat hot as a pudding (with cream or rum butter or egg custard), or cold, cut into squares.

Growing and storing apples and pears becomes more difficult as you go north. Perhaps this is why dried fruit pies, such as sly cake, Eccles cakes and these Cumberland squares are not just Christmas food, as mince pies tend to be further south. In Jane Austen's time in Surrey, when you went visiting friends in February or March, you would be offered baked apples to eat, the last of the winter's store. In the north-east, certainly up to the last war, we would eat this kind of thing. We loved it, and called it squashed fly cake, and giggled in a corner, while the family talked. No one realized that they were eating a cake with a history, and medieval ancestors.

Fruit Tea Loaf

¾ lb mixed dried fruit and peel   ½ lb self-raising flour
¼ lb dark brown sugar   1 egg
8 oz strained, cold Indian tea

Stir together the dried fruit, chopped peel, sugar and tea. Leave overnight, and next day beat in the flour and egg. Bake in a lined 9″ loaf tin for 1 hour at mark 4, 350°, then for a further 30 minutes at mark 3, 325°. Serve thinly sliced and generously buttered. For the best flavour, keep the loaf in an air-tight tin, or wrapped in foil, for two or three days.

The tea habit developed into a passion with the English in the mid-nineteenth century, when tea plantations were successfully organized in Assam and Ceylon. (The tea plant indigenous to India was discovered in 1823 in Assam; earlier attempts to introduce Chinese seeds and plants had not been successful.) It even came to have a meal to itself, rather than just a sociable hour after the main midday dinner. Elegant society drank tea between four and five o'clock; sandwiches and delicious cakes were served with it. For the working classes, 'high tea' became the full-scale evening meal after a long day's work; and it still is, though in many parts of the country it is just called 'tea' in spite of the fact that it consists of meat and two or more vegetables, followed by a substantial pudding—the tea itself will be drunk beforehand, or with the food. Yorkshire 'high tea' remains a real spread of the old-fashioned kind, in which ham, cheese, cakes, biscuits, tarts are all put on the table together as they might have been in the eighteenth century before meals were separated into savoury and sweet and cheese courses.

High tea, or a buffet meal with tea to drink, was soon recognized as a suitable event for church and chapel congregations. As Gervas Huxley remarked in *Talking of Tea*, it marched along hand in hand with the temperance movement which was so strong a part of chapel-going in the north. One of the favourite items of such occasions was fruit loaf made with tea. And the same fruit loaf was served at family gatherings, and at funeral meals, along with the inevitable ham (in Yorkshire, it is sometimes called 'slow walking bread'). It always makes me think of that Lancashire story, one of many about Eli, who in this instance was upstairs in his bed, dying: 'D'you fancy something?' asked his wife. 'I'd like some of that ham you're cooking downstairs.' 'Oh, you can't have that Eli. That ham's for the mourners!' No doubt she had already got her fruit loaf baked and put away—it tastes all the better for keeping a few days.

Banana Tea Loaf

8 oz self-raising flour
¾ level teaspoon mixed spice
½ level teaspoon salt
4 oz caster sugar
4 oz butter
1 tablespoon honey

4 oz sultanas
3 oz glacé cherries
2–4 oz blanched almonds, chopped, or walnuts
1 lb ripe bananas
2 eggs
Juice of 1 lemon

Sift the first four ingredients into a bowl. Chop butter into small pieces and add that, then all the remaining ingredients—remember to peel the bananas first and mash them with a fork.

Turn the mixture into a buttered 9″ loaf tin. Bake at mark 4, 350°, for 1 hour, then for a further half-hour at mark 3, 325°.

Remove from the tin and cool on a rack. Serve thinly sliced and generously buttered—like most tea loaves, it tastes all the better for keeping.

Deservedly, this has become a popular recipe at country teas during the last ten years. The long cooking does not at all spoil the scented flavour of bananas. And their moist texture enhances the keeping qualities of this recipe. Although almonds are most generally used, I think that walnuts give a more subtle flavour.

Doris Grant Loaf

3 lb stone-ground wholemeal flour
2 teaspoons salt
3 tablespoons water at blood-heat (98–100°F)

3 level teaspoons dried yeast
3 rounded teaspoons Barbados sugar, honey or black molasses
2 pts water at blood-heat

Mix the flour and salt. If the weather or your kitchen is very cold, warm the flour slightly in a tepid oven. Put the water into a bowl, sprinkle on the yeast and whisk it until it has dissolved. Add the sugar, honey or molasses. Leave the mixture to froth up—this takes about 15 minutes. Pour into the centre of the flour, and add the 2 pints of water. Mix well by hand until the dough leaves the side of the mixing bowl, and feels elastic. It will be a little more slithery than a normal white flour dough, but this doesn't matter as this wholemeal dough does not require kneading. Divide it between three warmed and greased loaf tins, each of 2 pint capacity. Cover the tins and put them in a warm place for 30 minutes, so that the dough can rise to within half an inch of the rim of the tins. Bake at mark 6, 400°, for 40 minutes.

I remember the sensation this recipe caused when it came out towards the end of the last war. Everybody was longing for good food, and was tired of the national loaf which was a pale fawn colour. Here was the real thing, and it took only a few minutes to make because no kneading was required. Nowadays everyone who cares about good food takes the loaf for granted—it is just 'wholemeal bread', and every member of the family can produce it successfully once they can read and measure. Doris Grant has been associated with food reform in Britain for over thirty years, but whether you share her preoccupations or not you will enjoy this superb bread. It goes particularly well with shellfish and smoked salmon.

Northumbrian Wholemeal Scones

1½ lb stone-ground wholemeal flour	3 tablespoons very hot water
1 teaspoon salt	¼ pt milk
2 oz lard	¼ pt boiling water
1 tablespoon golden syrup	1 oz fresh yeast

Sieve flour and salt into a basin, and rub in the lard. Make a well in the middle. Melt the syrup in the water. Mix the milk and boiling water, and add a little of this to the syrup so that there is about a teacupful. Into the syrup and milk, fork the yeast. Leave it to work for 10 or 15 minutes. When it is creaming and frothy, tip it into the flour, plus the remaining milk and hot water—go slowly with this, as you need a fairly soft but not sloppy dough. On the other hand you may need to add extra milk and water—if you add boiling water to the milk in equal quantity, you will end up with the right blood temperature of 98–100°F.

Leave to rise until doubled in volume. This should be done in a draught-free place; temperature doesn't matter—dough will rise in a refrigerator, it merely takes longer. Roll out the risen dough on a floured board, and cut out rounds with a scone cutter. Leave to rise again, to 'prove', for another 30 minutes, then brush with milk and bake in a hot oven, mark 7, 425°F, for 20 minutes. Eat hot with plenty of butter, honey, or a savoury mixture of chopped hard-boiled eggs and parsley.

Basic Bun Dough

1 lb strong plain flour	4 oz milk
¼ teaspoon salt	4 oz boiling water
1 oz fresh yeast	3 oz butter
2 oz caster sugar	1 egg lightly beaten

Put flour and salt into a large warmed mixing bowl. Crumble the yeast into a 3-pint pudding basin, add 1 heaped teaspoonful of the sugar and ¼ lb of flour from the bowl. Pour the milk into a measuring jug, and make up the 8 oz of liquid with boiling water straight from the kettle. With a wooden spoon mix this hot liquid into the yeast, flour and sugar—go slowly so as to make as smooth a batter as possible : leave it in a warm place to rise and froth up—this takes about 15 minutes, or a little longer. Meanwhile mix the rest of the sugar with the flour, and rub in the butter. Form a well in the centre, put in the egg and the frothy yeast mixture. Mix to a dough with a wooden spoon. Turn it out on to a floury surface and knead for 10 minutes, adding more flour as required, until the dough is a coherent, slightly rubbery ball, with a moderately tacky but not sticky texture. Any dough on your fingers should rub off easily.

Wash, dry and grease the large mixing bowl with a piece of butter paper. Place the dough in it. Cover it with a damp cloth, or put the whole thing inside an oiled polythene bag. Leave to rise to double its quantity. This can take anything from 1 to 12 hours depending on the temperature.

Now the dough can be used in various ways :—

Hot Cross Buns

Basic bun dough (page 262)
1 level teaspoon ground cinnamon
1 level teaspoon ground nutmeg
1 level teaspoon mixed spice
½ teaspoon ground mace
3 oz raisins
2 oz candied chopped peel

2 oz almond paste or shortcrust pastry
Beaten egg

Bun wash
2 oz sugar
2¼ oz (½ gill) water

When making the basic bun dough, mix the spices in with the flour at the beginning (see previous recipe). Break down the risen dough, knead in the fruit and peel. Roll the dough into a long sausage shape on a floured surface, and cut it down into 18 discs. Shape them into round buns, and then place them on baking sheets lined with Bakewell paper—leave them plenty of room to rise and spread in the baking. Roll out the almond paste or shortcrust pastry and cut it into thin strips. Brush the buns with beaten egg and lay 2 strips on each bun to form a cross. Leave the buns to prove for 15–30 minutes; this allows for baking in two batches—one should go in after 15 minutes, the second after 30.

Bake at mark 8, 450°, for 10–15 minutes, until nicely browned.

Meanwhile boil the bun wash ingredients together for 2 or 3 minutes until syrupy. Brush it over the hot buns when they come out of the oven: this makes them shiny and sticky. If you want a more opaque icing for other buns—it's unsuitable for hot cross buns—boil the bun wash a little longer until it's really thick.

To reheat, give the buns 10 minutes in a moderate oven—mark 3–4, 325–350°.

Until you make spiced hot cross buns yourself, or well-sugared Chelsea buns, it is difficult to understand why they should have become popular. Bought, they taste so dull. Modern commerce has taken them over, and, in the interests of cheapness, reduced the delicious ingredients to a minimum—no butter, little egg, too much yellow colouring, not enough spice, too few currants and bits of peel, a stodgy texture instead of a rich, light softness. In other words, buns are now a doughy filler for children.

Once, as long ago as the Middle Ages, buns came often in wedge-shapes, called for this reason wigs. The baker would slap down a circle of fine wheat dough, cut it across, and across again, and there were the wigs, the wedges. When breakfast became a light meal in the seventeenth century, with coffee or tea instead of ale, people realized that buttered buns or wigs were the best food to eat with the new drinks. The habit has lasted until today in Scotland, where children are sent out to the baker's before breakfast for fine white baps, hot from the oven, and in France, where croissants and brioches are ready first thing at the pastrycooks' and bakers' shops. At one camping site near our village in Touraine, the pastrycook even comes round the tents and caravans with his newly made croissants at eight in the morning. Hot cross buns became a speciality for Good Friday breakfast in the eighteenth century; they were made extra spicy and rich with fruit, and marked with a cross as a sign of the festival.

Chelsea Buns

Basic bun dough (page 262)
2 oz melted butter
3 oz dark brown sugar
3 oz raisins

2 oz candied peel
Beaten egg
Bun wash (page 263)
Extra caster sugar

Break down the risen dough, and roll it out on a floured surface to a large oblong about 12″ × 18″. Brush the butter over it. Sprinkle on the sugar evenly, then the fruit and peel. Starting with one of the long sides, roll up the dough fairly tightly. Cut it down into 18 pieces. Place these coiled pieces side by side in one or two well-greased oblong tins, one inch deep, leaving half an inch between them, and between them and the sides of the tins. Brush the buns over with egg, and leave them to prove for 15–30 minutes. Bake for 10–15 minutes until brown, at mark 8, 450°. The buns should rise and come together, so that when they are eventually separated the sides have a characteristically torn white appearance, which contrasts with the sticky brown, sugared top. However, leave them to cool down in the tin before doing this.

While the buns are still hot, brush them over with bun-wash and sprinkle them with sugar.

The best of all buns, on account of their buttery melting sweetness, and the fun of uncoiling them as you eat them.

Bath Buns

Basic bun dough (page 262)
4 oz sultanas
2 oz candied peel, chopped

Beaten egg
2 oz lump sugar
Bun wash (page 263)

Break down the risen dough, knead in the fruit and peel lightly and form into buns in the same way as hot cross buns, by making a sausage of dough and cutting it down into 18 pieces. Form them into buns, place them on Bakewell paper-lined baking sheets and brush them over with egg. Quickly reduce the lumps of sugar to large nibs—use a pestle and mortar, or put the sugar into a brown paper bag and crush it with a rolling pin. Tip the lot into a sieve, so that the fine powder falls away into a basin and is not wasted, and put the nibs on top of the buns. Bake as above, and brush carefully with bun-wash when they come out of the oven so as not to dislodge the crunchy sugar.

This crunchy sugar scattered over today's Bath buns is a last souvenir of the crushed caraway seed comfits which were used to flavour wigs and buns as late as the eighteenth century. Comfits were made by dipping aromatic seeds over and over again in boiling sugar, until they were thickly coated—there is a most carefully set out recipe for making them, complete with a list of equipment, given in Sir Hugh Plat's *Delight for Ladies* of 1605. Sugared almonds are made on the same principle. One may still buy aniseed comfits of an exactly Tudor kind at Flavigny in Burgundy—elsewhere they seem to have disappeared. A pity, for they were much used in decorating cakes and tarts and puddings like trifle, and provided a far more discreet note and elegant flavour than glacé cherries do nowadays.

Oatcakes

¼ lb medium oatmeal	*Glaze*
¼ lb plain flour	1 egg
2 oz lard or dripping or poultry fat	1 tablespoon milk
Level teaspoon salt	1 teaspoon sugar

Mix the oatmeal and flour in a basin. Rub in the fat, add the salt and mix to a soft but not a tacky dough with cold water. Roll out on an oatmeal-strewn board until ⅛" thick. Cut out circles with a scone cutter; and, if you like your oatcakes really thin, slap them out between your oatmealy hands (this is tricky as the edges begin to crack, but it's the old Welsh method and it does produce very good oatcakes). Alternatively, cut out a dinner-plate round, and quarter it.

Cook the oatcakes on an ungreased medium-hot griddle,

without turning them. The moment the first batch are in place, brush them over with the glaze—it will turn to a shiny coating as they cook. Store in an airtight box, and toast lightly before the fire before serving them.

Oatcakes have with most of us the reputation of being Scottish. We're used to triangular tartan packages of farls or quarters, that is, quarters of a large round bannoch (from the Gaelic *bannach* meaning cake), stacked one on top of the other. But oatcakes belong just as much to Wales, Ireland and the north of England. In the eighteenth century, sacks of oatmeal were as common a sight in Manchester market as sacks of wheat were in the south. Fine white flour was a luxury in the north until modern times.

After their cooking on the griddle, oatcakes used to be propped up to harden beside the fire against a toast-stone or oat-cake rack or plain block of wood (there is a fine collection of implements for making oatcakes in the Welsh Folk Museum near Cardiff, at St Fagan's). Nowadays the hotplate of an electric or solid-fuel stove, or a medium-hot grill or oven, has to do instead very often. It doesn't matter what you use, so long as the oatcakes are really crisp. Nowadays, too, they have to be stored in an air-tight tin, rather than in the meal-chest where they were kept buried in oatmeal.

I had a letter from Liverpool, lamenting the difficulty of buying oatmeal there. How odd that would have seemed to our ancestors. The writer lived as a child in the West Riding of Yorkshire and she remembers oatcakes which were about a

'foot long, oval, about eight inches wide across the middle; thin and soft like a piece of cloth. Certain people—some farmers—used to come around with a basketful and our mother would buy perhaps half a dozen. These were then spread on the bread-creel to dry [a creel is a wickerwork basket], and when they were crisp they were eaten, either with slabs of butter, or broken up in milk. Either way they were delicious! And I wish I knew how to make them!'
Here is the recipe:—

West Yorkshire Oatcake or Riddle Bread

1 lb fine oatmeal   Scant teaspoon salt
½ oz fresh yeast   Water at blood heat

Put the oatmeal and salt in a bowl. Cream the yeast with a
teacupful of water, and leave it to rise to a creamy froth. Mix
into the oatmeal and add more water until the batter is like a
thick cream. A ladleful is thrown on to the heated griddle or
'bak' stone, in a narrow strip. It immediately puffs up with
steam, which makes it smooth underneath and rough on top.
'When baked it is damp and flexible and is hung on the wooden
clothes rail before the fire to dry or on lines across the kitchen
ceiling. It must be crisped quickly immediately before it is to
be eaten'. The flavour is slightly bitter and very appetising.
'It can be used for soups, fish, fowl, cheese, butter, or any kind
of meat in place of any other kind of bread or biscuit.'

The quotations come from Florence White's *Good Things in
England*. In her day, oatcakes could be bought from an oat-
cake baker at Skipton, whose business was established in 1858.

Potato Cakes

1¼ lb potatoes   1 egg (optional)
1 oz melted butter   4 oz flour
½ teaspoon salt   1 teaspoon baking powder

Scrub, boil and peel the potatoes in the usual way (left-over
potatoes may be used, but newly-cooked ones taste better).
Weigh out a pound of them and mash thoroughly, or put
through the coarse blade of a vegetable mill. Mix in the other
ingredients quickly, using enough flour to make a coherent and
not too sticky dough. Roll out thinly and cut into saucer-sized
rounds. Bake on a griddle greased with lard, beef suet or bacon
fat, and eat immediately, rolling the cakes like pancakes round
little sticks of salty butter.

Or: roll the dough out to a $\frac{1}{2}''$ thickness, and cut with a scone cutter. Cook on the griddle, and eat with bacon, eggs and so on. They will need 15 minutes' cooking time.

Or: in the Welsh manner, add 2 tablespoons of brown sugar and 1 tablespoon granulated sugar to the mixture. Cut into $\frac{1}{2}''$ rounds with the scone cutter—15–20 minutes' cooking time on the griddle, greased with suet or lard.

Muffins

1 lb flour (preferably strong flour)	1 egg
$\frac{1}{2}$ pint milk	Teaspoon salt
$\frac{1}{2}$ oz fresh yeast	1 oz butter

Break the egg into a bowl. Warm the milk and butter together to blood heat, and beat it with the egg. Cream the yeast with 4 tablespoons of warm water.

Put the flour into a warm bowl, and make a well in the centre. Pour in the yeast, and then the egg-butter-milk liquid. Knead thoroughly, adding more flour, or more water if necessary (different kinds of flour absorb different amounts of moisture). The dough should be soft but not sticky. Cover the bowl with a damp cloth and leave in a warm place for about $1\frac{1}{2}$ hours, or until the dough has doubled in size.

Roll out the dough to a $\frac{1}{2}''$ thickness on a floured board. Cut out the muffins with a large scone cutter—about $2\frac{1}{2}''$ across. Knead the trimmings together, and roll and cut them out in the same way.

Immediately you have finished this, start cooking the muffins on a lightly greased griddle, turning them over when they are floury and slightly brown on the base. Alternatively, cook them in a very hot oven, with plenty of bottom heat, and turn them over after 6 or 7 minutes.

The muffins will rise and swell to look rather like a puffball fungus. They should not cook too fast, so the centre of the griddle may have to be avoided, and they should keep a floury look. Toast them by the fire, then pull them apart and put a big knob of butter in the middle; muffins are never cut, always pulled apart. Keep them warm in a muffin dish, as you toast the rest, turning them over after a few minutes so that the butter soaks into both halves.

Crumpets

1 lb plain flour	Teaspoon salt
1 pt milk	Good pinch bicarbonate of soda
½ oz fresh yeast	About 4 tablespoons warm water

Warm the flour in a bowl in the plate-warming part of the stove, or stand it in a rack above the cooker. Heat the milk to body temperature (a clinical thermometer can be used if you do not have a kitchen one), then fork up the yeast with 3 table-spoons of the milk. It will soon cream and swell into frothiness. Make a well in the centre of the flour and pour in both the yeast mixture and the warm milk. Beat for a good 5 minutes (an electric beater can be used—3 minutes will be enough). Cover the bowl and leave the dough to rise in a warm place for an hour. Dissolve the bicarbonate of soda in the warm water, add it to the mixture, beating it in thoroughly, then leave it to rise for another hour.

Grease the griddle with lard or suet, and grease the crumpet rings (Tala make them, but they are not essential). Place the rings on the griddle and heat it when the dough is ready. Pour spoonfuls of mixture to half-fill the rings, and leave for a few moments to cook. Turn them over when the top part loses its liquid appearance, and finish the cooking. Ease off the rings and start again with some more dough.

Eat these crumpets toasted in the usual way, with plenty of butter. They make a good base for fried eggs, or scrambled eggs with anchovies. Some people like them with syrup as well as butter.

Singin' Hinnies

1 lb flour
4 oz butter
4 oz lard
$\frac{1}{4}$ teaspoon bicarbonate of soda
$\frac{1}{2}$ teaspoon cream of tartar

$\frac{1}{2}$ teaspoon salt
6 oz currants, raisins or sultanas
Milk to mix
Piece of lamb or mutton fat for the griddle

Sift together the flour, raising powders and salt. Rub in the butter and lard, then mix in the fruit. Add enough milk to make a firm dough. Roll out, then cut into rounds of about $2\frac{1}{2}''$ in diameter. Spear the mutton fat on a fork and grease the heated griddle with it thoroughly. Put on the cakes, and turn them when the underneath is a nice mottled brown. Cut in half and put a big knob of butter in the middle. Keep the singin' hinnies warm in the oven until they are all cooked. If you are making them for a children's party, or at Christmas, put silver sixpences, washed and wrapped in greaseproof paper, in the middle of some of them.

People who have left behind them a north-eastern childhood should be forgiven for insisting that singin' hinnies are the best of all girdle cakes (in fact I think the Welsh *pice ar y maen* are better, but it's a close thing). The affectionate name recalls the warmth of home and community life—'hinny' being the local pet name, a charming corruption of honey and the equivalent, more or less, of 'luv' and 'ducks' in other parts of the country. The singing comes from the way the cakes sizzle with richness as they cook.

This is one of the few regional dishes that can compare with, say, the regional dishes of France. Not in substance, but because they are—or were, to my knowledge, until the fifties—eaten by everyone in the area, rich, middling and poor. I remember as a child, going to birthday parties at one shipyard owner's house in the thirties. The food was lavish, but we always started off with hot singin' hinnies; he could afford to put many silver sixpenny and 'thruppenny' pieces inside, their greaseproof wrapping transparent with melted butter. When we went for a large family tea-party on Sundays to our great-aunt's house, there would be great-uncle Bob in his seaman's jersey making sure we started with plenty of singin' hinnies. One way and another we were lucky in that depressed time. Other people remember singin' hinnies 'as substitutes for the birthday cake we could not afford, and the paper enclosed coins being halfpennies, and few at that. I have known when the birthday child was carefully guided to choose the only scone containing a coin.' Moreover the singin' hinnies made less of a song for many people, as they could not afford the full complement of butter and lard.

Cacen-gri (Girdle Cakes)

1 lb flour	4 oz lard
1 teaspoon baking powder	3 oz dried fruit and peel
½ teaspoon salt	2 standard eggs
4 oz butter	A little buttermilk or milk

Sift the flour, baking powder and salt together into a bowl. Rub in the butter and fat. Add the fruit and peel, then mix to a soft dough with the eggs, adding a little buttermilk or milk. Roll the dough into two balls, and pat them out to the thickness of half an inch. Bake these rounds on a moderately hot griddle. Split and butter them lavishly before serving them hot for tea.

Pice ar y Maen (Welsh cakes on the stone)

1 lb flour	¼ lb currants or raisins
1 teaspoon baking powder	6 oz sugar (optional)
Generous pinch salt	2 large eggs
1 teaspoon mace	Milk to mix if necessary
4 oz butter	Extra sugar
4 oz lard	

Mix and bake as above. When cooked, do not butter them but turn them in the extra sugar. The richness of a second egg, and the delicate unmistakable flavour of mace, makes these the most delicious of all the girdle cakes.

Gloucester Pancakes

For 4

6 oz flour	3 oz chopped suet
Pinch of salt	1 egg, beaten
1 teaspoon baking powder	A little milk
	Lard

Mix the flour, salt and baking powder together in a bowl. Stir in the suet and mix everything well together, using the beaten egg and a little milk to make a firm dough.

Roll out the dough on a lightly-floured board until it is about $\frac{1}{2}''$ thick. Cut out $2''$ rounds with a glass or scone cutter. Fry the little cakes in hot lard on both sides until golden brown. Serve hot with golden syrup. (These cakes can be cooked on a lard-greased griddle, but are best done in a frying pan.)

Gloucester pancakes have a delicious, richly sandy texture inside, which comes from using suet. No other fat will achieve the same result. It is also important to fry them in lard, on account of the flavour.

Pancakes for the Rich, or a Quire of Paper

$\frac{1}{4}$ lb butter	2 tablespoons brown sherry
$\frac{1}{2}$ pt single cream	1 teaspoon rose water or orange-flower water
3 oz flour	
1 large egg	$\frac{1}{2}$ grated nutmeg

Melt butter over a low heat. Add to the cream, and with remaining ingredients make a pancake batter. If it seems a little thick, don't worry—the butter cools in contact with the other ingredients, but will melt again in the hot pan making the mixture more liquid.

Rub an omelette pan over with a butter paper and heat it. Pour in a tablespoon or a small ladleful of the liquid (depending on the size of the pan), and tilt the pan so that it runs evenly over the base. The edges of the pancake will be thin and lacy, so ease them up with a knife before attempting to turn it. There is no need to keep greasing the pan, as the mixture is rich enough not to stick. These elegant, thin pancakes—paper-thin as the charming eighteenth-century name indicates—are like the French *crêpes dentelles*, and can be dressed up in the Suzette style (recipe on pages 275–6). The English way was simply to sprinkle them with sugar and serve them very hot.

Rose water and orange-flower water can be bought at good chemists' shops. Channel Island milk can be substituted for half, or all, of the cream.

It is sad that this kind of recipe should survive as a common-place in France, but not in England. We have let it vanish from our tables, and cling masochistically to the poor man's recipe (page 277). This shows the different attitudes to food. The farmer from whom this particular version of the recipe came labelled it firmly as being for the rich. In France, in Brittany, Normandy, Touraine, it would be regarded as a recipe for Sundays or other feast days; the poor man's version as an every-day family dish. Obviously the poor would eat the simpler pancakes more often than the richer, thinner kind, but they would not feel that the latter were not for them.

There is another, more sensible way of looking at these two kinds of pancake. The plain, thick batter produces a pancake which is more suitable for the strong flavours of meat and fish, for cheese and for eggs. This has nothing to do with the house-keeping money: or with frugality. You might, after all, choose to make a lobster filling. It would be quite wrong to wrap it up in the thin laciness of this recipe. For the dessert course, which should come lightly at the end of a meal, this 'rich man's' recipe is the one to choose, whether you serve it with nothing more than sugar and lemon juice, or whether you raid the brandy and liqueur bottles.

Like the Bretons who have a repertoire of pancakes still, the Welsh cling sensibly to a fine variety of girdle or bakestone cakes and pancakes. This may be a primitive style of cooking by origin, but with the subtle addition of a number of extra ingredients—extra, that is, to the basic mixture of flour/eggs/milk—the results can be elegant. This recipe would surprise the Viking housewife whose stone griddle, a true bakestone, was dug up in the excavations at Jarlshof in the Shetlands:—

Welsh Light Cakes or Pancakes

6 rounded tablespoons flour	½ teaspoon bicarbonate of soda
2 rounded tablespoons sugar	1 rounded tablespoon cream of
3 tablespoons soured cream	tartar
Pinch salt	2 oz water
3 eggs	About ¼ pt buttermilk or milk

Beat together the first five ingredients. Mix the bicarbonate of soda and cream of tartar with the water—it will froth up rapidly—and add it to the batter. Dilute to a bubbly, not too thick consistency with the buttermilk or milk, adding it gradually. Cook a small pancake—the batter should spread out fairly easily as the pan is tilted, and the surface should rapidly become netted with holes. If the mixture seems too thick, add some more of the buttermilk or milk.

Apart from a preliminary greasing with a butter paper, you will not need to do more than brush the pan occasionally with a little oil or melted butter.

To turn the pancakes, ease the delicate, lacy edge from the pan with a thin, pointed knife, before pushing in the slice.

The Welsh way of eating these deliciously light pancakes is to spread them with Welsh butter and pile them up, one on the other. The butter melts in the heat and falls through the holes, so that the whole thing is rich and succulent, as well as light. To serve, cut the pile of pancakes in quarters.

If you wish to serve them with Suzette sauce—which is not in

the least English, but invented by a French chef, Henri Char-
pentier, for Edward VII—here is his recipe :

1 heaped tablespoon vanilla sugar	1½ liqueur glasses maraschino
1-inch square lemon peel	1½ liqueur glasses kirschwasser
1-inch square orange peel	2 liqueur glasses curaçao
4 oz unsalted butter	

Put the vanilla sugar into a small screw-top jar a day or two
before you need it. Cut the peels into thin strips, and add them
to the sugar. Shake the mixture about, after closing the jar
tightly.

When you make the pancakes fold each one in half, then in
half again to make a quarter-circle. For four people you need
eight large ones. Dispose them on a plate in two circles, one on
top of the other. They can, like the sugar, be prepared in
advance, and stored in foil in the refrigerator.

Just before serving the dish, cut the butter into even-sized
pieces. Mix the liqueurs together. Melt the butter in a pan, pour
just over half the liqueur mixture into the butter, stir it about
and tilt the pan towards the heat so that it catches fire. As the
flames die down, put in the sugar, and then the pancakes to
reheat. Turn them over so that they are bathed in the delicious
sauce, but be careful not to disturb their triangular folds. Finally
add the remaining liqueur, allow it to flame again and serve
the pancakes. This last part is usually done at table in restaurants—a bit flashy, and you pay far too much for the spectacle.
Such a simple dish is best made at home.

Crempog Las

¼ lb flour	1 heaped teaspoon finely chopped
1 large egg	shallot
1 dessertspoon chopped parsley	Pepper, salt
	Milk to mix

Mix and cook in a greased pan, like a pancake, keeping the
batter on the thick side.

The Welsh eat *crempog las* hot, with butter; but when Mrs Freeman ran the Compton House Hotel in Fishguard she served them at breakfast time with sausages and bacon, and found they were a popular dish on the menu.

Harvest Pancakes for the Poor

Eighteenth-century ingredients	*Modern translation*
1 pottle wheat flour	4 oz flour
2 quarts new milk or mild ale	8 oz milk or mild ale
4 eggs	½ egg (1 is better)
Powdered ginger to taste	Half a teaspoon powdered ginger
Lard for frying	Lard to grease the pan

Mix flour to a batter with milk or ale, and the egg. Flavour with ginger, and fry in lard in a heavy pan, a ladleful at a time.

Chopped apple was sometimes added to enliven the pancakes.

A pottle was a measurement of bulk, equivalent to half a gallon (that is, 4 pints). As far as flour is concerned, it means 2½ lb in weight. The word pottle was also used for small, conical chip baskets of strawberries or mushrooms.

This mixture—particularly when only half an egg is used— makes solid, heavy pancakes, which were ideal for the labourer's family at harvest, the busiest time of the year when everyone was needed in the fields. They were quickly cooked, which saved on firing as well as time. They were easy to carry, like a Cornish pasty or an apple turnover. They were reckoned to be an adequate substitute for both meat and bread—and they were thought of as a treat, 'a pleasant Part of a Family Subsistence'.

They make much better picnic food than a sandwich, particularly if you wrap them round a fried sausage, or a finger length of pâté, or cream cheese beaten up with chives and parsley. A Breton habit still, a habit which we once shared, of using the pancake as portable food, with embellishments when they could be afforded. Another Breton habit is to break an egg on to the pancake when it has been turned once, and leave it to cook. Delicious.

Grasmere Gingerbread

½ lb plain flour or fine oatmeal, or   1 teaspoon ground ginger
  ¼ lb of each   ¼ teaspoon baking powder
¼ lb pale soft brown sugar   5 oz lightly salted butter

Mix the dry ingredients together. Melt the butter over a low heat, and when tepid use it to bind the mixture. Line a roasting pan or oblong tin with Bakewell paper. Spread the mixture over the tin in a ¼″ layer, pressing it down lightly. Bake until golden brown, at mark 4, 350°, for 30 to 35 minutes. Mark into oblong pieces straightaway, but leave to cool in the tin.

This is a good mixture for fruit crumbles, see page 201.

In spite of the name, Grasmere gingerbread is a crumbly biscuit, not in the least like our usual soft dark gingerbread. You can buy it in a cottage by the churchyard at Grasmere, where William and Dorothy Wordsworth—and members of their family, and friends—are buried. In those days fine-ground oatmeal would have been used rather than wheat flour, which was a luxury as it had to come from the south.

Gingerbread of the past, the gingerbread of fairgrounds, the gingerbread that might lose its gilt, was not in the least like this recipe. For one thing, it was made of honey, not treacle, which until the sixteenth and seventeenth centuries was regarded as a medicine—particularly as an antidote for poisons—rather than a cheap sweetening substance. (Golden syrup was not made until the 1880s: even then black treacle remained popular in the north of England where gingerbread and parkin are still among the most commonly made cakes.)

A medieval recipe, from about 1430, gives a good idea of what this early gingerbread was like. You warmed a quart of honey and skimmed it, then added breadcrumbs until the mixture was thick enough to be shaped into a square loaf without further cooking. Before the crumbs were added, the honey might be coloured yellow with saffron, or red with sanders which was a preparation of sandalwood from India. It was also flavoured with black pepper and cinnamon, and presumably with ground ginger too, although this is not mentioned, presumably because whoever copied the manuscript overlooked it—such slips were commonplace in those days and they are still the nightmare of modern cookery writers, who have printers and editors to help them check their manuscript.

This solid square was decorated with box leaves held in place by cloves. Sometimes the cloves had gilded heads, and were used to pattern the top of the gingerbread, which was eventually cut into slices for eating. The nearest thing to medieval gingerbread is the French *pain d'épice*, which is made from flour, honey and spices, including ginger. It has an odd, slightly leathery texture—odd, at least to our modern English tradition —and is made in huge squares. They are then cut into long bars, wrapped in plastic and sold in every grocer's shop in northern France, but especially in the honey-producing areas above Orléans or in Alsace.

I made some gingerbread to this medieval recipe, and found that you needed about 1 oz of breadcrumbs to one heaped dessertspoonful of honey. The size of a cake made with 2 pints of honey must have been enormous. Some kind of colouring was needed, because the mixture would have been too pale without it: I used powdered saffron. By stirring the crumbs into the very hot honey, I made a thick paste which could easily be handled and moulded into shape, like almond paste though rather more grainy. When the cake was cool, we ate it in slices and found it a little close in texture, but the spices and the pepper in particular combined well with the honey sweetness and made it good to eat.

Mereworth Biscuits

¼ lb plain flour	Pinch salt
1 oz butter	Hot milk

Rub the first three ingredients together. Then mix to a dough with hot milk—it should be firm but soft. Knead it well. Roll out small bits of the dough to paper thinness: it will look and feel like a piece of cloth. Cut into approximately 2″ rounds with a plain scone cutter and bake at mark 7, 425°F, for about 5 minutes, until they are slightly browned and puffed up. Cool and store in an air-tight box.

This recipe makes a huge number of light biscuits, which taste delicious with butter alone, or with butter and a soft cheese. The thinner you can roll them the better. Some will puff up into a balloon; others will have two or three bubbles.

We once looked down on the perfect Greek cross of Mereworth Castle through young beech leaves, not long after we had visited the Villa Capra at Vicenza, which stands right up on a dusty hill surrounded by long grass. And here in the spring countryside of Kent was this perfect replica, with the same collected elegance, far below in a valley. I should like to see the kitchens of Mereworth, where these biscuits were made in the nineteenth century. The recipe is so simple, the results are so good—quite in keeping with the ambience. It comes from Lady Sarah Lindsay's *Choice Recipes*, published in 1883.

Elegant Sugar Thins

8 oz butter	½ teaspoon salt
8 oz caster sugar	1 teaspoon baking powder
1 egg	Vanilla essence (or lemon juice or
1 tablespoon double cream	ground ginger)
10 oz plain flour	Extra sugar

Cream the butter and sugar, then add the egg and cream and the remaining ingredients. If you like, divide the dough into three, and flavour each part differently. Form the dough into a long roll or rolls, about 2" in diameter, and wrap in foil. Put into the refrigerator until next day. Shave off the dough in the thinnest possible slices. Put them on a baking tray, sprinkle them with sugar and cook them for 5 minutes at mark 5, 375° : they should remain pale in colour. There is no need to bake the dough all at once : cut off what you need and put it back in the refrigerator.

Walnut Biscuits

7 oz butter
5 oz caster sugar
8 oz self-raising flour

1 large egg
3 oz shelled walnuts, chopped

Mix in the same way as the Elegant Sugar Thins, but bake them for 10 minutes as it is not possible to cut them into such fine rounds. Particularly good with coffee. A crisp, rich biscuit.

Almond Fingers

Pastry
1 oz butter
3 heaped tablespoon icing sugar
1 egg
1 tablespoon lemon juice
6 oz flour

Filling
Apricot jam
5 oz butter
5 oz vanilla sugar
2 eggs
4 oz ground almonds
1 heaped tablespoon flour
2 tablespoons rum
2–3 oz blanched, slivered almonds

To make the pastry, cream butter and sugar together. Beat in egg next, and then the lemon juice and flour. Leave to rest for one hour in the refrigerator. Roll out and line a 7" × 11" tin.

Spread the pastry base evenly with apricot jam. Cream the butter and vanilla sugar together from the filling ingredients. Add the eggs, then the flour, ground almonds and rum. Spread evenly over the pastry. Sprinkle the top with almonds. Bake for 35–40 minutes at mark 4, 350°. The top should be a light golden brown and the almonds slightly coloured. Leave to cool in the tin, and cut into fingers when cold.

One sees many commercial brands of almond slice. They are made with a view to profit and long shelf-life. Try this recipe instead; the difference in flavour is startling—principally because it is not mean with butter and almonds and eggs.

Mazarines

Pastry	*Filling*
2 oz butter	2 egg whites
1 tablespoon caster sugar	4 oz caster sugar
1 egg yolk	2 oz blanched, flaked almonds
4 oz flour	1 tablespoon grated plain chocolate
1 oz ground almonds	Apricot jam

To make the pastry, cream butter and sugar, then add egg yolk, and finally the flour and almonds. Roll out and cut into strips about 2" wide. Lay them on a baking sheet lined with Bakewell paper, and bend the edges up slightly. Spread the apricot jam down the strips. To make the rest of the filling, beat the egg whites until stiff, then fold in the sugar, almonds and chocolate. Put into a saucepan and heat to boiling point, stirring as you do so. Spoon this mixture quickly along the pastry strips. Bake at mark 4, 350°, for about 45 minutes. Allow to cool, then cut the strips diagonally into little fingers.

A recipe from *Come Cooking!* compiled by the West Sussex Women's Institutes in 1969.

The name is a puzzle. It may derive from France's Cardinal Mazarin, or from the Duchesse de Mazarin who died in Chelsea in 1699. In a dictionary of 1706, mazarines are defined either as little dishes which can be set in the middle of a larger dish, or—which is more relevant to this recipe—as 'a sort of small tarts fill'd with sweet-meats'.

Brandy Snaps
Makes 20–30

4 oz butter	2 teaspoons ground ginger
4 oz golden syrup	1 teaspoon lemon juice
4 oz granulated sugar	2 teaspoons brandy
Pinch salt	½ pt double cream, whipped
4 oz flour	

Melt butter, syrup and sugar over a low heat in a medium-sized pan, stirring until you have a smooth mixture. Do not allow it to become really hot. Remove the pan from the heat, and when the mixture is barely tepid, stir in salt, flour, ginger, lemon juice and brandy.

Spread baking sheets with Bakewell paper and put teaspoons of the mixture on to it, allowing room for them to spread a great deal. About six teaspoons a sheet is right—although this will depend on whether the teaspoons were generously measured. Bake at mark 3, 325°, for 8–10 minutes.

Press the brandy snaps round the handle of a wooden spoon into cigarette shapes while they are still hot. If they cool and become difficult, replace them in the oven to regain their suppleness. When cold store them in an air-tight tin. Fill them with whipped cream, piping it in at both ends, not long before they are required.

There are many versions of these biscuits in English cookery, because they were popular as fairings—along with eel pies and gingerbread. Indeed at some fairs, like the Marlborough Mop, you can still buy them in flat, irregular, lacy rounds, much better than candy floss to sustain you on the Big Wheel or at the boxing booth. Old versions use black treacle—golden syrup, a refined product, did not come in until the 1880s.

Stuffings, Sauces & Preserves

Oyster Stuffing for turkey and other poultry

2–3 dozen oysters
10 oz white breadcrumbs made from stale bread
5 oz chopped suet
2 tablespoons heaped parsley
Grated rind of a lemon

2 heaped teaspoons thyme
¼ teaspoon each mace, nutmeg
A pinch Cayenne pepper
Salt, pepper
2 large eggs beaten

Open the oysters. Save their liquor for the oyster sauce which is usually served at the same time. Chop the oysters in four, so that the pieces are quite large. Mix them with the remaining ingredients, adding salt and pepper to taste.

This quantity is enough for a 14 lb turkey.

Oyster Sauce

2 dozen oysters
2 oz butter
2 tablespoons flour
½ pt milk

¼ pt cream, preferably double cream
Grated nutmeg
Pinch Cayenne pepper
Lemon juice to taste

Open the oysters, saving their liquor carefully. Put it with the liquor from the stuffing oysters. Chop the oysters themselves into fairly large pieces. With the butter, flour, milk and cream make a smooth béchamel sauce; add the oyster liquor and simmer for 20 minutes. Season to taste, and sharpen with a little lemon juice. Just before serving the sauce, stir in the chopped oysters

—they will dilute it slightly. The sauce should be about the consistency of double cream or a little thinner.

This sauce is to go with the oyster stuffing for a turkey. For a large chicken, halve the quantities of both recipes.

If you cannot manage to buy oysters, try the recipes with mussels. It would be wise to start with a chicken, to see how you like the flavours together.

Herb Stuffing

1 medium onion, chopped	4 oz breadcrumbs
2 oz butter	1 egg
2 oz chopped ham or bacon	1 egg yolk
1 tablespoon chopped parsley	Salt, pepper
1 teaspoonful thyme	

Cook the onion gently in the butter until softened, and golden, but not in the least brown. Put it into a bowl with the juices. Mix in the ham and remaining ingredients, seasoning the mixture to taste.

A good general stuffing for veal, poultry, and stuffed tomatoes. It can be used as a basis to which extra flavourings may be added to suit the occasion.

Parsley and Lemon Stuffing

1 large white loaf	1 teaspoon lemon thyme (optional)
Grated peel of two lemons	1 teaspoon dried marjoram
Juice of 1 lemon	½ lb lightly salted butter, creamed
4 oz parsley	3 eggs
	Salt, freshly ground black pepper

Cut the crusts from the bread, and reduce it to crumbs. Spread them out on baking sheets and dry them in the oven—they should not colour, so keep the temperature very low. Weigh out half a pound, and put into a basin. Mix in the lemon peel and juice. Discard the parsley stems and chop the leaves into the breadcrumbs. Add the lemon thyme if used, and the marjoram. Amalgamate thoroughly with the creamed butter and beat in the eggs.

Enough for the centre cavity of a 12 lb turkey. Remember that stuffing should never be packed in tightly—it must have room to swell. And to be cooked through properly.

Hazelnut Stuffing for poultry or lamb

1 large onion, chopped	Juice of 1 lemon
2 oz butter	Grated rind ½ lemon
4 oz fresh white breadcrumbs	1 large egg, beaten
2 oz hazelnuts, lightly grilled, chopped	Salt, freshly ground black pepper
4 knobs preserved ginger, chopped	2 tablespoons chopped parsley

Cook the onion until soft and golden in the butter. Keep the lid on the pan so that it doesn't brown. Mix with the remaining ingredients in the order in which they are given. Taste and correct the seasoning.

For a turkey, double or treble the amount, according to its size, remembering (see previous recipe) that stuffing should always be loosely packed. The ginger adds a chestnut-like texture and a subtle flavour which is difficult to place.

It is important to choose good hazelnuts. They need not be large, but they must have a fine flavour. The most delicious I have tasted were served with wine in Avellino, behind Vesuvius. They had been baked very slowly to a pale golden brown, and they were the same colour all through: I wish I had brought some home to make this recipe with as they had the most delicious crispness. Avellino has been known for its hazelnuts since the Roman era (the botanical name is *Corylus avellana*), and you come to it through miles of hazel woods.

Kentish cobs are another variety (cobs, cobbles, that is, small stones): children used them, incidentally, in playing conkers, before the introduced horse-chestnut tree became common. Filberts are a different species—*Corylus maxima*—their name anglicized from French *noix de Philibert*, in other words, Saint Philibert, who was abbot of Jumièges in Normandy 1300 years ago. In much of France filberts ripen around the time of his feast day of August 22nd.

Hollandaise Sauce

3 tablespoons white wine vinegar	3 large egg yolks
2 tablespoons water	6 oz unsalted butter, cut into 12
10 white peppercorns, slightly crushed	pieces
	Salt and lemon juice to taste

METHOD ONE

Boil the first three ingredients together in a small pan, until there is a tablespoon of liquid only. Strain it into a pudding basin and leave it to cool. Beat in the egg yolks. Set the basin over a pan of not-quite-simmering water and beat in the butter, piece by piece, using a small wire whisk, or wooden spoon. The sauce should never be overheated, or the egg will scramble, and you will have to start again mayonnaise-style with a fresh egg yolk. At the end flavour with salt and lemon juice to taste.

METHOD TWO

Boil the first three ingredients down to a tablespoon in the same way. Strain into the blender, add the eggs and switch on. Gradually add the butter, which should be melted and tepid but not hot. Finally season with salt and lemon juice. Place in a bowl to reheat over a pan of almost simmering water, stirring gently but steadily.

A French sauce, which has also become part of the English

repertoire. Delicious with asparagus and other fine vegetables, or with fish.

Mayonnaise

3 egg yolks	½ pt olive or corn oil
1 teaspoonful French mustard	Salt, pepper
Lemon juice or wine vinegar	

Beat the egg yolks with the mustard and a dash of lemon juice or vinegar, until they begin to thicken; beat in the oil drop by drop at first until the sauce begins to emulsify—then you can go a little faster. Finally flavour with more lemon or vinegar, and salt and pepper. Be sure that eggs and oil are at warm room temperature before you start; rinse the bowl out with hot water, too, and then dry it. This way you will never have a failure. But *if* you do—one sometimes makes a careless slip with the oil—either put another egg yolk in a clean basin, or a table-spoon of mustard, and add the curdled sauce drop by drop, then the remainder of the oil. The mustard is a useful tip, if you are short of eggs, and if the food you are serving the sauce with can stand it.

Mayonnaise can be made successfully in a blender (use 1 whole egg and 2 yolks), or with an electric beater. The method is the same.

Mayonnaise, like Hollandaise Sauce, was first made in the eighteenth century. There are many legends about its origin and name: it seems to have become popular in England in the middle of the last century. Eliza Acton, who published her *Modern Cookery* in 1845, felt the need to reassure her readers about it; by 1861 Mrs Beeton took it for granted. Both writers include Hollandaise Sauce under the heading 'Dutch sauce', which, in spite of its name, it is not.

Mayonnaise and Hollandaise are the cold and hot versions of the same principle: they are the ideal partners for simply cooked food of quality.

English Salad Sauce

2 small hard-boiled egg yolks	1 teaspoon water
1 raw small egg yolk	$\frac{1}{4}$ pt double cream
Salt, freshly ground white pepper	Chilli, shallot or tarragon vinegar,
Pinch Cayenne pepper	or lemon juice
$\frac{1}{4}$ teaspoon sugar	

Sieve the hard-boiled yolks (keep the whites to decorate the salad) into a basin. Stir in the raw yolk, the seasonings and water. Stir in the cream gradually. Finally flavour with vinegar or lemon juice.

Apart from the extra egg yolk, this is Eliza Acton's recipe from *Modern Cookery* and it cannot be bettered. Anyone who remembers the unpleasant salad sauces we were reduced to making in the last war, or who had a baptism of bottled salad creams and 'mayonnaise' as a child, can feel safe with this recipe. It really is good, and lighter than mayonnaise. Nothing to be ashamed of at all. It can be used as a basis for extra flavourings appropriate to the salad, just as mayonnaise can—crushed anchovies, chopped green fresh herbs, capers, tomato concentrate and so on. It is not a sauce for plain green salads of lettuce, but for mixed salads of fish, meat, rice and so on.

French Dressing

1 clove garlic, finely chopped	Freshly ground pepper
$\frac{1}{4}$ teaspoon sugar	1 tablespoon wine vinegar
1 teaspoon French mustard	5 tablespoons olive oil
(optional)	Salt

Crush the garlic down in the bowl with the sugar, and mustard if used. Sprinkle with pepper and mix to a paste with the vinegar. Whisk in the olive oil, and when everything is properly amalgamated, taste it and add salt—and more of any of the other seasonings that seem a good idea.

Fresh green herbs are a good addition to this sauce—parsley

and chives are the usual ones, but tarragon, chervil, and savory can be added when they are appropriate.

The ideal sauce for green salads, and salads of fine vegetables which are being presented on their own. Tomatoes, cooked asparagus, purple-sprouting broccoli, new potatoes and so on. If you intend to dress a salad with mayonnaise, mix it first with a few spoonsful of French dressing then drain off any surplus. The mayonnaise will mix in much more easily, and the result will be lighter.

We call this most useful of sauces, French dressing or vinaigrette, and occasionally talk about it as if it was something Elizabeth David brought to England (like Raleigh and potatoes to Ireland) at the end of the 1940s. In fact it has been around since the eighteenth century, and Hannah Glasse gives what might seem a very modern salad—broccoli, boiled and served cold with a dressing of oil and vinegar. 'Garnish with Stertionbuds' (Nasturtium buds were pickled as a substitute for capers). She is referring to purple or green-sprouting broccoli, which does make an excellent salad.

Bread Sauce

1 small onion, stuck with three cloves	Mace or nutmeg
	Salt
¾ pt rich milk	Freshly ground white pepper
3–4 oz fresh breadcrumbs from a good loaf (not from factory flannel)	Pinch Cayenne pepper
	1½ oz butter, or 2 tablespoons double cream

Put the onion and milk into a basin and bring it to just below boiling point—this can be done over a pan of simmering water, or in a slow oven. The point is to infuse the milk with the flavour of onion and cloves, so the longer the milk takes to come to boiling point the better.

Remove the onion and whisk in the breadcrumbs until the sauce is thick with all the milk taken up. Keep the basin over the boiling water until the sauce is heated through. If it seems on the thin side—bread sauce should not spread very much when put on to a plate—add more crumbs. If it seems so firm that a spoon stands up in it, add a little more milk. Season with mace or nutmeg, with salt and the peppers. Finally stir in the butter or cream and put into a sauce tureen. Scatter a small amount of Cayenne pepper on the top.

In the Middle Ages many sauces were thickened with bread. This wasn't because cooks failed to realize that flour or egg yolks could do the job, but because sauces had on the whole to be coherent enough not to run off the bread trenchers which were used as plates, and not to sink into the trenchers too quickly or completely. With flour, thickening beyond a certain point turns a sauce to glue. With a lot of egg yolk, the sauce turns to custard. Bread is the thing for an agreeable un-sloppy moistness of texture, providing the crumbs are allowed to retain a certain identity, and are not beaten back into a floury paste.

English bread sauce (and a mushroom soup still made in the Bresse district of France) are two survivors of this old cookery practice. Another, which older readers may remember from their childhood, is the supper dish of bread and milk, which declined into a dish for children and invalids, before it disappeared altogether under the onslaught of patent cereals. Like the sauce given above, bread and milk is delicious when bits of first-class baker's bread, and not factory flannel, are crumbled into hot creamy Jersey or Guernsey milk.

In some early recipes, stock is used instead of milk. Serve with poultry—roast chicken, turkey, guineafowl—and with game. Or with sausages. Or with sweetbreads, page 132.

Sawce noyre for roast capon

1 lb chicken livers	1 slice of bread
Chicken fat	Cider vinegar or lemon juice
Aniseed, ginger and cinnamon	Salt, pepper

Fry the livers in chicken fat for about 4 minutes, until they are brown outside but still pink inside. Add aniseed, ginger and cinnamon to taste—start with $\frac{1}{4}$ teaspoon each. Cut the crusts from the bread, and reduce it to crumbs with the liver (if you have a Moulinex chopper). Otherwise put the liver through the fine plate of the mincer and mix it with the crumbs. Sharpen the reheated sauce to taste with vinegar or lemon juice. Season with salt and pepper. This sauce is more of a spreading than a runny pouring consistency, as you would expect from a medieval recipe. (This one comes from a manuscript of 1439, now in the Bodleian Library at Oxford.)

Chicken livers were used to make a favourite European sauce in the Middle Ages, and recipes still bob up in unexpected places in France and Italy. The Italians use white wine and lemon juice as a flavouring, and include dried ceps (mushrooms), a slice of Parma ham, onion and garlic, all cooked in together. I like the flavour of aniseed with poultry : it may sound odd, but the famous chickens of Le Mans are fed a proportion of aniseed to give them their delicious flavour.

In France *sauce noire* or *sauce infernale* is served with game (the game livers are included in the sauce) and spread on croûtons of fried bread placed under the birds as they are served. In Italy it comes to the table on its own, as a first course, with thin toast : or spread on slices of hot roast veal interspersed with pieces of toast also spread with the sauce. It's called *salsa di fegatini*—sauce of little livers.

Apple Sauce I

$\frac{1}{2}$ lb Bramley's Seedlings	1 strip orange rind
1 small or moderate quince	1 oz butter
$\frac{1}{4}$ pt water	Freshly ground black pepper
1 heaped tablespoon sugar	

Cut the apples up roughly, and slice quince rather more finely. Do not peel or core the fruit. Put with water and sugar and orange rind into a pan, and simmer, covered, until soft. Sieve into a clean pan, and cook briskly for a few minutes until the purée is lightly coherent, not sloppy and wet. Stir in the butter, and, last of all, a little freshly ground pepper.

Apple Sauce II

¾ lb Cox's Orange Pippins or Laxtons or James Grieve apples
3 oz water

1 strip lemon peel
1 oz butter
Freshly ground black pepper

Cook in the same way as Apple Sauce I and serve with pork, salt pork, sausages, duck, goose.

Apple Sauce III

1 lb Cox's Orange Pippins, Laxtons, or James Grieve
Clarified butter

3 oz cider or dry white wine
3 oz double cream
Lemon juice

Core and dice the apples (peel them, too, if you like, but it's not necessary). Fry them gently until they are golden and slightly softened in some clarified butter. Remove the apples to a serving dish. Deglaze the pan with cider or wine, scraping in all the apple juices and brown bits and pieces. When this liquid has reduced to a concentrated essence, stir in the cream. Heat through, sharpen with lemon juice and pour over the apples. For veal and chicken.

Spiced Apple Sauce

1 lb Bramley Seedlings
1 oz butter
2 tablespoons water
2 tablespoons white wine vinegar
¼ teaspoon grated nutmeg

¼ teaspoon cinnamon
¼ teaspoon freshly ground black pepper
About 1 oz soft dark brown sugar

Peel, core and cut up the apples. Put them in a pan with the butter, water, vinegar and spices. Cover and cook until soft enough to beat to a purée. Add sugar to taste, and more spices if you like.

A good recipe, with chutney-like overtones. Ideal for boiled salt pork, and duck or goose.

Cumberland Sauce

2 Seville oranges, or 1 sweet orange and 1 lemon
½ lb redcurrant jelly
1 teaspoon Dijon mustard

½ gill port (2½ oz)
Freshly ground black pepper, salt
Ground ginger

Peel the oranges, or orange and lemon, thinly. Cut the peel into matchstick strips and blanch them for 5 minutes in boiling water. Drain them in a sieve.

Meanwhile heat the jelly and mustard together over a low heat, whisking them to a smooth thickness. Add the juice of the oranges, or of the orange and the lemon, and the remaining ingredients, with plenty of black pepper, and a little salt and ginger to taste. Stir in the peel, and then simmer for 5 minutes. Pour into a glass dish or a jar and serve cold with cold or hot ham and tongue, with venison and game, duck and goose.

If Cumberland sauce is stored in a covered jar in the refrigerator, it will keep for weeks quite satisfactorily.

In *Spices, Salt and Aromatics in the English Kitchen*, Elizabeth David has a long and interesting discussion on the origins of Cumberland sauce (one thing is sure—it didn't come from Cumberland).

'What basis there is for the story that it was named after Ernest, Duke of Cumberland, that brother of George IV's who became the last independent ruler of Hanover, nobody has ever explained. Still, as legends concerning the origin of dishes go, it's as good as another, and better than some : the sauce itself being as obviously German in origin as was its supposed royal namesake of the House of Hanover.'

Then she goes on to point out that there is no recipe for it in any of the standard nineteenth-century cookery books, where one would expect to find it. Its rise to popularity occurred at the beginning of this century, when fruit sauces with game and so on became popular in England (see Black cherry sauce, page 300). There are earlier, similar sauces—Francatelli gives a German sauce for boar's head and brawn in an edition dating from his *Cook's Guide* of the early 1880s. The major difference is that it contains an inordinate amount of horseradish (it takes Teutonic courage, I think, to grate 'a large stick of horseradish' into half a pot of redcurrant jelly).

Some modern recipes add the unnecessary embellishment of glacé cherries, which really strike a false note. Another thing to avoid is a stiffening of cornflour or gelatine : the sauce thickens quite enough as it cools, and its flavour should not be blunted with such things.

Caper Sauce

1 tablespoon butter
1 tablespoon flour
¾ pt stock from cooking the main ingredient, eg, mutton or lamb, or fish
Salt, pepper

1 extra ounce butter
1 egg yolk
2 tablespoons cream
1 heaped tablespoon capers (or more)
½ tablespoon chopped parsley

Melt the butter, stir in the flour and cook for a few moments. Moisten with the stock, which should be hot. Allow to simmer down to a smooth sauce the consistency of single cream. Season with salt and pepper. Mix the extra butter, then the egg yolk beaten with the cream, and keep the heat very low as you stir the sauce for a little while longer until it thickens. Add the capers and parsley at the last minute—if you know the tastes of your company, you can add more capers.

Capers are the pickled flower-buds of the caper plant, *Capparis spinosa*, which is native to the Mediterranean region. They have been imported in barrels of vinegar since the Tudors; their first written record in English goes back to the fifteenth century.

Caper sauce is served with boiled leg of mutton or lamb, with skate and with salmon. Capers on their own go well with scrambled egg when it is being served cold, as part of an hors d'oeuvre; arrange them in a diamond pattern over the surface.

Mint Sauce

Mint-leaves (see recipe)	3 level teaspoons sugar
3 tablespoons boiling water	4 tablespoons wine vinegar

Chop enough mint leaves to fill a small jug of a size to hold ¼ pt comfortably. Pour on the boiling water and leave the mixture to infuse. When it is almost cold, stir in the sugar and then the vinegar. Mix well and adjust the seasonings to taste. Serve with roast lamb.

The first point is not to be mean with the mint. The second is to use boiling water, which releases the fragrance of the mint into the sauce. The third is to avoid malt vinegar, which is harsh and can ruin any wine which is being served.

Mint with lamb and new potatoes is one of the pleasures of summer. Mint jellies which try to hold this pleasure for winter eating, I find disgusting, because they are too sweet, too green.

Horseradish Sauce

2 tablespoons grated horseradish root, or a good proprietary brand of horseradish	6 oz double cream Sugar salt Juice of half a lemon

When grating horseradish remember that the outside of the root is the hottest part, so that a tablespoon from the outer root will have far more punch than a tablespoon grated across it.

Whip the cream, then fold in the horseradish to taste. Add salt and sugar, and, finally, lemon juice to sharpen it.

Horseradish sauce goes with beef in English cookery, as everyone knows. The surprising thing is that it goes well with fish, too (Charles Cotton, Izaak Walton's friend the poet, gives a recipe for cooking trout in a stock flavoured with horseradish which works very well).

Anyone who has observed the tenacity of a colony of horseradish plants in their garden may be surprised to learn that it's a comparative newcomer to northern Europe, being a native of west and south-east Asia. This hot-climate plant was first named in England in 1597 by Gerard in his *Herball*. By then it was already well established in Germany, where people had become as fond of its pungent taste as we were of mustard. They called it *meerettich*, sea root, meaning root from over the sea. The English confused *meer*, sea, with *mähre*, mare, and arrived at horseradish.

White Devil Sauce

1 teaspoon French mustard	1 teaspoon sugar
1 teaspoon anchovy sauce	½ teaspoon Harvey Sauce
1 teaspoon wine vinegar	½ teaspoon Worcestershire Sauce
1 teaspoon salt	¼ pt double cream

Mix all the ingredients together, except the cream. Whip the cream until it is fairly stiff, then add the seasoning mixture to taste.

This can be used as a sauce to be served with cold chicken, game, etc. Better still, spread the cold meat with French mustard lightly, having cut it into nice pieces. Arrange them in a small ovenproof dish, and pour over the sauce. Place in a hot oven, mark 6, 400°F, till thoroughly heated through and lightly browned.

Mustard of the Dijon type would be the normal thing to use for this recipe, but I like the grainy *Moutarde de Meaux* which has an especially good flavour. The recipe comes from *Food for the Greedy*, by Nancy Shaw, which was published in 1936.

Venison Sauce

2 tablespoons port wine
¼ lb redcurrant jelly

Small stick of cinnamon, bruised
Thinly pared rind of a lemon

Simmer all the ingredients together for about 5 minutes, stirring to break down the jelly (this may require the addition of a tablespoon or two of water, if commercially made redcurrant jelly is used). Strain into a hot sauceboat.

A simple version of the many varieties of port wine sauce for venison. It was invented by Queen Victoria's chef, Francatelli.

Hard Sauce or Brandy Butter

8 oz unsalted butter, cut in pieces
4 oz icing sugar
3 tablespoons brandy

Squeeze of lemon juice
Grated nutmeg

Put the butter in a warmed bowl and cream it, either with a wooden spoon or an electric beater. Tip the remaining ingredients, except for the nutmeg, into the bowl and mix everything together with your hands; grate in a good amount of nutmeg, mix again, taste and adjust the seasoning. The flavours combine much better in the warmth from your hands than they do with a spoon or beater.

Cumberland Rum Butter

8 oz unsalted butter, cut in pieces
6 oz soft brown sugar

3 tablespoons rum
Grated nutmeg

Follow the method given above. Sometimes the butter is melted rather than creamed, but the result is a little on the close, heavy side.

In our family, these butters were always made with half the usual quantity of sugar as in the recipe above, and tasted all the better for it, particularly when they were being eaten with Christmas Pudding and mince pies which are sweet. (A Frenchman visiting the court of Queen Elizabeth I, was shocked to see that most people's teeth were black and rotten from eating too many sugary things—our national sweet-tooth has a long history.)

In Cumberland, rum butter and oatcakes were given to friends who called at the house to see a new baby. In turn they would leave 'a silver coin, and on the day of the christening, when the butter bowl was empty, the coins were placed in it. A sticky bowl, with plenty of coins sticking to it meant that the child would never be wanting.' There are many people still alive today whose birth was celebrated with rum butter, oatcakes and silver sixpences.

Vanilla Sugar

The simplest thing is to put four vanilla pods in a 2 lb bottling jar, and keep it filled up with caster sugar. Although the pods seem expensive, they are a good investment: they can be used whole in cooking, for instance, when making a custard or stewing fruit, and afterwards they can be washed and dried, before being returned to the sugar jar. This process can be repeated for quite a long time.

On occasions when you must have vanilla essence, look closely at the label first before buying it to make sure you are getting the real thing, not a synthetic imitation (McCormick is the brand to look for).

Vanilla comes from the Spanish word *vaina,* meaning a scabbard or sheath, and so a pod.

Concentrated Vanilla Sugar

Tip 4 oz of granulated sugar and 2 vanilla pods, cut into 1″

lengths, on to the whirling blades of a liquidizer (top speed).
Do this through the hole in the lid, quickly replacing the stopper
because the sugar disintegrates to a cloud of white dust. After
a few seconds sugar and pods will have turned to a slightly
sooty-looking mixture. Don't worry about tiny black specks.

Mix the powder with 8 oz caster sugar, and keep in a
separate, tightly-closed jar from the ordinary vanilla sugar. This
concentrated sugar is ideal for ice-creams, sweet soufflés and
custards when you want vanilla to be the predominating flavour.
Always add it gradually to whatever you are making, and stop
when the taste is right, making up the total weight of sugar with
ordinary vanilla sugar.

Cherry, Plum or Damson Sauce

8 oz stoned morello or amarelle cherries, plums or damsons	1-inch piece cinnamon
¼ pt red wine	2 tablespoons red currant jelly
¼ pt port	Juice of 3 oranges
1 tablespoon sugar	Juice of 1 lemon
2 cloves	Black pepper
	1 oz butter

Put the fruit, wine, port, sugar, cloves and cinnamon into a
pan. Bring to the boil and simmer for 10 minutes until the fruit
is tender. Add jelly, fruit juices and season with pepper. At this
stage plum or damson sauce may be sieved and sweetened a
little more : cherries are best left whole. When the sauce is well
amalgamated, remove it from the heat and whisk in the butter.

Serve immediately with hot boiled tongue, page 134, venison
and game.

Canned morello cherries may be used. And in any case avoid
using sweet dessert cherries as they do not have the right acidity
of flavour.

An early version of this sauce is given by Francatelli. It is
related to other fruit sauces such as Cumberland Sauce, and
the very simple venison sauce on page 298. They are obviously

German in origin, though whether we owe them to the Hanoverian kings or to Prince Albert's influence is uncertain. Their great popularity occurred in Edwardian times, although, as I have said, a few earlier recipes of the kind do appear occasionally.

Cornel Cherry, Rowanberry, Bilberry or Cranberry Jelly

Weigh the berries, freed of stalks and leaves, and put them into a pan with an equal weight of tart apples (windfalls do very well) cut into pieces. Do not peel or core the apples. Cover them with water and simmer gently, covered, until the apples and berries are reduced to a soft pulp. Strain the juice through a muslin-lined sieve, without pressure if you want your jelly to remain clear (personally when I have a very few cornel cherries I do not want to waste a drop of the flavour, so I squeeze the pulp as hard as I can and expect everyone to overlook the opaque appearance of the jelly in the interests of flavour).

Measure the juice, put it on to boil with 1 lb of sugar to every pint. When the jelly reaches setting point, pot in the usual way.

These jellies are the ideal accompaniment to game and turkey or guineafowl, to roast lamb as well. Their tart flavour is good, too, with thin bread and butter.

Quince, Medlar, Sorb or Crab Apple Jelly

Although quinces should be ripe, medlars and sorbs are best used before they get to the softened, bletted stage when they are pleasant to eat as a dessert fruit. Crab apples should be used when they are just ripe.

Cut up the fruit after washing it. Cover it with water, and continue as in the recipe above. Precious quinces can be eked out with a proportion of windfall apples—in very thin years, I have used ½ lb quinces to 1½ lb of apples and the jelly has still been delicious.

These jellies are not quite so tart as the ones above, but they go well with pork. Medlar jelly is good with poultry and game.

Orange Sauce for duck and game

1½ oz butter	1 tablespoon sugar
1 rounded tablespoon flour	Any meat juices available from
¾ pt hot duck, game or beef stock	cooking duck or game
2 Seville oranges, or 2 sweet oranges and 1 lemon	2 oz port (can be omitted for duck)

Melt the butter in a small pan and let it turn a delicate golden brown colour. Stir in the flour, cook for 2 minutes, then moisten with the stock. Allow this sauce to simmer gently for at least 20 minutes—the longer the better. Meanwhile remove the peel thinly from the oranges, cut it into matchstick strips and simmer in water for 3 minutes. Drain and add to the simmering sauce. Add the juices of the oranges, and lemon if used, and stir in sugar to taste; start with a little and add more if necessary. Finally pour in the meat juices from roasting duck or game, which should be well skimmed of fat, and finally the port.

An English version of the French *sauce bigarade*, which goes back to the eighteenth century. The meat can be served with a garnish of orange slices heated in a little of the sauce : the main thing is not to make the whole dish too sweet, as it sometimes is in some restaurants.

Spiced Redcurrant Jelly

3 lb redcurrants	1 teaspoon cinnamon
1½ pts water	8 oz malt vinegar
3 cloves	3 lb granulated sugar

Put the redcurrants into a large pan as they are—do not remove stalks, leaves, etc. Add the water and spices. Bring to the boil and simmer until the redcurrants are soft. Strain through a jelly bag (or put through a sieve, if you do not mind cloudy-looking jelly). To the liquid, add the vinegar and sugar and boil until setting point is reached. Pour into sterilized jam jars; cover while still very hot.

An unusual recipe from *The Llandegai Recipe Book,* which was first published in 1958 to help raise money for the organ and bells of St Tegai's Church at Llandegai (*llan* means 'church of'). These local pamphlets and small books of recipes, brought out to raise money by schools, monasteries, the Women's Institutes, often contain a handful of regional recipes which have been popular for centuries, although they have never quite reached the main cookery books. Often, one hears an echo of some medieval or Tudor dish, undimmed by additions of baking powder, or the substitution of margarine and vegetable fats for butter and lard.

Apricot and Pineapple Jam

1 lb dried apricots	3 lb sugar
2½ pts cold water	¼ lb blanched, sliced almonds
12-oz tin pineapple	

Wash and then soak the apricots in the water for 24 hours. Remove any stones and crack them to get at the kernels which should be put with the almonds. Simmer the apricots in their soaking liquid for half an hour. Meanwhile drain the pineapple —keep the juice—and chop it fairly small. Add the pineapple, the juice, the sugar, the almonds and any kernels to the apricots. Bring back to the boil and cook for about twenty minutes until the jam reaches setting point. Pot in the usual way.

I have included this recipe for jam because it is one I have never come across outside England—most jam recipes are common to all the countries of northern Europe and America. My mother used to make it when I was a child for special occasions, but she lost the recipe during the war. Then, quite unexpectedly, someone sent me the recipe because he, too, had associated it with the splendid teas provided by his mother in the days before calorie-counting became a national passion. He recalled the puff pastry rolls filled with various savoury mixtures, the sandwiches, angel cakes with cream and jam, coconut pyramids and other small cakes, then larger cakes for filling up the gaps—and this magnificent jam.

Lemon Curd

2 large lemons	½ lb loaf sugar
3 oz butter, cut in bits	3 large eggs

Either grate the lemon rind finely into a basin, or rub the skins all over with half a dozen sugar lumps to remove the fragrant zest and oils, and put the lumps into a basin (the first method gives a slight graininess to the lemon curd which many people prefer). Add the strained lemon juice, the butter and the sugar. Stand over a pan of simmering water and stir occasionally until the sugar is dissolved into the juice and butter. Meanwhile beat the eggs, and pour them through a strainer into the basin. Stir steadily until the mixture becomes thick. Do not allow it to boil. Pour it into clean pots and cover in the usual way.

If you like a milder flavour, add an extra ounce of butter and another egg to the ingredients above.

When using lemon curd for tarts, sprinkle a layer of crushed sponge finger biscuits over the pastry before adding the lemon curd. 4 oz of almonds, ground to a coarse powder with their skins on, are even better than sponge finger biscuits.

Quince Comfits

Quinces are precious, to be used sparingly, but try and set aside six or seven for these delicious sweets. Wash them, and rub off any of the grey fluff which may still be clinging to their yellow skins. Cut them up roughly, put them into a pan with about an inch of water. Cover and simmer until they are soft enough to sieve. Weigh this pulp, and put it with an equal weight of sugar into a clean, heavy pan. Bring to the boil and boil slowly for at least an hour, until the mixture is very thick indeed and leaves the side of the pan. Stir fairly frequently so that the bottom doesn't catch. It will splatter from time to time with a soft explosive plop, so keep your stirring hand wrapped in a cloth.

Pour into metal baking trays or swiss roll tins, lined with Bakewell paper. Dry for 3–4 days over the solid fuel or oil cooker, or in the airing cupboard. Cut into squares with a knife dipped into hot water and dried. Put these squares into an air-tight box with caster sugar and shake them about so that they are well coated. The surplus sugar will prevent them sticking together, but in fact the mixture should be so firm that this is not likely.

Try to keep them stored away for Christmastime desserts. They can be put on top of grilled pork chops, and left under the heat for a few moments, too.

A recipe for those who have wisely planted a quince in their garden. This best of all fruit trees has flowering globes of pink in the spring, and in autumn fruit of such golden fragrance that they scent the house when you bring them in.

An old recipe popular throughout Europe. 'Quyncys in comfyte' were served at Henry IV's coronation banquet in 1399. By the eighteenth century, this 'marmelade' of quinces was a standard household recipe. If you cook the above mixture less, or add less sugar—say ½ lb to each 1 lb of sieved quinces—you will end up with a softer quince 'cheese' or 'butter'.

Preserved Spiced Oranges

10 large thin-skinned seedless oranges, or 18 smaller ones	1 pt white wine vinegar
2½ lb granulated sugar	1½ sticks cinnamon
	¼ oz cloves
	6 blades mace

Wipe the oranges. Cut into slices at least ¼″ thick, and remove any pips if the oranges are not as seedless as they might be. Put into a pan and cover them with water. Put a lid on the pan, and simmer gently for 40 minutes, or until the peel is soft. Be careful not to overcook the slices, or they may disintegrate.

Meanwhile dissolve the sugar in the vinegar, put in the spices and bring to the boil. Simmer for 3–4 minutes.

Drain the orange slices, but keep their cooking liquor; place them in a shallow pan and cover them with the vinegar syrup —if there is not quite enough, add some of the orange cooking liquor. Simmer with a lid on the pan for another 30–40 minutes, or until the slices look clear. Again do not overcook, or allow the syrup to boil hard. Remove the pan from the heat and leave for 24 hours, slices and syrup together.

Drain the orange slices and put them into jars. Cover them with the syrup. Keep topping up with the syrup for 3 or 4 days. The jars can then be sealed, and should be left alone for six weeks. Serve the orange slices with pork, duck, ham, either hot or cold. Syrup left in the jars when the slices have gone, makes a good orange sauce for duck.

Rich Orangeade

6 large, sweet oranges	Orange-flower water
1 Seville orange	Juice of 1 lemon (see recipe)
½ lb sugar	

Remove the peel in thin strips from all the oranges. Be careful not to include the white pith. Put the strips into a large pan with 1½ pints of cold water. Bring slowly to simmering point, and keep at this temperature for 5 minutes; do not allow the

water to boil or it will draw too much bitterness from the peel.
Leave the pan to cool down. Bring sugar to the boil with 1
pint of water, and boil for 3 minutes to make a syrup. Cool it
down, too. Finally mix together the strained peel water, the
syrup and the strained juice of all the oranges. Add a light
flavouring of orange-flower water, and a little lemon to sharpen
the flavour if this seems a good idea. Serve well chilled.

A Victorian recipe, which must have been popular at dances
towards the end of the winter when Seville oranges are in season.
It can be made without them, and without orange-flower water,
but it will not be such a delicious drink.

Follow exactly the same principle for making lemonade. More
sugar may be needed, but this is the kind of thing that can
always be adjusted at the end. Omit the orange-flower water.

Metric Conversion Tables

Conversion tables for measurements and temperatures

Weight

1 oz — 28·35 g	1 kilogramme — 1000 g — 2 lb 3 oz approx
2 oz — 56·7 g	500 g — 1 lb 1½ oz ,,
¼ lb — 113·4 g	250 g — 9 oz ,,
½ lb — 226·8 g	125 g — 4¼ oz ,,
12 oz — 340·2 g	100 g — 3½ oz ,,
16 oz — 453·6 g	25 g — 1 oz ,,

Liquids

¼ pt (1 gill)	— 142 ml
½ pt	— 284 ml
1 pt	— 568 ml

1 litre	— 1000 g — 1¾ pt — 35 fl oz approx
½ litre	— 500 g — ¾ pt plus 4½ tablespoons ,,
¼ litre	— 250 g — ½ pt less 2 tablespoons ,,
1 decilitre	— 100 g — 6 tablespoons ,,
1 centilitre	— 10 g — 1 dessertspoon ,,
1 millilitre	— 1 g — a few drops ,,
5 millilitres	— 5 g — pharmaceutical teaspoon ,,

Temperatures

Electricity and Solid Fuel	Gas	Degrees Fahrenheit	Degrees Centigrade
Cool	¼–½	250	121
Very slow	1	275	135
Slow	2	300	149
	3	325	163
Moderate	4	350	177
	5	375	190
Moderately hot	6	400	205
Hot	7	425	218
Very hot	8	450	232
	9	475	246

309

Some Source Books

Acton, Eliza, *Modern Cookery . . . for Private Families* (1845; reprinted by Elek Books, 1966). See also *The Best of Eliza Acton*, ed. Elizabeth Ray with an introduction by Elizabeth David (Longman, 1968; Penguin, 1974).

Beeton, Mrs, *The Book of Household Management* (1859; facsimile of 1861 edition published by Cape, 1968).

Bunyard, Edward Ashdown, *Anatomy of Dessert* (Dulau, 1929).

Carême, (Marie-Antoine) Antonin, *Le Cuisinier parisien, ou l'Art de la cuisine française au dix-neuvième siècle* (1828).

—, *L'Art de la cuisine française au dix-neuvième siècle*, 5 vols (1833–44).

Cobbett, William, *Cobbett's Cottage Economy* (1822; reprinted by Cedric Chivers, 1966).

David, Elizabeth, *English Potted Meats and Fish Pastes* (Elizabeth David, 1968).

—, *English Cooking Ancient and Modern*, vol. I, *Spices, Salts and Aromatics in the English Kitchen* (Penguin, 1970).

De Salis, Harriet Anne, *Savouries à la mode,* revised ed. (1890).

Digby, Sir Kenelm, *The Closet of the Eminently Learned Sir Kenelm Digby, Kt, Opened* (1669; reprinted by Philip Lee Warner, 1910).

Farley, John, *The London Art of Cookery* (1783).

Francatelli, Charles Elmé, *A Plain Cookery Book for the Working Classes* (1861).

—, *The Cook's Guide* (1862).

Gerard, John, *The Herball, or General History of Plants* (1597), ed. M. Woodward (Minerva Press, 1971).

Glasse, Hannah, *The Art of Cookery Made Plain and Easy* (1747; 1796 edition reprinted by S.R. Publications, 1971).

Gunter, William, *Gunter's Modern Confectioner* (1861).

Hall, Augusta, Baroness Llanover, *Good Cookery Illustrated* (1867).

Hartley, Dorothy, *Food in England* (Macdonald, 1954).

Heath, Ambrose, *Good Sweets* (Faber, 1937).

Huxley, Gervas, *Talking of Tea* (Thames & Hudson, 1956).

Jenkinson, Eleanor L., *The Ocklye Cookery Book* (Cassell, 1909).

Kitchiner, Dr William, *Apicius Redivivus, or the Cook's Oracle* (1817–1843).

'A Lady' (Maria Rundell), *Domestic Economy and Cookery, for Rich and Poor* (1827).

Lindsay, Lady Sarah, *A Few Choice Recipes* (1883).

The Llandegai Recipe Book (1958).

Lucas, Dione, and Hume, Rosemary, *Au petit Cordon Bleu* (Dent, 1936; revised ed., 1953).

Markham, Gervase, *Country Contentments, in Two Books* (1615), bk II, *The English Hus-wife.*

Le Menagier de Paris (1393). Translated by Eileen Power as *The Goodman of Paris* (Routledge, 1928).

Oxford High School Cook Book.

Plat, Hugh, *Delight for Ladies* (1605).

'A Potter', *Pottery, Home-made Potted Foods, Meats and Fish Pastes, Savoury Butters and Others, by a Potter* (Wine and Food Society, 1946).

Raffald, Elizabeth, *The Experienced English Housekeeper* (1769; facsimile edition by E. & W. Books).

Shaw, Nancy, *Food for the Greedy* (Cobden-Sanderson, 1936).

Smith, E., *The Compleat Housewife; or Accomplished Gentlewoman's Companion* (1727).

Smith, Michael, *Fine English Cookery* (Faber, 1973).

Soyer, Alexis, *Shilling Cookery for the People* (1855).

Taylor, Harold Victor, *The Apples of England* (Lockwood, 1936).

West Sussex Women's Institutes, *Come Cooking!* (1969).

White, Florence, *Good Things in England: a practical cookery book for everyday use* (Cape, 1932; reprinted 1951).

The Whole Duty of Women (1737).

Wilson, Anne, *Food and Drink in Britain* (Constable, 1973).

Woodforde, Rev. James, *The Diary of a Country Parson, the Reverend James Woodforde, 1758–1781*, ed. John Beresford, 5 vols (Oxford University Press, 1924–31; reprinted 1968).

Index

FOR THE BEST IN PAPERBACKS, LOOK FOR THE

In every corner of the world, on every subject under the sun, Penguin represents quality and variety – the very best in publishing today.

For complete information about books available from Penguin – including Pelicans, Puffins, Peregrines and Penguin Classics – and how to order them, write to us at the appropriate address below. Please note that for copyright reasons the selection of books varies from country to country.

In the United Kingdom: For a complete list of books available from Penguin in the U.K., please write to *Dept E.P., Penguin Books Ltd, Harmondsworth, Middlesex, UB7 0DA*

In the United States: For a complete list of books available from Penguin in the U.S., please write to *Dept BA, Penguin, 299 Murray Hill Parkway, East Rutherford, New Jersey 07073*

In Canada: For a complete list of books available from Penguin in Canada, please write to *Penguin Books Canada Ltd, 2801 John Street, Markham, Ontario L3R 1B4*

In Australia: For a complete list of books available from Penguin in Australia, please write to the *Marketing Department, Penguin Books Australia Ltd, P.O. Box 257, Ringwood, Victoria 3134*

In New Zealand: For a complete list of books available from Penguin in New Zealand, please write to the *Marketing Department, Penguin Books (NZ) Ltd, Private Bag, Takapuna, Auckland 9*

In India: For a complete list of books available from Penguin, please write to *Penguin Overseas Ltd, 706 Eros Apartments, 56 Nehru Place, New Delhi, 110019*

In Holland: For a complete list of books available from Penguin in Holland, please write to *Penguin Books Nederland B.V., Postbus 195, NL–1380AD Weesp, Netherlands*

In Germany: For a complete list of books available from Penguin, please write to *Penguin Books Ltd, Friedrichstrasse 10 – 12, D–6000 Frankfurt Main 1, Federal Republic of Germany*

In Spain: For a complete list of books available from Penguin in Spain, please write to *Longman Penguin España, Calle San Nicolas 15, E–28013 Madrid, Spain*

JANE GRIGSON

FISH COOKERY

There are over 50 species of edible fish; and Jane Grigson feels that most of us do not eat nearly enough of them. If anything will make us mend our ways, it is this delightful book with its varied and comprehensive recipes, covering everything from lobster to conger eel, from sole to clam chowder. Many of her dishes come from France, others are from the British Isles, America, Spain, Italy – any country where good fish is cooked with loving care and eaten with appreciation.

CHARCUTERIE AND FRENCH PORK COOKERY

Although it could be said that European civilization has been founded on the pig, this unfortunate animal has encountered much prejudice and degradation in the past. But ever since Charles Lamb stated that there was no other taste comparable to that of roast pork, the pig has never looked back. And it is hoped that this book – the first of its kind – will further its popularity in the English kitchen. Together with a guide to *charcuterie* and a host of French pork dishes, it gives new and unusual information on the history and growth of this art. Certain to delight both adventurous housewife and diffident traveller to France, this book allows you to make a true pig of yourself.

GOOD THINGS

Bouchées à la reine, civet of hare, Mrs Beeton's carrot jam to imitate apricot preserve, baked beans Southern style, wine sherbet . . .

These are just a few of the delicious and intriguing dishes in *Good Things*: Jane Grigson is a firm believer in the pleasure food gives. Echoing the great chef Carême – 'from behind my ovens, I feel the ugly edifice of routine crumbling beneath my hands' – she emphasizes the delights and solaces of a truly creative activity.

and
THE MUSHROOM FEAST
JANE GRIGSON'S VEGETABLE BOOK
FOOD WITH THE FAMOUS
JANE GRIGSON'S FRUIT BOOK

Mediterranean Food   Elizabeth David

Based on a collection of recipes made when the author lived in France, Italy, the Greek Islands and Egypt, this was the first book by Britain's greatest cookery writer.

The Complete Barbecue Book   James Marks

Mouth-watering recipes and advice on all aspects of barbecuing make this an ideal and inspired guide to *al fresco* entertainment.

A Book of Latin American Cooking   Elisabeth Lambert Ortiz

Anyone who thinks Latin American food offers nothing but *tacos* and *tortillas* will enjoy the subtle marriages of texture and flavour celebrated in this marvellous guide to one of the world's most colourful *cuisines*.

Quick Cook   Beryl Downing

For victims of the twentieth century, this book provides some astonishing gourmet meals – all cooked in under thirty minutes.

Josceline Dimbleby's Book of Puddings, Desserts and Savouries

'Full of the most delicious and novel ideas for every type of pudding' – *Lady*

Chinese Food   Kenneth Lo

A popular step-by-step guide to the whole range of delights offered by Chinese cookery and the fascinating philosophy behind it.

The Best of Eliza Acton   Selected and Edited by Elizabeth Ray
With an Introduction by Elizabeth David

First published in 1845, Eliza Acton's *Modern Cookery for Private Families*, of which this is a selection, is a true classic which everyone interested in cookery will treasure.

Easy to Entertain   Patricia Lousada

Easy to Entertain hands you the magic key to entertaining without days of panic or last minute butterflies. The magic lies in cooking each course ahead, so that you can enjoy yourself along with your guests.

French Provincial Cooking   Elizabeth David

'It is difficult to think of any home that can do without Elizabeth David's *French Provincial Cooking* . . . One could cook for a lifetime on the book alone' – *Observer*

The National Trust Book of Traditional Puddings   Sara Paston-Williams

'My favourite cookbook of the year. Engagingly written . . . this manages to be both scholarly and practical, elegant without pretension' – *Sunday Times*

The New Book of Middle Eastern Food   Claudia Roden

'This is one of those rare cookery books that is a work of cultural anthropology and Mrs Roden's standards of scholarship are so high as to ensure that it has permanent value' – Paul Levy in the *Observer*

The Adventurous Gardener   Christopher Lloyd

Prejudiced, delightful and always stimulating, Christopher Lloyd's book is essential reading for everyone who loves gardening. 'Get it and enjoy it' – *Financial Times*

The Magic Garden   Shirley Conran

The gardening book for the absolute beginner. 'Whether you have a window box, a patio, an acre or a cabbage patch . . . you will enjoy this' – *Daily Express*

The Cottage Garden   Anne Scott-James

'Her history is neatly and simply laid out; well-stocked with attractive illustrations' – *The Times*. 'The garden book I have most enjoyed reading in the last few years' – *Observer*

Growing Fruit   Mary Spiller

From blossom to harvest, through planting, pruning, picking and storing, in a small or large garden, plot or pot, here is an illustrated step-by-step guide to growing fruit of all kinds.

The Illustrated Garden Planter   Diana Saville

How to choose plants for your garden – to cover a wall, creep between paving, provide colour in summer – and to plan for collective effect or to overcome a difficult site. 650 plants are illustrated, in all over 900 described.

Organic Gardening   Lawrence D. Hills

The classic manual on growing fruit and vegetables without using artificial or harmful fertilizers. 'Enormous value . . . enthusiastic writing and off-beat tips' – *Daily Mail*